Best Wishes

BOB HOPE'S
OWN STORY

DRAWINGS BY TED SALLY

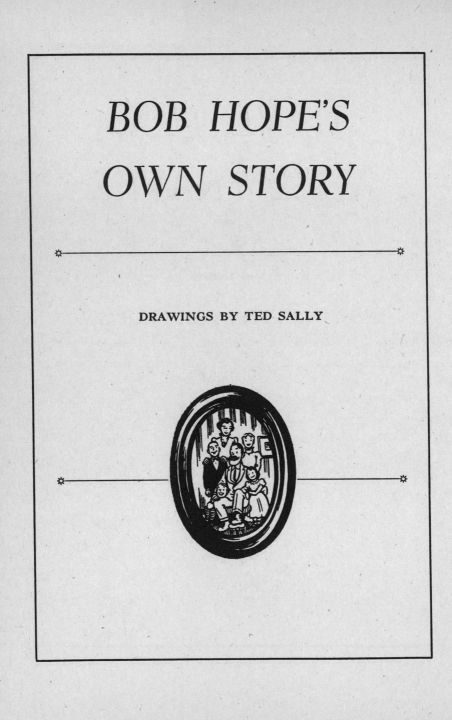

HAVE TUX,
WILL TRAVEL

AS TOLD TO PETE MARTIN

SIMON AND SCHUSTER
New York   London   Toronto   Sydney   Singapore

SIMON AND SCHUSTER
Rockefeller Center
1230 Avenue of the Americas
New York, NY 10020

First Simon & Schuster trade paperback edition 2003

SIMON AND SCHUSTER and colophon are registered trademarks of Simon & Schuster, Inc.

Parts of this book have appeared in the *Saturday Evening Post*
under the title "This Is On Me."

For information regarding special discounts for bulk purchases,
please contact Simon & Schuster Special Sales at 1-800-456-6798
or business@simonandschuster.com

Manufactured in the United States of America

10 9 8 7 6 5 4 3 2 1

The Library of Congress cataloged the hardcover edition as follows:

Hope, Bob.
Have tux, will travel: Bob Hope's own story, as told to Pete Martin. Drawings by Ted Sally
p. cm.
"Parts of this book have appeared in the Saturday evening post under the title This is on me."
1. Actors—correspondence, reminiscences, etc.
I. Martin, Pete. II. Title.
PN2287.H63 A3
927.92   54-13312
ISBN 0-7432-6103-8

WARNING!

I'VE GOT A FRIEND *who knows the entire book-writing scam. When he heard that I was doing a book about myself, he packed some K-rations, a sleeping bag, a spare can of gas, and headed for my house in North Hollywood. He took off on the Hollywood Freeway. The Hollywood Freeway—that's a road on which you blow both your horn and your top. Neither one does any good.*

His face was gray with fatigue when he checked in. He borrowed my razor, gulped a few mouthfuls of my brandy and unwrapped the surprise he'd brought along for me. It was a bundle of advice.

"Look, chum," he said. "If you're doing a book about yourself, you've got to probe deep in your insides. You've got to strip off the layers of the Hope the public knows and put that other Hope down on paper. Let's not be shallow and surfacy about this thing, chum."

I'm going to level with those who're thinking about reading this. I don't know what other kind of Bob Hope my adviser meant. Maybe he meant a crazy-mixed-up-kid Bob Hope. Maybe he was day-dreaming about a deep-domed, Walter-Lippmann-type Bob Hope. Could be he was conjuring up a sensitive, introverted Bob Hope.

I've got news for those who're hoping to read With Bob Hope in a Platinum-Lined Snake Pit. That breezy Hope—that Hope with a bounce you see on the screen or on your TV set—is me.

I get peeved as easy as the next guy—unless the next guy is Donald Duck. Occasionally I'm disillusioned with people I've liked and trusted. But I don't make a hobby of mental turmoil. If I did, it would be out for this story. I don't think most people want that.

So I'm just putting down the Bob Hope I know. I'm no one-man Moral Rearmament Movement. I don't go around giving out with monologues about my sense of inner guilt and the pretzel bends in my soul. Nor do I go for sleeping pills or lying on a psychiatrist's couch to have my head shrunk. I'm not a baby who sucks soothing syrup from a booze bottle.

Maybe this makes me less interesting. I notice that most of the books are written about people whose insides look like road maps. Those roads lead to frustration.

When I feel a spell of brooding coming on, I lie down and knock off some uninterrupted sleep.

Maybe there's supposed to be something glamorous about folks whose personalities are split like a bundle of kindling. But I notice they spend most of their time getting an analyst to glue them back together.

It wouldn't be hard to arrange that out here in California. We grow more neuroses than hibiscus. We've got even more psychiatrists than actors' agents. Our psychiatrists have Cadillac fins on their couches.

I have a warning signal that saves me lots of psychiatrists' fees. If I pick up a golf club at the Lakeside Golf Club—or at any golf club in the world—and the stick seems heavy, that means my barometer is dropping. When that happens, I know I'm a little tired. I ought to get some rest. If I'm ragged at golf, that's it. If it wasn't for that, I wouldn't know I'm tired.

I know it's hard for people to believe a man in my business is normal emotionally and mentally. If they don't, there's nothing I can do about it.

Not long ago I got on a plane to fly north to play Letterman Hospital in San Francisco. I sat next to a kid about sixteen. He recognized me when I sat down. I was trying to put some routines together to use at Letterman and at Oak Knoll Hospital. I pulled out a pile of material to look at. This kid said to me, "Do you have to memorize all that?"

"No," I said, "I'm just looking through some jokes."

The kid gave me a third degree. He didn't use the glaring, unshaded light in my eyes and the hose, but he did a thorough job. He just kept asking me questions.

Finally he asked, "Did you ever make a picture with Bing Crosby?"

"Didn't you ever see any of the Road pictures?" I wanted to know.

"No," he said.

He asked me how I put my stuff together. He wanted to know how long I'd been in show business. He tried to squeeze it out of me whether it had been a lot of trouble getting a start.

WARNING

The woman sitting behind me asked me for my autograph. I gave it to her. The kid asked for my autograph too. He held it up and studied it. He said to the woman back of us, "What do you know? Signs it the same way every time."

He turned back to me. "Boy, you must have a pretty tough life."

I wasn't feeling abused. I said, "I feel pretty good."

There was a pause. Then he asked, "When did you have your last breakdown?"

"What gave you the idea I've had a nervous breakdown?" I wanted to know.

"Don't all comedians have nervous breakdowns?" he asked.

"Some of them may," I said; "I feel fine."

I still do. Most of the time it's my audiences that have the nervous breakdowns. See how you make out.

—BOB HOPE

HAVE TUX,
WILL TRAVEL

Chapter 1

O NE OF MY WRITERS, Larry Klein, looked at me one day and said, "You know, if you had your life to live all over again, you wouldn't have time to do it." I wouldn't want to live it over again. It's been pretty exciting up to now. The encore might not be as much fun.

Among other things, Larry meant that I travel a lot. Hoofers, comedians and singers used to put ads in *Variety*. Those ads read: "Have tuxedo, will travel." This meant they were ready to go any place any time. It meant that they were "available" for

1

picnics, weddings, clambakes, one-night stands, extended engagements. It also meant that they would be dressed classy when they showed up.

I've been traveling ever since I can remember. I've been "available" ever since I did my first Charlie Chaplin imitation when I was nine or ten. But I haven't always had a tux. I bought my first one out of savings when I was nineteen. It was real sharp, but it was secondhand and a tight fit. It cost me fourteen bucks at Richman's in Cleveland. It would cost more than that now to have it let out enough at the seams.

I'm still traveling. I'm the only hit-and-run comedian in the business. My wife, Dolores, complains that I'm always taking off for Alaska, London, Korea, Cleveland, Denver, or Washington, D. C., without giving her warning. I'll say this for Dolores: No one can handle being married to a traveling-salesman type better than she does. She's very sweet about my absences, although I notice that the towels in our bathroom are marked Hers and Welcome Traveler. But when she gets a certain look in her eye, I take her on my next trip.

Of course, Dolores is much too good for me. She was raised on the right side of the tracks. We Hopes lived *under* the tracks.

Last year the Friars threw a testimonial dinner in New York for me. During the evening several tributes were paid to me as a show-business pro. It was nice to hear all that flattery. I was glad Dolores was there to hear it too. Up to then, she'd thought I was a pilot for United Air Lines.

The well-known autobiographer and *littérateur*, Bing Crosby, once sent a letter to a friend in which he tried to explain me. "People are always asking me how Hope survives the schedule he sets for himself," he wrote. "The truth is he couldn't survive without it. Applause, laughter and commendation are food and drink for him. There's no tension felt when he walks on stage—not by him, anyhow. He expands, he mellows, he blooms, he beams. When he tells his first gag and the place falls apart, his life is complete. How can a fellow like that weaken physically? I once talked him into a vacation and he never forgave me. He had hives, shingles and a spastic colon when he returned. Never again, he vowed."

That phrase "not by him, anyhow" is sheer jealousy. But actually, I'm the one who should be jealous of Bing. He's the luckiest man I know. Anything he touches turns to gold. Everything I touch yells for the police. But I understand why my weakness for knocking myself out made him think me an interesting case for analysis. Bing would rather do anything than work. It's a delight to be with that fat baritone in a film or a radio show. He's as smooth as the oil from one of his collection of gushers. But his idea of a perfect script is one that opens with him looking through a knothole. The rest of the picture is what he sees through it.

At that, Bing may be right about what keeps my motor turning. But the ugly problem staring me in the face now is trying to remember my life for publication. Not that it doesn't seem worthwhile. Ben Franklin and Giovanni Jacopo Casanova did it, and their stuff still sells, doesn't it?

I'll never forget the first time I met Fred Allen. He was catching my act in a theater. When he came backstage afterward, I rushed up to him and asked, "What did you think?"

He propped his eyebags open, and drawled, "You reek with confidence." Now that I'm breathing down Franklin's and Casanova's necks, I could use some of that reek.

In the past, I've used the story of my life as a springboard for launching gags. Once I've used them, I file them away in steel cabinets. When she ordered those filing cases, my secretary, Marjorie Hughes, specified "airtight." It was either that or a chlorophyll spray.

Here are a few samples:

I lived in a very tough neighborhood. I'll never forget the morning I got the new wrist watch . . . and the afternoon I got the new teeth. You could tell if a kid in my block was a sissy. If he couldn't fight, he didn't have any ears. I always had mine. I wore them tied behind my neck.

I went out to my old grammar school yesterday. There was the same old desk, the same old inkwell, the same old shaving kit.

I wouldn't say I was smart, but the teachers thought I was an unusual student. They studied me.

Mark Twain might have envied that sort of thing, but something tells me that they're not what this project calls for.

I don't say that my mind is an orderly one. When I try to remember dates and names, I bang my forehead with my fists so hard I have to have my head reblocked. But I've learned a thing or two from radio and TV shows. I do better if I warm up for them beforehand on stage, in front of the audience. Then when I'm on the air, I feel good out there. So I'll shadowbox around with my memories before I go into my Ben Franklin-and-Giovanni Jacopo routine.

I'll start with my mother. After all, that's where most people start. What a job she did with her seven rockhead sons. She was so great. One of my memories is her Saturday-night routine. She'd get out a big washtub and give us baths in the kitchen. She took us in order of our conduct for the week. If we'd been good, we got fresh water. That's why I was tan until I was thirteen. Nowadays when I walk into a luxury hotel and see those gleaming bathroom fixtures, I remember that galvanized job in the kitchen, soap in my eyes and mother dunking us.

One of the great things about my mother was that she never stopped encouraging us. When I began to grow up and had theatrical ambitions, she took me to Keith's 105th Street in Cleveland to see Frank Fay. Frank was vaudeville's top monologist. He must have been pulling down $2,000 to $2,500 a week. That would be two or three times as much today. He just stood there and talked to the audience as if they were old friends.

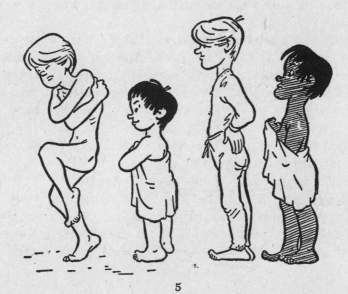

After Frank had worked for a few minutes, Mother looked at me and said loudly, "He's not half as good as you."

"Sh-h-h," I said; "Ma; please, Ma!"

"I don't care," she said. "He can't sing or dance." Later in his act, Frank did both of those things, but she hadn't given him a chance to do either. The people near us looked at us as if we were goofy. Mom looked back at them defiantly and stared them down. Years later I had one of my biggest thrills when I came back to Cleveland and played that same theater. Mother was still alive then. She was sitting out front. I knew she was saying to herself, *It's about time. They should have recognized his genius sooner.*

Another memory that floats into my head involves Joe E. Lewis, the nightclub genius. Once when I was in Chicago, I dropped in at a night spot, the Chez Paree, to catch Joe's last show. I was too late for it, but I saw Dottie Lamour sitting at a table. I sat beside her. A woman walked over to the table, took my chin in her hand, and turned my face toward another woman she'd left back at her table.

"This is it, Julie," she said, handling my head as if it were a cabbage.

Dottie and I laughed so hard we almost fell under the table. The woman didn't say "Pardon me." She just walked over and used me for demonstration purposes. She'd probably said to her friend, "There's Bob Hope over there," and her friend had said, "I don't believe it." So she walked over, took my head and twirled it around a couple of times to prove her point.

When I'd pulled myself together, I asked her, "Where do you get your material, honey? It's great."

"I listen to you every Monday night," she said.

I stopped laughing. I'd been on Tuesdays for four years.

Taking my memories as they pop into my mind brings up my brief career as a pug. It was a career so condensed it was engraved on a pin head—mine. I took up pugilism because Whitey

Jennings, my best pal in Cleveland, said to me in the Alhambra Poolroom, "I'm going to fight in the Ohio state amateurs."

"Oh, yeah?" I said jeeringly.

He was serious.

"No fooling," he said. "I signed up today." He showed me his entry card. It read: "Packy West fighting in the featherweight division." Packy was an impressive name for a fighter to have in those days. It had been used by an outstanding boxer of that era, Packy McFarland. Next day I went downtown and registered in the lightweight (one hundred and thirty-five pound) division as Packy East. The gang Whitey and I hung around with thought the name I'd chosen whimsical. It was a rib on Whitey's fighting name. "That Hope," they said, "he's a card."

I was sixteen, I weighed one hundred and twenty-eight pounds and the featherweight class had a top limit of one hundred and twenty-six. I just missed getting into it. If I'd taken the apples out of my pockets, I could have qualified as a featherweight. If I had, I'd have made out better. As it was, I creamed my first-round opponent. He was constantly looking over his shoulder toward his corner for instructions. When I hit him, he turned to his second, asked, "What'll I do now?" and his second yelled strategy back to him. I finally tagged him while his head was turned.

Having won that contest, I put on a turtle-necked sweater and began to swagger when I walked. In my next bout I drew a bye. That put me into the semifinals. We'd fought the prelims at Charlie Marotta's Athletic Club. We moved to Moose Hall downtown in Cleveland for the semifinals.

The Sunday before my next fight I was looking at the rotogravure section of the *Plain Dealer*. In it were pictures of the Ohio state amateur champions. My eyes went to the picture of the kingpin of the lightweight division. He was a fellow named Happy Walsh. He was called Happy because he just smiled back when he was slugged. Nothing bothered this fellow—fists, knives, guns, nothing. He was happy about everything. He looked as if he even had muscles in his hair. I looked at him, awestruck. I never dreamed that I'd meet him in the ring. The following Wednesday I went down to Moose Hall with my manager, Red Walsh—no relation to Happy.

As we walked in, Red said crisply, "Packy East reporting. Who's he fight?"

The man in charge said, "He fights Happy Walsh."

I turned plaid. It was like saying, "Tomorrow you fight King Kong."

"Don't sag like that," Red told me. "Get up off your knees. You can lick him!"

"I'm not on my knees," I said with dignity. "I just knelt down to tie my shoes."

When I went into the ring I was numb. Red kept looking at Happy Walsh and smiling. Happy kept smiling back at him. Everybody was smiling except me. All my friends were there. The Alhambra Poolroom was represented. Eighty or a hundred of my pals had come down from the corner of 105th and Euclid. In the first round I played cozy. Happy examined me as if trying to see what was holding me together. When I found out I was still alive, my footwork got fancier. I pranced around on my toes. In the second round I threw my right. I never got my arm back. Happy hit me on the chin. I fell in a sitting position, bounced and fell over. I got so much resin in my hair, I can still play two verses of "Humoresque" in it with a comb.

Red threw a bucket of water over me and carried me out. I was the only fighter in Cleveland's history who was carried both ways: in and out of the ring. That ended my fighting days—in the ring. I had other, more informal fights.

Those gags I quoted a while back about our tough neighborhood weren't exaggerated. Late one afternoon I was walking through Rockefeller Park with Whitey Jennings when we saw two girls we knew. The girls said, "Hello there."

We said, "Hi. How does it feel to look like Clara Bow?" What with such sparkling jests, we had quite a chat.

A gang of young, second-generation hoodlums hung out in that park. When the girls left, one of the members of the gang came up and asked Whitey, "What do you mean by talking to my gal?" Without waiting for an answer, he poked Whitey. Whitey swung back and another member of the gang began to work on me. In no time, seven of the mob were chopping away at us. The odds seemed large for us, so Whitey and I took off.

On our way home we found that the gang had used knives on us. Those knives were so sharp that we hadn't noticed them until Whitey's blue shirt turned a funny dark color.

"What's that?" I asked.

He put his hand up, looked at it and said, "Blood!"

I felt myself. My hand came away red too. So we went over to Mt. Sinai Hospital and they sewed us up. We were a mess. They took fourteen stitches in my back and upper arm. I still have that scar. It's a beaut. We got home late from the hospital. I went right to bed without telling anybody what had happened. I didn't want to alarm them.

Next morning the papers reported that two thugs had attacked two youths named Hope and Jennings in the park. My mother read it and came tearing up the stairs to my bedroom. She was calling out, "Where's my boy? Where's my boy?" She used the quavering tones actresses use in a road-company *East Lynne*—bless her heart. When she saw that I was still all in one piece and that I even had my ears, she did a fast shift into a tongue-lashing because (A), I'd got in a fight, and (B), I hadn't told her about it. Mothers are wonderful people. Everybody ought to have a spare.

My brothers made up a posse to clean up the gang. But they couldn't find them.

I have another scar I got falling out of a tree. When I was about fourteen or fifteen I was working in the summertime with a line gang stringing wires for electric lights. We were clearing trees out of a place so we could string wires through a wood. They had me up the tree tying on a rope so they could pull the tree down when the boys with the axes and saws had cut part way through it. The beavers gnawing below worked so fast that the tree started to fall with me in it. I rode it down.

But it's not true my nose is the way it is as the result of having been broken in an accident. It came the way it is from the manufacturer. My brother Fred's nose is even ski-snootier than mine.

Chapter 2

B UT ENOUGH of this warming up. I was born in 1903 at Eltham
in England. Eltham is about ten miles from London's Char-
ing Cross Station. It's pronounced without the *h*. When I was
about two years old, my father and mother moved to Bristol. My
mother was the daughter of a Welsh sea captain. Her name was
Avis Townes Hope. My dad's name was William Henry Hope. In
an effort to be funny, I've sometimes cracked, "When I was born,
my mother said, 'William, get the doctor back. He's taken the
baby and left the stork.'"

The only thing I really remember about my life in England is
being clonked on the noggin by a rock. I was defending my dog
from a gang of Bristol kids. I've been leery of dog acts ever
since. The rock throwers must have been cads or they wouldn't
have flung a dornick at that small bundle of pink-and-white loveliness: Leslie Townes Hope.

That was me. I'd been named for a relative who'd been with
Chinese Gordon in the Sudan. Gordon was the British general
who fought one of Britain's little wars in China in the early

1860's. Later he was killed at Khartoum by the African tribesmen. The rescuing force was too late getting there.

My oldest brother, Ivor, remembers a lot about the Hopes in England. In fact, he seems to have complete recall about me. Shake a bottle of charged water at Ivor or rattle a few cubes of ice in a glass at him, and he's off on a reminiscent binge. He remembers in three dimensions. There are times when I think he ought to be given both a lie-detector and a saliva test. He remembers when I almost drowned while the Hopes were at Herne Bay, a watering place near Canterbury. I was pulled out from under a pier, taken to a nearby hotel, wrung out and dried. Ivor doesn't say who saved my life. He's modest. But it's all right with him if you guess that my rescuer's first name rhymes with fiver.

According to Ivor, we Hopes lived in a stone house at Eltham. It had a conservatory in back. With an Englishman's passion for privacy, my dad had encrusted the high brick wall surrounding the place with broken glass. Dad was a master stonemason and builder. He was a sporting man. He raised gamecocks and he fought them against the leading rivals. It may not seem sporting today, but it was considered so then to toss a gamecock into a barrel with a ferret to see which would win. The chicken always did. But my dad had his softer side. He was also a flower hobbyist. He specialized in chrysanthemum culture. He grew mums as big as soccer balls.

The only thing I remember about England (singlehanded) is that rock bouncing off of my noggin. Later when I went back to our old home in Bristol I went to see the street I'd lived on. I'd vaguely remembered that there was a park in back of the house. Sure enough, there it was. But I don't remember anything about a big back yard with a high fence with broken glass on top and bantam roosters.

Ivor also remembers Father teaching us to box down in our cellar, and holding out his chin at us and saying, "Hit it!" Ivor also recalls Grandpop Hope putting me up on a table and making me dance or sing or play a tune on a comb covered with tissue. Ivor says he heard me recite "The Burial of Sir John Moore" for Grandpop when I was four.

Grandpop made his living as a general contractor. He had fourteen sons and three daughters. He trained all of his sons to be subcontractors. I've already said that my dad was a master stonemason. In addition, my Uncle Fred was a steamfitter, my Uncle Sid was a carpenter, my Uncle Jack was a specialist in brickwork, Uncle Frank was a master plumber. My aunts were taught trades, too. One of them learned to be a corsetmaker, another a dressmaker. They learned the hard way, serving as apprentices.

Grandpop's youngest son, Uncle Percy, wasn't much older than my oldest brother, Ivor. In spite of his name—or perhaps because of it—Percy was a hard citizen. He'd ask us small Hopes, "Is there anybody you don't like?" If we mentioned anyone, Perc socked him on the nose.

The Hopes at Eltham not only had a house complete with conservatory and fighting cocks, we also had a basket-weave trap, or pony cart, and a pony to pull it. It was one of those vehicles you enter from the back. Somebody gave Uncle Perc and Ivor a shilling and they drove me into London in the pony cart looking for a delicacy known as "fagots and peas." A fagot looked like a long hamburger.

Tying Ginger, the pony, outside the fagot-and-peas joint, we went in. When we came out with the wrinkles out of our bellies, Ginger and the basket-weave trap had disappeared.

We started home. But unknown to us, Ginger had arrived home, dragging the trap upside down. The London police had been alerted to look for us. When they found us and took us home, my grandmother led Uncle Perc out into the stable, took down a buggy whip and let him have it. My mother begged her to let him off, but she said sternly, "Stand aside or I'll thrash you too."

Grandmother came from rugged Devonshire folk.

Another posy from Ivor's bushy corsage of memories is one of my dad perching me on the handlebars of his bicycle and pedaling off to the Crystal Palace to join the rest of the family. They were listening to a musical concert. Somewhere along the way the bicycle fell into a ditch. Dad and I arrived at the Crystal Palace covered with bandages. To my mother, the most shocking thing about the accident was the fact that between home and the Crystal Palace Dad had shaved off the mustache he'd worn for years.

Dad was not only an artist with the stone-cutting tools, he was a happy man. He loved to live it up. He was popular, and a great entertainer. He was also well read. Later, when we'd moved to Cleveland, professors from Case Institute and Western Reserve dropped in to talk history with him.

He had only one fault. It was his theory that as a result of his occupation, stone dust collected in his throat. He stopped off at pubs to sluice it out. The trouble was that once he'd washed the inside of his throat, he stopped at a few more places for something to "steady" himself. Sometimes he got so steady he couldn't move. The day he fell off the bicycle with me must have been one of those times when his throat was dusty. I was too young to know it.

I was also too young to know that while Dad made a lot of money as a stonemason-builder, he lost most of it on the horses. He got in with a fast sporty set. Then the horses and high living got into him. When he lost his bundle, he came to the United States to make a fresh start.

I don't remember my grandfather or my grandmother from those days. Grandpop had built a row of houses in Eltham. We lived in one of them. They were put together like stone battleships. Another of Grandpop's projects was building Letchworth, a town of 700 homes. Letchworth was called the Garden City of England. He was a great one for "ribbon" building. In this country we call it row-house building. He'd have had a ball in the early days of Baltimore or Philadelphia. Sometime in the 1890's,

Grandpop came to the U.S.A. and built churches in Detroit and in Cleveland. But Grandmother said she wouldn't come to America until they built a bridge across the Atlantic, so he went back home to be with her.

It wasn't until I went back to England in 1939 that I got to know him. It was the first time I'd been there since I was four. The English papers reported: "One-time shoeshine boy and ironmonger's assistant comes home." The English are supposed to be conservative and not given to exaggeration, but they hooked one there. How could I have been a shoeshine boy or ironmonger's assistant when I was only four when I left there?

I took Dolores with me. We threw a party for my relatives at a pub in Hitchin, where Grandpop was living. Forty of them showed up. After they'd had dinner they looked at me as if saying, "Get up and do something. We hear you're funny!" I got up on a little stage in the pub dining room and told a few jokes. Grandpop sat there and looked at me, deadpan. It made me nervous, so I said, "Now let's get Uncle John up here. They tell me he whistles."

"You're doing it wrong," Grandpop said. "You don't know these people. You've been a tourist. Let me do the introducing." He was ninety-six then, but on his feet he was a ball of fire— George Jessel or Alben Barkley with an English accent.

I got a kick out of him. He had so much moxie. He was still riding a bicycle. Later, when they took it away from him, he kept on ambling down to the pub for his shot of nourishment and to say hello to the boys. When he felt perky he did a clog dance. One of his eyes had started to go. His hearing was going too. He claimed that he could hear through his eyes, so I yelled into them. He said that he could hear me fine that way.

In 1943 I was playing a fighter base an hour and a half's ride from Hitchin. When I walked into the theater, they told me Grandpop was out front. I called him up on the stage. He came up the aisle, leaning on a cane. I introduced him, that audience of fliers gave him a cheer and he made a little speech. He said that it was nice to be there, that he wanted to wish them luck in their missions, that he hoped they would help bring peace to the world. Those slow words from an old gentleman leaning feebly on his cane packed quite an emotional wallop. Then he went back to his seat.

Three weeks later, when he was ninety-nine years and eleven months old, he died. I was playing Birmingham and I got a call to rush to Hitchin. I got there just in time to see him before he left us.

The second memory I'm sure I remember myself (and not something somebody told me) is an incident that happened on shipboard while crossing the Atlantic. Everybody was lined up to be vaccinated. I was only two away from getting the scratch when I decided that I didn't like it. I headed a Keystone-cop chase around the decks with everybody after me. They finally cornered me and scraped me with the scalpel. That was the way they let you have it in those days.

After it was over, my mother tried to wipe the vaccine away from my arm with her hand. She must have had a cut on her thumb; some of that vaccine must have gotten into it. Anyhow, she had a vaccination scar on her thumb which she carried to her grave.

If I had known the things that were waiting for me once I'd

passed through Quarantine at Ellis Island, I'd have been more scared than I was of the doctor who jabbed my arm. It's a good thing nobody stepped up to young Master Leslie Townes Hope and told him about a place called Hollywood and a street called Broadway, and informed him that when he grew up his voice and his ski snoot would go out over the air with no wires to carry them. These things were tough enough to wrestle with when they did come along.

Chapter 3

Looking back at my Cleveland boyhood, I know now that it was grim going. But nobody told us Hopes it was grim. We just thought that's the way things were. We had fun with what we had. We ate regularly, although sometimes when we'd eaten everything on the table, we sat there staring hungrily at each other.

We didn't live it up, but we lived breezy and we had our share of the laughs.

As a boy I spent most of my time trying to get my hands on a buck. I don't think I was any greedier than anybody else—note to certain movie and stage producers who complain that I drive a hard bargain: Down boys, down!—but it was up to all us Hopes to get in there and pitch. Dad had come over to the United States to start from scratch. It was a scratchy start, all right. In March, 1908, when the small Hopes came up out of the steerage at Ellis Island, each of us wore two suits of sandpapery underwear under two suits of clothing to save luggage space.

Things weren't much better for Dad in Cleveland than they'd been in England. Occasionally he was called upon to go to New York to put a rose window in a church—but the skilled stone-cutting he knew how to do was going out. Jobs were hard to find. At times he was so discouraged he acted as if he were thinking of giving up stonecutting and becoming a tester for a distillery.

Mom nursed him and fed him chicken broth when he came out of his periods of backsliding. In his defense, he had a lot of friends who invited him to have a friendly glass. In those days it was an insult to say "no" to such invitations.

Mom took up part of the slack by moving into a series of big houses and filling them with roomers. Nobody ever told the young Hopes it was up to us to take up the rest of the slack. We saw that for ourselves. I remember Dad saying, "The United States is a fine place for women and dogs. It's a poor place for horses and men." He had trouble adjusting himself to this country. I don't think he ever did.

For one thing, every time he seemed to get going, he'd have a setback. He became a partner in a cut-stone company, and he and his partner bid on a Cleveland high-school contract. The high school was to be built of flat-faced stone and embellished with two stone towers. The bid of Dad and his partner was low. They got the job. Unfortunately, somebody forgot to figure in the two towers. So Dad and his partner lost their shirts. This was one of the times when we moved into a bigger house so Mom could take in more roomers.

19

She not only took in roomers, she was a wizard at altering cast-off clothing and making it fit her next smallest son. Each garment went right down the line. She kept us fully clothed and we usually looked clean. Washing, ironing and cooking were the story of her life. When we were kids we used to fight for a turn washing and drying the dishes. But we couldn't keep up with her or make her relax. Even after we grew up and came home for a holiday, Mother would want to wash our ears, just as if we were kids again.

She had her own ideas about meeting the family's obligations. She paid the butcher's bill when it came due, even if it meant walking through snow and sleet to do it. One of her blackest times was when she left her purse in a phone booth. It had eighty bucks in it. That eighty bucks was all the rent her roomers had paid her that week. She sent my brother Jack to look for it. While he was gone she prayed. Jack came back with the purse, but it was empty. Somebody had scooped it out and left it there. That was a rough blow. But no matter how rough things were, she clung to her standards, and they were higher than ours. All we cared about was getting our hooks on some dough to help her out.

While I was still in short pants, Whitey Jennings and I were the whiz kids of the Alhambra Pool Palace. My specialty was three-cushion billiards. Whitey was a pool flash. Sometimes we even hustled the hustlers. A hustler was a sharpshooter who walked into a poolroom and asked, "Anyone want to bet a couple of dollars?" If he got you interested, he'd throw a couple of games to you. When you were puffed with pride, he'd raise the bets, turn on his real game and knock you off. Whitey and I weren't hot enough to take on all of the visiting pro hustlers, but we did real good with the semipro locals.

My oldest brother, Ivor, says that I came home one day with eighty-five bucks clutched in my fist, and when my mother asked me, "How did you get that?" I told her, "I won it at the Alhambra." According to Ivor, she handed this loot to him and said,

"Give it back to those Les won it from. It's tainted." Ivor says that I met him down at the corner and we split it. I hate to spoil that one for Ivor, but nobody had that kind of money around the Alhambra. We played for a dollar or two dollars, *if* we thought we had a sure thing. But Mother could be tolerant too. When my Aunt Lou said to her, "I saw Les standing in front of the Alhambra Poolroom. I don't like that," Mom said, "Les is down there finding himself; he'll work out all right." It never occurred to her that when I found myself I might not like my type.

Whitey and I were always prospecting around for ways to raise pocket money. The richest pay streak we hit were the picnic foot races. We were pretty good runners. Few kids our age could outfoot us. We'd look through the papers to find out what organizations or industrial outfits were having their picnics, and where.

Sometimes there'd be a picnic at Luna Park and another at Euclid Beach the same day. We couldn't be at both places at once, but we figured a way to lick the problem. If the grocers were having their picnic at Luna Park, we called up a number of the grocers-picnic committee and asked, "What time are you having your foot-racing events?"

The fellow might say, "Two-thirty. Why?"

"We're from the Cleveland *Press*," we'd say. "We wanted to take some photos. But two-thirty is too late."

"What time would you like the foot races to be put on?" he'd ask.

We'd tell him, "If you put them on at two o'clock, we'll send our cameraman out."

"Sure," he'd say. "Fine. Glad to have you."

Then we called the organization which was holding the competing picnic at Euclid Beach and arrange to have the races there postponed until three-thirty. When we arrived at Luna, the fellow in charge of the program would be waiting for the cameraman, but Whitey and I'd pressure him into starting the races without a photographer. "Let's get them over," we'd say. "We want to go swimming." So after a while he'd say, "O.K. We can't wait for that photographer all day."

Next we'd find out who was to start the races. Then we'd ask him, "How do you do your starting?"

"How does anybody start races?" he'd say. "On your mark, get set, go, of course."

When we'd caught his rhythm and were familiar with the interval between his "get set" and his "go," we started in that interval. That way we could count on a two-yard lead. With such a start, even Charlie Paddock couldn't have caught us. In a college AAU meet they'd have called us back. Not at a picnic. They didn't care. They were smoking fat cigars and drinking beer. Nobody was technical. The first prize was fifteen dollars; the second ten. Whitey and I usually won first and second. Then we hurried out to Euclid Beach and knocked off the same prizes there. No one ever believed more in the beneficial results of taking part in athletics than we did.

Our No. 1 rival was a boy named Henry Thomas. Henry was a fine athlete who also played the picnic foot-racing circuit. He was faster than we and was getting too many prizes. So we took steps. Someone had told us that the motto of the Olympic coach, Mike Murphy, was: "A man who won't be beat can't be beat." We didn't want to let Mike Murphy down. I bumped Henry at the start and Whitey bumped him at fifty yards.

Whitey and I also dug starting holes. None of the other sprinters did that. They weren't sure it was ethical. They accepted bumping, but they thought starting holes a prostitution of sport. This is the kind of thing which comes back to me when I nudge my mind and dig down into it under the layers of fat.

Saturday mornings one lucky boy in our family was chosen to go shopping downtown with Mom. The call would go to the son who was in favor that day. Mom would take a reading to see how many Oak Leaf Clusters we had on our Good Conduct

Medal for the week—if she could find a Good Conduct Medal in the whole tribe of us. She'd buy lunch for the one she'd taken along, at the Bailey Company, a big Cleveland department store. After lunch, Mom and her youthful escort spooned up a gooey ice-cream sundae, then took the Cedar Avenue streetcar home. It was a kick to go with her. I still can't forget how she lugged her market basket around to the different stalls, to save pennies for us.

My first day in school in Cleveland the other kids asked me, "What's your name?" When I said "Les Hope," they switched it to Hopeless. It got to be quite a rib and caused some scuffling and a few bloody ski-snoots for me. I'd gone to school dressed in an Eton jacket and a stiff, white, turned-down collar. This didn't help matters. I was quite a sight coming home from school with my book in one hand and two front teeth in the other.

Uncle Frank and Uncle Fred were already living in Cleveland when we got there, so my two older brothers went to stay with Uncle Frank. The rest of us moved in on Uncle Fred and his wife, Aunt Alice. Her small son, Francis, used to complain, "Those Johnny Bulls are wearing all my clothes." When he went out on Sunday he wore a coat, a little red coat with a velvet collar. I thought it was real snazzy and I insisted that he let me wear it instead. But first I had to fight him for it.

Mom scouted around for a house for us. The first place we lived by ourselves was Standiforth Court. We were always on the move. We lived at 2029 Euclid. After that we moved behind the Cleveland Express barns. They weren't trolley barns. Express in those days meant Adams Express or Wells-Fargo vans, and horses to pull them. It was a long walk between the barns and our house. And if we got home after dark, it was scary. If we were barefoot, we stubbed our toes or got stone bruises in the darkness. I went barefoot a lot when I was a kid. I looked forward to taking off my shoes and feeling the cool mud under my feet and the dust squirting between my toes.

Next we lived at 1925 East 105th, then at 1913, then at 2029—

all on Euclid. We didn't move very far, only to bigger houses which had more rooms for roomers. I remember one of those roomers, a Mrs. Florence Lethridge. She was a friend of Mom's who'd come from England to live with us for a while. She was about twenty-five, and I had a crush on her. She'd been in show business and smoked Sweet Caporals. So she seemed attractive and sophisticated to me. Girls my own age didn't bother me then. That's because I hadn't found out they were girls.

Mom gave our ears a scrubbing on Sunday mornings—till I was ten years old I didn't know whether I was a boy or a kitchen sink—and after making sure we were clean and uncomfortably dressed, she sent us off to Sunday school at the Euclid Avenue Presbyterian—a church Dad had helped build. We had to go until we got a medal for perfect attendance before she let us off the hook. We couldn't stop along the way and skate, either. When we went by Wade Park and looked at the kids ice skating, we drooled. The white flag was up and they'd be out there cutting fancy figures, but we Hopes had to truck on down to church.

Although we used to get dressed up on Sunday, we still had to have ice in the icebox and there was no Sunday delivery. One of us had to go get it. There was always a contest to see who'd go. For one thing, it took the curse off of having on your Sunday clothes. For another, my mother gave whoever got it an extra piece of lemon pie. The lucky one would go up Frank Street, all the way up the hill with the wagon, get fifty pounds or maybe a hundred, bring it back and put it in the box.

In those days Dad's figure varied from medium stout to happy stout. He was a five-tenner. He weighed a hundred and ninety. Mom was a little woman, five or five-one. She had dark eyes, and a soft voice. Only it wasn't so soft when she sent us out to cut switches for her to use on us. But there came a time when she told each of us in turn, "You're too big to whip now; I'll never do it again."

Dad wasn't much for disciplining us. He didn't touch us until

24

things got tough. But when he made a move there was action. He'd take off his belt and salt us good. My father taught me if you do something wrong, life can be painful. At the same time, I learned that a woodshed can be drafty.

A haircut then didn't cost as much as it does now. But even two bits was worth saving when multiplied by seven. So Dad cut our hair. He followed a system of his own. He lined three or four of us up at a time and kept his scissors hot. He left a high-water mark on our necks, but there was no point in squawking. We just took it and disliked it. Afterward our hair jutted out above our necks until we looked like Dutch boys. Some of our unkind friends called our hairdos "suicide leaps."

With the exception of Ivor, there wasn't a kid in our family who didn't give Mom some kind of worry. You'd never know we'd come from England—we didn't have much British self-control and reticence. When my brother Jack got mad, he walked out of the house and didn't come back for days. It worried Mom to death and she'd send me to look for him. Not that he headed straight for an opium den. I usually found him holed up at the Y.M.C.A. Jack was a member of the Y, and they were lenient with their credit to him. Nevertheless, when he paid for a night's lodging out of paper-selling earnings, it made his financial structure shake like a tuning fork.

Through Mom, we had Welsh blood in us. She was a great singer of Welsh songs. The annual Cleveland Welsh picnic at Euclid Beach was a must for the Hopes. All of us had to appear there and sing it up with the Welshmen. I can still hear my mother's voice giving out, *"Till the sands of the desert grow cold."* She was just great. Later on, when I was in vaudeville, I joked about the singing Hopes. "We had to sing in our house," I said. "We didn't have any lock on our bathroom door."

An extra pint or two of Mom's Welsh blood must have filtered into me, because if there was one thing I could do, it was sing. I was the pet of Miss Bailey, my singing teacher. Singing was far and away my best subject in school. I'd look at an arithmetic book and dare it to teach me anything, but singing was my pigeon. I wouldn't say I was smart in any other subject.

I didn't make college until I played a Harvard man in *Son of Paleface*. Even in this movie version of a college, Latin was Greek to me. So was Greek. In the film I was voted the Man Most Likely to Remain. I wasn't as lucky as Phil Harris, who was graduated from U.S.C. (University of Southern Comfort). Most people go four years. Phil stayed for a fifth. It made his mouth very dry.

I've always been the restless type, the kind who gets nervous staying in one place. My feet began to itch early in life. I couldn't roam far enough in the daytime, so I walked in my sleep. Once I walked downstairs at two in the morning and strolled out of doors wearing a nightshirt that came midway down my hips. It was shorter than the nighties the gals wear today (known as "shorties"), so I must have been quite sexy in a minor way.

Still asleep, I walked two blocks and a half to the corner of 105th and Euclid and rapped on a drugstore door. What I had on my mind I don't know. Maybe I dreamed I was having an affair with a double-dip sundae. A policeman recognized me, covered me with his raincoat and led me home. I woke up under his raincoat. Cops had taken me home before that as a result of forays, but this was the first time I was ever grateful to one for doing it.

Mom tried to cure me of sleepwalking by tying one end of a rope around my leg and the other end to one of my brother Jack's legs. It was her theory that if I rambled, it would wake him. It was O.K. as a theory but Jack was unpleasant about being pulled out of a deep sleep and finding himself being towed around the bedroom floor like a Christmas toy on a string.

Ropes were always getting mixed up with my sleep. Jack and I slept on the third floor. My pal Whitey had a paper route with me. Whitey talked me into knotting a rope around my foot and dangling the rest of it from the window, so he could yank it and wake me on cold, dank mornings when all I wanted to do was burrow under the covers and sleep in.

I tried so many different ways of raising a dollar Horatio Alger could have used me for a technical expert. I don't remember whether the paper route was my first job or my tenth. Any job that needed a strong back and a weak mind was where you'd find young Les Hope, pointing the profit motive like a bird dog trying out his nose for distance.

At one point I sold papers on one of the corners of 102nd and Euclid. Three of my brothers had stands on the other corners. I had the Southwest Grocery Store corner, Jack had the Cleveland Trust Company corner, Sid had the Marshall Drugstore corner, Fred the Standard Drugstore corner.

I had one regular customer whose name I didn't know; all I knew was that he snapped his face open and shut like a wrinkled old coin purse. Not that he talked often. I sold him his paper every night when he went home from downtown in a chauffeur-driven brougham automobile. But we weren't chatty about it. We made our deal with gestures on my part and grunts on his. I'd hand him his paper and he'd hand me two cents. One night he gave me a dime. I told him I was fresh out of pennies, but he didn't say, "Keep the change. Pay me tomorrow." It was my rush hour, but I said, "I'll run and get your change," and I hotfooted it into the grocery store on my corner.

It was one of those stores with the cashier in the rear and the change going back and forth in little baskets whipping along on overhead wires. When I came back, my customer said, "Young man, I'm going to give you some advice. If you want to be a success in business, trust nobody. Never give credit and always keep change on hand. That way you won't miss any customers while you're going for it."

I was turning that over in my mind when a streetcar inspector asked me, "Do you know who that was?"

I said, "No."

"He is only the richest man in the world," the inspector said. "That's John D. Rockefeller, Senior." He was living in Forest Hill, just outside of Cleveland. There have been times since when I wish I had taken his advice.

Among other things I did, I pulled taffy at a taffy store, Humphrey's, at 105th and Euclid. It was done by hand in those days. You'd get a big loop of the stuff and throw it around a hook and pull it. At twelve I was a delivery boy for Heisey's Bakery. I attribute never having been nominated for a motion picture Academy Award to the fact that I put too much acting into that job and it burned me out. I delivered packages in well-to-do residential sections, where the citizens sat around asking themselves, "What do you suppose the poor are doing on a day like this?"

I'd go up to a door, deliver cookies, bakery goods, or whatever, then I'd say, "Did I have a tough time finding this house! I spent all my carfare looking for it."

The lady of the house asked, "How are you going to get back?" and I said wearily, "Don't worry about me. I'll walk."

"You can't do that!" she'd say. "My goodness!" Then she'd give me ten or twenty cents for carfare back to Heisey's Bakery.

I was knocking over quite a stack until I got absent-minded and pulled my exhaustion scene twice at the same house. The housewife called Heisey on the phone and ratted on me. When Heisey discovered that I was making more than he was, he suggested that I submit my resignation. "O.K., Mr. Heisey," I said, cuttingly, "if you feel that way about it."

During lean times I bootlegged my way into the Western Reserve or Case football games disguised as a lump under a football player's blanket. I remember going to League Park with my brothers to watch Tris Speaker or Napoleon Lajoie play for the Indians. If we were stopped by an overzealous ticket taker, we used a knothole.

One thing we could do free was go swimming down on the

lake front. I understand that's been fancied up now. The boys wear bathing suits.

When I was thirteen, I had a job in a flower stand at Luna Park. Luna was an amusement place with roller coasters and love tunnels. That flower stand had a tie-in with one of the games built around tossing celluloid balls into a hole; three balls for a dime. If you tossed one in, you won a flower; if you sank two, you took home half a dozen; if you bull's-eyed three, they gave you the whole stand.

My job was selling balls and handing out flowers. I seldom had to hand out more than one. Somehow those holes were a little snug for the celluloid balls.

I also worked as a drugstore delivery boy and as a soda jerk. When I grew a little older—in my late teens—I was a shoe hustler. I pushed shoes in the shoe department of Wm. Taylor Sons and Co. department store. They'd give shoe salesmen a "premium" if they sold a certain hard-to-move style they had in stock. We were supposed to gain the confidence of a customer, then sell him those boots. It was good training. There's still a premium for selling an old routine to a TV sponsor.

I can't recall what came between the Taylors and me. Something did. The Taylors still remember it. When I went back to Cleveland last October to do a TV show, the Taylors hung signs in their windows. Those signs said:

WELCOME BOB HOPE. ALL IS FORGIVEN

When I was eighteen, I went to work nights for the Chandler Motor Car Company. My job was filling out stock orders in the service department. The foreman, named Whitehouse, was a baritone singer. It wasn't long before we held a men's-room audition and assembled a quartet of service-department employees. We'd grudgingly stop singing barbershop long enough to fill a few orders. There was a boom on, zillions of Chandlers were selling, and life was a fat and sassy affair. I guess it was sassy of us to record our singing on the day manager's dictating machine, then stand and listen to ourselves, entranced.

We did several numbers this way. But we made a mistake. One night, after admiring our voices, we forgot to break the record. Next morning, when the day manager switched on his machine to begin his "Dear Sir: Yours of the sixteenth received and contents noted," he not only found himself listening to a quartet he didn't know he had, but he heard a few remarks about what a jerk he was.

Somehow, a coolness arose between us. That was the end of my association with the Chandler Motor Car Company. Afterward, I got so I could kid about being fired from a job. I had a joke about the manager of a theater who told me I was "going places." "After the first show I did for him," I said, "he stood out in the alley and pointed out those places."

In addition to our paper route, Whitey and I worked up a chirp routine. Whitey had a good voice, but I was something special, a combination soprano-tenor who knew no range limit. We sang for kicks around the neighborhood and down at the corner after supper when the arc lights hissed and sputtered over our heads. When we sang in front of the apartment buildings on 101st street—a classier residential neighborhood than ours—the cliff dwellers there threw coins down at us. It was probably a bribe to get us to go away, but we didn't know that. We just stood there with our eyes shut and our mouths open, happily singing "Let Me Call You Sweetheart"; "Sweet Adeline"; "Dear Old Girl"; and "Back Home Again in Indiana."

We also cashed in on our singing in another way. We stood outside of Pete Schmidt's Beer Garden singing, then shoved the smallest member of our gang over the fence to pass his cap. If Schmidt was feeling mellow or if business was rushing, he walked outside and threw us a quarter himself.

Sometimes we took one of the nickels flung at us from an apartment and blew it on sitting in a nickelodeon and worshiping Doug Fairbanks. Doug was our boy. We even tried to grin like him. The way I did it, little girls yelled for their mammas when I smiled at them.

For an hour or two after a Doug Fairbanks picture, I *was* Doug. Inspired by his gymnastics, Whitey and I jumped from the top of the two-story-high Alhambra Theater building. We used a delivery-wagon umbrella as a parachute. Fortunately, we were loose-jointed physically as well as mentally, and we landed in a pile of sand. Aside from having our teeth jarred, we weren't hurt. In addition we had another big deal on behind the theater. We had a rope hung from the limb of a tree and we'd jump off one side of a big barn, fly through the air and land on another barn on the other side, Doug-style.

I went for Wally Reid too. Man, he was it. He used to jump into his low-cut speedster with the top down, then stop his car and jump out. I tried it with a Model-T one day and it was such a long way to the ground, I almost broke my leg.

Before I sign off on the crazy things Whitey and I used to do, we were great at hopping freights. The trains ran about three or four blocks from my house, so we'd run up there and climb on and ride a few blocks, then get off. The habit grew on us. Before long we were riding all the way to Willoughby, about twenty miles. Then we rode back. Finally, we rattled as far as Ashtabula, which was fifty miles away.

We didn't ride the brake rods. We sat on top of the cars or in a coal-car gondola. We were a tremendous worry to our mothers because two kids about twelve or fourteen years old flying around were bound to have a lot of close calls jumping on and off.

Once we went out to Ashtabula wearing shirts, pants, and tennis shoes. Ashtabula had a big train yard. The Twentieth Century came through there and stopped. So Whitey said, "Why don't we ride the blind back on the Twentieth Century?"

The blind was the car right behind the engine. It's also called the blind baggage. You can crawl into the space that separates the blind from the combination water and coal tender. We edged over near the track and Whitey, who was fearless—I was the coward of the twosome—waited until the train got in. When everything was clear, we ran alongside, jumped on, the engine snorted and we were gone.

One of the things about that space between the two cars is that it widens when the engine's pulling and narrows when it's stopping. The engineer picked up water on the run going back through Willoughby and we were drenched, but the wind of the train's rapid movement dried us in about three minutes.

The train began to slow down about ten miles out of Cleveland, so we thought we'd better get ready to jump off. When the space opened up I got out, but when Whitey started to come out it closed on his knee. He screamed horribly, frightening me to death.

He groaned, "My knee, my God, my knee!" and fell backward. I held onto him and said, "How is it?" And he said, "I don't know. I think my kneecap is crushed." I thought, *Well, we're going to stop at 105th Street and I'll get off and get the station master.*

I wasn't too large at that time, but when we stopped I got off and took Whitey over my shoulder, stumbled over to the side of the tracks, and laid him down. One of his aunts lived five blocks from the station and I ran all the way to her candy store on St. Claire Avenue and said, "Whitey's been hurt; he's crushed his knee. He's over there by the tracks at the station. Good-bye."

When I ran out I ran home instead of back to Whitey, I was so scared.

Luckily the station master noticed something lying beside the track and they picked Whitey up and took him to the hospital. They put him back together in one piece and eventually he joined the gang on the corner once more. He was even a flash foot racer.

But the next day I was still so scared that I just went around saying, "Whitey's dead. He's dead."

I've never been that frightened before or since. I was terrified with the panicky fear that grabs you when you're small and shakes you like a dog shaking a bone. It can only happen to you like that before you grow up and learn to pretend you're not scared when your insides quiver with fright.

Whitey and I were members of the Fairmount gang. There was also a gang called the Cornell gang. Its members lived on Ford Drive. One of them was John McClain, who is now a columnist and critic for the New York *Journal-American*. We used to have gang fights, using sticks for spears and swords. One day the Cornells brought their grandfather's Civil War flags with them but we were unimpressed and we chased them two miles and took their flags away. I remember when we hit Johnny Mc-Clain over the head and took his flag, he cried. I kept those flags for quite a while. They made wonderful souvenirs, until various fathers came around and were nasty about getting them back. It seemed that they were real battle flags.

Cut now to twenty-five years later. I'm sitting with Dolores in the old Hollywood Restaurant, run by Joe Moss on Broadway. John McClain is there too. At the next table a man is using obscene language. I turn to him and say, "Watch your language, Buddy. We have a lady here."

When he stands up he's a huge, ape-like character, and he asks, "Whadda ya gonna do about it?"

He's a little large for me so John McClain stands up too and says, "Sit down, Buddy."

The guy takes a look at John, who's six-two and solid. Then he sits down. I thought it was pretty nice of a guy we used to lick.

One job Whitey and I had when I was a kid was delivery boy at the Standard Drug Store. We worked there at Christmas time when there were a lot of deliveries to make. Whitey and I were stationed in the basement where the store kept its stock. When people bought stuff we made it up into packages. We'd yell up the dumbwaiter to the fellow at the soda fountain, "Send down a chocolate sundae." Or we'd sing up the dumbwaiter and it bothered him so much he finally sent a sundae down to keep us quiet.

If we had a little spare time we had toilet paper fights. The store had hundreds of rolls down there. Some of it was imported from Japan and was real fancy. It made no difference to us. It was just ammunition. One day when we were pelting each other, some of it had come loose and was flying around the place. The manager walked down the steps. That finished the fight and our jobs too.

Chapter 4

EVEN BEFORE THAT money tossed at me from apartment-house windows, Charlie Chaplin imitations had made me show-business conscious. I'd put on my Chaplin make-up and walk duck-legged down to the corner past the fire-house. I twirled a rattan cane and wore flapping oversize, battered shoes. Amateur Charlie Chaplin contests had broken out in the country's theaters like a rash. I was so good at it that I was persuaded to enter a contest at Luna Park. To make sure I won, my brothers rounded up all the neighborhood kids and took them along to applaud. The man running the contest held his hand over the head of first one contestant, then another; then he cocked his ears for the volume of acclaim. When he held his hand over my head, the noise sounded like Indians screeching around a wagon train. The result was the No. 1 prize, a new cooking stove for Mom.

Thinking of pocket money brings still another memory. This one has chicken feathers, sweetbreads, and a cute little trick named Mildred Rosequist mixed up in it. My brother Fred, who was and is a genius at hustling a buck, ran a butchershop in a stall he leased in the Center Market. When I was seventeen and was beginning to have rolling eyeballs over curvy bits of femininity, Fred offered me and another pal of mine, Johnny Gibbons, stepping-out money if we'd pick and clean chickens for him. So Friday nights we dipped his chickens into boiling-hot water, then plucked and disemboweled them.

One great thing about working for Fred in the meat market was the chance it gave Johnny and me to practice pugilism. At noon we'd go out in the backyard and spar a couple of rounds. We couldn't decide whether we were going to replace Benny Leonard or Vernon Castle. To make sure, we'd practice dance steps between each round. No wonder Fred wondered why we were dead all afternoon.

Fred's stand was one of fifty or more in a building that looked like a giant Quonset hut. The market housed vegetable, meat and fruit stalls. The butchers in the market liked music, so they hired a band and built a stage for it over the stalls. The band was a string-swing outfit with a couple of saxes. They urged Fred and me to get up and swing with the band, but if we wandered off key, the butchers banged the refrigerator pipes with their cleavers in anguished protest.

Working for Fred wasn't all dancing, boxing and singing on a platform above the stalls. Nature study was involved, too. During one rush hour Fred tossed me a key and said, "Run down to the locker in the basement and bring me up a hind quarter of beef."

I galloped down, found the locker and was reaching up to lift a hind quarter of beef from its hook when I felt something fuzzy on my shoulder. Turning, I found myself staring into the face of a small animal. He looked as if he hated everybody. I don't remember whether his eyes were red or not. All I knew was it seemed to have nine of them.

I ran upstairs yelling. The butchers and customers were thinking of throwing a net over me and sending for a man in the little white coat to take me away, when they found out what had thrown me into such a panic. The butchers had chipped in, had bought a ferret, and had put him in the basement to keep down the rats. All I can say is, if you've never met a ferret socially, you've missed nothing.

"Imagine you being scared of a little animal like that!" Fred said to me. "He doesn't take up much room."

"It's not only overcrowded down there," I said, "but he thinks I'm a rat. Get yourself a lion tamer with a pistol full of blanks, a kitchen chair and a whip to bring up your beef for you."

I was paid on Saturday nights. If I didn't think Fred had paid me enough, I wrapped up some sweetbreads and took them over to my sweetheart, Mildred Rosequist. She cooked them and we had a feast. It was a chivalrous gesture, if I do say so myself. After all, how many fellows bring sweetbreads to their girls today?

Fred had a diabolical way of embarrassing me before my girl on Saturday nights. About seven-thirty Mildred would come over to the market to wait for me. I'd be trying to talk her into a session of watching the moonlight on the lake when Fred would ask in conversational tones, "Les, would you mind taking the chicken guts downstairs?"

To say that this upset Mildred (and also my plans for a late date) is putting it mildly. Somehow, it didn't seem to fit in with romance, and it would have been a pleasure to boil, pluck, and disembowel Fred too.

I'll never forget the first time Mildred and I kissed. She didn't really mean to kiss me. I tricked her into it. We were drinking from the same fountain and I turned the water off. She was wearing braces and I was wearing braces. When we kissed our braces locked. After that we went everywhere together.

Mildred was tall, blonde, willowy, graceful, and a slick dancer. I thought she was beautiful. She looked as if she'd done her hair with an egg beater. But I loved it that way. Girls then wore their hair puffed out on each side and they stuffed those puffs with wads of false hair they called "rats." The resulting bulges were known as "cootie garages." They looked as if they'd stopped at a filling station and said to the man, "I'll take thirty-five pounds of air in my head."

Thinking of Mildred brings back the first pass I made at show business. More than anything else, my story is the story of show business, especially vaudeville and tab shows. Tab shows were miniature musical comedies which traveled around the country —"tab" being short for tabloid musical comedy.

I took some of the money I earned and tried to improve my dancing by taking lessons from a colored man named King Rastus Brown on Central Avenue. He did a machine-gun routine with a cane that was a honey. He'd point his cane at the audience and make a rapid rat-tat-tat with his feet. After working with him for a while, I went in for amateur nights, hoping to pick up a first prize of ten dollars or a second prize of five dollars. I did all right, except when my teacher was one of the entries. I finished second then.

I also took dancing lessons from an old vaudeville hoofer named Johnny Root. When I was nineteen, Johnny Root went off to California for his health and let me take over his dancing classes. I remember the cards I had printed: LESLIE HOPE WILL TEACH YOU HOW TO DANCE—Clog, Soft-Shoe, Waltz-Clog, Buck and Wing, and Eccentric.

The upshot was the last year that I worked for Fred at the butcher stand I wasn't much use to him Saturday nights—the only night the stand was open. I was torn between two different kinds of ham.

At seven o'clock I put on my derby, snapped its curling brim into place with my forefinger, and announced in superior tones, "I have an appointment with my public." Then I'd saunter off to play a vaudeville date, with Mildred under one arm and my music under the other.

Mildred and I had worked up a dance act and we played a few dates at such places as the Superior Theater. We'd make seven or eight bucks and I split it with her. "This is a little dance we learned in the living room," I'd tell the audience. Then we'd do that one, and I'd say, "This is a little dance we learned in the kitchen." Then we'd do that. We ended with, "This is a dance we learned in the parlor." The parlor dance was a buck dance. We saved it for last because it was our hardest and it left us exhausted.

That seven or eight bucks a performance was heady stuff. The applause went to my head even faster. I decided that the stage was my dish. Once I decided that, I was a pushover for it. I'd gone to Fairmount Grammar School, to Fairmount Junior High, then to East High. After a year and a half at East High I quit.

I'm proud of my state. Ohio has a lot of schools. I know. I avoided most of them. I kid a little now about my leaving Cleveland. I say, "My mother wanted me to go to Ohio State. My father just wanted me to go."

I planned to take Mildred with me when I left Cleveland to become Mr. Marvelous of the Footlights. But Mildred's mother was small-minded about it. (Another way of putting it is to say that Mildred's mother got the notion that I wasn't the divinity-student type and she refused to trust her daughter on theatrical tours with me.) So before long I gave Mildred up.

Mildred's mother said that even if we got out-of-town bookings—which she seriously doubted—her daughter couldn't go on tour with me unchaperoned. I should never have let her see the act, but she did, and she hid Mildred until she was sure I was out of town. Having lost one partner, I picked up another one, Lloyd Durbin, a kid I'd known around 105th and Euclid.

When we were breaking in our act around and about in Cleveland, the boys from the pool room came over to the St. Claire Theater to catch us. As I walked out, everybody in the first two rows pulled out newspapers and began to read. I was fearless about it. I went down, tore the newspapers from their hands and told the audience not to mind my needlers since, after all, they were fugitives from the morning police line-up.

Lloyd and I were lucky to wangle a booking into the Bandbox Theater in Cleveland. There we met Fatty Arbuckle, who was trying a comeback in a small revue. One of the local agents, Norman Kendall, had suggested us to the manager of the Bandbox. Norman wanted some cheaper and leaner talent, because Fatty was fat both physically and financially. So Lloyd and I stepped cockily into the spot on our Haney plates. Any tap dancer will know what I mean when I say that we had Haney plates screwed into the toes of our shoes.

Lloyd and I also did a soft-shoe and a buck-and-wing dance in the revue. Then we sang Sweet Georgia Brown and went into our big number, which was a comedy Egyptian dance. Later, I was to do the same dance with Hal LeRoy on the first Frigidaire television show. The Egyptian flavor was all in pantomime. We didn't wear Egyptian costumes. We wore brown derbies. We pretended to go to a well near the Nile, dip some water in a derby and bring it back. The gag was that afterward we poured actual water out of the derby. It was real crazy and it fetched a boff.

Before Fatty left Cleveland, he introduced us to Fred Hurley and asked him to "do something" for us. Fred produced tab shows, and he put us in one. Our tab bore the cheery title "Hurley's Jolly Follies."

Frank Maley, from Alliance, Ohio, managed the Jolly Follies. He was the blackface comic, the manager of the show, and ran things. He'd take off his blackface real quick and collect the money at the box office, and he was in charge of scenery. He was

40

not only efficient, he was a real guy. His wife, a beautiful blonde girl, was the show's piano player. I think her name was Lillian. She played piano in the pit.

Hurley was the tycoon, the Mr. Big. He had several shows out on the road. He stayed back home, being an executive.

The Jolly Follies opened in East Palestine, Ohio. From there we went into Ottawa, Ohio. Being in a tab show in the 1920's was an education in show-business—not a higher education, but a practical one. Tabs were a slightly better grade than burlesque. For one thing, they weren't so smutty. They lasted an hour and a half and fell into two classifications: there were script tabs with a plot, and bit tabs. A bit tab was a lot of blackouts strung together.

Blackouts were a famous device in revues and vaudeville. Right on the punch line of a sketch the stage lights were switched off to accent the end of a skit. The curtain was lowered during the blackout, then went up on another scene. It was the equivalent of a dissolve in a motion picture.

We traveled by bus. The audiences were tough. So were the living conditions. We were paid off in lean bellies and laughs. We were sitting on the stage in Ottawa at five o'clock when I asked, "What time is the rehearsal?"

"We rehearse at five-thirty," the house manager said, "the butcher shop doesn't close until five-fifteen."

"What's that got to do with the rehearsal?" I asked.

"The fiddle payer works at the butcher shop," he said.

Tab shows were a special part of show business. They had a flavor all their own. There's no dollars and cents way I can measure the seasoning, the poise, the experience that being with Hurley gave me. Years later, when I went into the Broadway musical, *Roberta*, I was given the juvenile comedy lead. I went on and played it without fainting, freezing, or falling into the footlights with first-night jitters. The director, Edgar MacGregor, eyed me in surprise.

"How do you know enough to play a part like this?" he asked. I asked what seemed a natural question after the years I'd spent with Hurley: "Is this supposed to be hard?"

Getting up in front of people and doing my stuff was the most natural thing in the world after working for Hurley. You could go to dramatic schools all your life and never get any easy feeling in front of an audience. Some of the comedians who're doing all right on television today: Skelton, Jack Benny, Fred Allen, Burns and Allen and Groucho (and even a youngster like Red Buttons) are the product of similar proving grounds.

When the Jolly Follies played Orangeburg, South Carolina, the theater was equipped with a street drop that Sherman hadn't bothered to burn when he'd passed through the town looking for a shore dinner. You don't see street drops like that any more. They were roll curtains which came down with a crash at the end of an ensemble. Afterward, a single or a double act walked out in front of them and did a number. The buildings and stores on one side of an imaginary city street were painted on a street drop. Billboards were painted on them too. These billboards were reserved for advertisements by the local merchants.

The buildings painted on the drop in Orangeburg were only a few feet high. They'd been kept small to leave more room for the ads. I remember it gave me a funny feeling to turn around and see a ten-story building right behind me that only came up to my knees.

That theater had only two dressing rooms. There was one for gals and one for guys. The boys' dressing room only held six men. My partner and I weren't important enough to make it. We dressed downstairs in the coal bin after we'd cleaned it and put up a couple of tables. There was still a lot of coal dust in the air, but it didn't help since we weren't doing blackface at that time.

Hurley's Jolly Follies played a famous show circuit called Spiegelberg Time. It also played Gus Sun Time. Gus Sun is a great name in vaudeville. Everyone who's ever been in vaudeville remembers him. The Sun Circuit was smaller than the

Orpheum or the Keith Circuit, but it was important in our business. Sun paid headliners good money and he supplied talent for so many theaters that he could work an act all year. For that matter, you could stay on Sun Time for five or ten years. You wouldn't make a fortune, but you'd make a good living.

I was making forty dollars a week and sending twenty home to my mother to help out. I don't know how I lived on twenty dollars a week, but I did it. For one thing, the dollar went a long way in those days. It goes a long way now too—all the way to

Washington, D.C.—but in those days you were allowed to feel it, see it, even use it.

Sun booked tab shows into such theaters as the Dixie in Uniontown, Pennsylvania, and the Lyric in Morgantown, West Virginia. There were never any wildly enthusiastic crowds to greet us when we arrived in a town. Our bus didn't have to pull in in a protective crouch.

Morgantown was the home of Kathleen O'Shea. Kathleen was a pretty girl who was also in the Jolly Follies. I never gave a woman a second thought in those days. My first one covered everything. When I sighted Kathleen, I filed Mildred Rosequist and coined a phrase for the way I felt about Kathleen. It was a phrase nobody had ever used before. "This," I said, "is different."

There may be homely dolls named Kathleen or cold types named O'Shea. If so, I've never met one. There seems to be a law that girls with such names must be pert, bright-eyed, irresistible. Chances are if Kathleen had been muddy-cheeked and thick-ankled, I wouldn't have had the run-in I had with the manager of a hotel in Bedford, Indiana.

There'd been another tab show in Bedford ahead of us the week before. This other troupe had tossed a wing-ding every night. As a result, the hotel manager was disgusted with show folk. When we arrived, he told our manager, "Keep your people quiet and let my tenants sleep, or it's out into the street for you."

I got a bad chest cold in Bedford, and Kathleen suggested that I come up to her room so she could give me some hot salve to rub on my chest. That night, after the show, I went upstairs to her room. She was just giving me the salve when there was a knock on the door. I opened it. There stood the manager, small-eyed and suspicious. He had his hands behind his back.

"What's the number of your room?" he asked.

"Two twelve," I said.

"What number's this?" he asked.

"Three-twenty-four," I said.

"Get downstairs!" he said.

"You got me wrong," I said. "I just . . ."

He pulled a gun and let it dangle by his side. Then he repeated, "Get downstairs!"

I don't remember whether I used that salve or not. Things were plenty hot the way it was.

After Bedford, we played Brazil, Indiana. We had trouble finding a place to live, because the local hotels didn't have regular accommodations for the troupe. We waited outside while our manager, Frank Maley, went inside to ask if they "took show folks." The hotel was a converted store. We could look right through the window. We could see Maley moving his lips and saying, "Do you take show people?" and the manager shaking his head and saying, "No!" as if we were social lepers.

We sneered at him through the window and then moved on to the next place.

In all fairness, that Hurley outfit was orderly. Some of them, like Gail Hood and Bud Brownie and Frank Maley, were married and had their wives with them. There were only a couple of hoofer characters who went for paper hats and noise-makers.

Next year I went out with another tab, Hurley's Smiling Eyes. The Jolly Follies had lasted only one season. That was longer than the team of Durbin and Hope had lasted. Tragedy broke up our act. During our first season together, Lloyd dropped into a restaurant in Huntington, West Virginia. He tucked away a harmless-looking wedge of coconut-cream pie. That place must have been snubbed by Duncan Hines, for Lloyd complained of pains in his stomach. We took him to a local doctor and the doc said he had food poisoning. Next day we put him on a train on a stretcher and sent him home to Cleveland in the baggage car. When we reached Cleveland, he was rushed to a hospital. They pumped him out. But it was too late. Also I think he was weakened by other illness. Anyhow he never got up alive from that hospital bed.

As Lloyd's replacement Hurley hired a boy named George Byrne from Columbus, Ohio. George was pink-cheeked and naïve. He looked like a choir boy. He was real quiet. Real Ohio. He was a smooth dancer and had a likable personality. We became good friends. We still are.

The new team of Hope and Byrne weren't together long before we asked Frank Maley if he wouldn't let us try comedy as well as dancing. We were doing all right the way we were. We were stopping the show with our dancing. In addition, I sang in the quartet and did juvenile leads and character parts. But we were ambitious. We wanted to do better.

"We have one script tab, 'The Blackface Follies,' we can put on," Maley said. "We'll find out how funny you are in that."

The Blackface Follies opened in McKeesport, Pennsylvania. Somehow, George and I got hold of a can of black grease paint (instead of burned cork) and, not knowing any better, we slathered it on. We felt real proud when Maley said, "My, you look glossy." It was an understatement. We shone like neon lights.

But after the show, when we tried to remove the stuff, it sank in instead of coming off. I've still got some of it in my veins. We stayed in the theater, working with wash basins and cold creams, until two in the morning. At one point we were thinking of using a blowtorch. After that we told Maley we thought we'd skip the blackface.

"It breaks into our sleep," we said. "We don't get home and get to bed until time for the next show."

Not all of the comedy connected with tab shows happened in the theater. During our second season we were in Braddock,

Pennsylvania. My brother Jim lived in Pittsburgh, and one night after the show I decided to go to see him. A local character who'd been hanging around the stage door—there were always such hangers-on, especially if there were girls in the show—heard me say I wanted to go. "I'll drive you," he told me. "I'm going to Pittsburgh too."

He showed up in a beautiful car and George and I got in. He took off down the main street. Presently we head a siren. He looked in the rear-vision mirror, then he began to drive like crazy. By this time he was doing fifty or sixty per down the main street.

"What's up?" I asked.

"Cops!"

He pulled into an alley and put on the brakes. The car rolled down into a gulley. Then he ran into the bushes, leaving George and me standing there. The cops got out, walked up to us and said, "Put up your hands!"

"Well—" I said.

"Shut up," they said. "You're in a stolen car."

Cut now to the Braddock jail. I'm saying to the copper, "We're playing the theater here. Ask anybody. I tell you we're playing—"

But the cop said, "Get in that cell. You can read us your clippings in the morning."

George and I stayed in the cell all night. We shared it with a wife beater. We knew he was a wife beater because he told us about it in detail. Now and then, the turnkey came in and said, "Why don't you promise to be nice, Joe? If you do, we'll let you go home."

"Nah," the wife beater said. "Da hell with da wife. Next time I fix her good."

He got on our nerves. We were afraid that he's go to sleep and dream that one of us was his wife. George and I spent the night huddled together. We swore to defend each other. We promised each other we would go down fighting to the death. We were afraid our cell mate had a piece of pipe in his pocket. In the morning, when Maley came around and identified us, we were a bedraggled pair.

It turned out that the guy who'd rolled the car into the gulley worked for a local doctor. He was a chauffeur man-of-all-work. The doctor was out of town, and the chauffeur had taken his car without telling the owner's wife. When she noticed that the car was gone, she'd reported it to the police. When the chauffeur heard the police sirens, he'd lost his head. He could have lost ours too.

Kathleen finally quit the show. She went home to Morgantown, West Virginia, and opened a dress shop. You might say that we opened it together. I helped finance her. When Hope and Byrne finally hit the big town to make it easy for fame and fortune to tag us, I pinch-hit as her New York buyer. I'd get on the phone to Morgantown and ask, "What do you need?" When she told me, I cruised up and down Seventh Avenue picking out the $10.75 and $16.75 items.

I had a vaudevillian's sense of style. "Chic" meant snappy to me. Some of those Morgantown girls must have looked unusual when they dolled up in numbers I'd selected for them. Nobody knows about this dress-buying period of my life except an elderly busybody named Crosby. I don't know how he found out. It's supposed to be a deep secret. But when I do a bad scene at Paramount he's apt to remark, "That was pretty good for a dress buyer."

Between tabs, George Byrne and I went back to Cleveland to pad our frames against another campaign on the boards with some of Mom's home-cooked food. I'm afraid we gave her plenty of anxious moments when we rehearsed our dance steps. We made the house bounce. We placed ourselves in front of a big mirror over the fireplace and clattered through our routines, watching our reflection to see if we were working smoothly together. Between rehearsals I taught myself to play "Yes, Sir, That's My Baby" on an upright piano, while George stood on top of the piano, plucking a banjo strung like a uke.

When I wasn't practicing, I'd get in my old Model T Ford and whip down there to Morgantown to see my gal every chance I got. Distance was nothing to a young coot in love. It took four or five hours to drive from Cleveland to Morgantown. I had a way to get around Pittsburgh and save about an hour. I remember flying down there with the upper half of my windshield turned down. Model T's used to have a windshield that was divided all the way across. If you wanted to look real dashing you lowered the top half.

Once I was about fifty miles out of Cleveland, hurrying to my girl, when I ran into a swarm of bees and they burrowed inside of my clothing. I pulled over to one side, ran into a farmer's barn, took off my pants and beat at my tormentors. The farmer came out of his house to see what was going on. At first he thought I was a lunatic, but when I explained that I was trying to get shut of a swarm of bees so I could see my girl, he understood.

"I've been stung when I was trying to get some honey myself from time to time," he said. So he pitched in and helped me slap at my knees and elbows.

George and I not only brushed up on our dancing, we polished our comedy lines until they sparkled—or so we thought. We worked up a joke in which George walked across the stage with a suitcase, put it down, then stepped over it. I'd ask, "How are you?"

And he'd say, "Fine; just getting over the grippe."

He'd walk across again with a woman's dress on a hanger, and I'd say, "Where you going?"

He'd say, "Down to get this filled."

Or he'd walk across with a big plank under his arm. I'd say, "Where you going?"

"To find a room," he'd say. "I've already got my board."

Then there was one where George looked down inside his

49

pants and I'd ask, "What are you doing?" and he's say, "The doctor told me to watch my stomach."

Or I'd walk out and say, "I was coming in the theater and a fellow stopped me outside and says, 'Pardon me, would you give me a dime for a cup of coffee?' and I said, 'A dime for a cup of coffee? I'm an actor.' And he said, 'Are you an actor?' and I said, 'Yes,' so he says, 'Come in and I'll buy you a cup.'"

And we sweated out a saxophone duet which could have ruined show business all by itself. Later, when I grew older and cagier, I thought of all the ways we could have cashed in with those saxophones. I'm sure we could have gotten the Buscher people, who made them, to send us a hundred dollars apiece not to play them any more.

In my two seasons with Hurley's tabs, I didn't double in brass. I did double in quartet. The quartet was Frank Maley; Gail Hood, the second comic; a guy named June Hoff and me. Gail was so deaf he couldn't hear a sour note if we sang one. When we hit a clinker, we stared at each other reproachfully as if wondering who the guilty party was in the way quartets have done ever since time began. Everybody but Gail. Not knowing that anything was wrong, he kept right on singing as happy as a cricket.

It was so funny that it fractured me. Frank Maley would come up to me afterward and say, "Okay, so it's funny. But don't ruin the number with your hyena laughing."

The next time he was even more severe. "Stop your laughing, Hope!" he said.

Finally he said, "If you don't stop your guffawing you're out of the show."

Not to laugh when somebody clinkered in the middle of "That Old Gang of Mine," and everybody but old Gail accusing each other of hitting the stale note, was one of the hardest things I've ever tried to do. But I made it. It was either that or an ad in *Variety*: "Les Hope available. Songs, Patter, and Eccentric Dancing."

In my second year with the *Smiling Eyes* company we had a

comic named Bud Browning. Bud did a hick act. The routine he used was invented by a comedian named Britt Wood, who still does it today. It was a fast monologue, and it went something like this: "This fellow from out of town stopped at a hotel and he stepped up to the manager and asked him if he had a room and bath, and the manager said, 'I can give you a room,' and this fella said, 'I asked for a room and bath!' and the manager said, 'I can give you the room but you'll have to take the bath yourself.' And right then he seen he had him."

Stuff like that.

Then Bud would go on, "I got in that elevator and they had a little light in there. It looked like fireflies caught in a bulb. I tried to cut that little old wire that held them in and I never did see so much hell in one piece of string in my life."

This kind of thing fitted right into *Over the River, Charlie* which was a melodramatic stock show we used to do. We played it straight, but with actors cast as yokels delivering corn like a Niblets factory, we got quite a few laughs out of it.

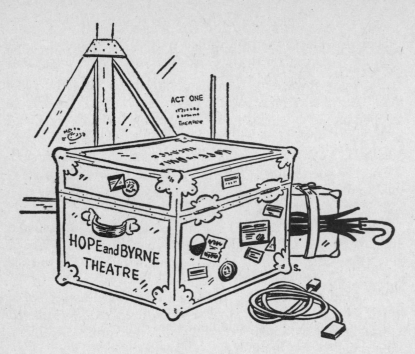

Chapter 5

AT THE END of our second season with Hurley, George and I broke away from tabs and moved into Detroit to play the State Theater. We were booked into the State at two hundred and twenty-five dollars a week, by Ted Snow, a Detroit agent. That kind of money was like a trip to the moon to us. In our second year with Hurley, we'd gotten only one hundred dollars.

George and I had made up our minds to work up an act hot enough for the big time. We wanted to be like two of vaudeville's all-time greats, Duffy and Sweeney. Sweeney's first name is Fred. I still see him around Paramount from time to time. I don't remember Duffy's first name, but they were a fabulous team. They were noted for their offbeat doings offstage as well as on.

Sometimes after their turn, they started an argument in the wings, then carried the dispute into the dressing room with them. After they'd closed the door, you could hear them yelling and screaming. Then there'd be a shot, followed by a thud and silence. When Duffy reappeared and stalked out through the stage door with a tragic look on his face, the other actors crept up to the dressing-room door and opened it, fearful of what they'd see. There'd be Sweeney taking off his make-up and whistling happily under his breath.

Every new place they played, one of them tried to get to the theater manager first.

If Sweeney won, he'd say, "Don't give Duffy any money. He drinks."

If Duffy won, vice versa. The winner would draw the whole week's pay for the act.

Show people loved Duffy and Sweeney's routine. They lay under the piano and sucked lollipops and did things nobody else had nerve enough to do. But they were too crazy for the average audience. I remember seeing them once at Loew's American in New York. They did their first show at ten o'clock in the morning. They came out with a few eggs, a frying pan and an electric toaster. They removed one of the footlight bulbs, plugged in the toaster, fried eggs on it in the pan and ate their breakfast while they did their act.

There is a famous show business story about a time when they played Birmingham, Alabama. They laid a bomb in Birmingham. The Birmingham people just didn't get them. This is no knock for Birmingham because they were over the heads of the average audience anywhere.

In Birmingham Duffy made a little speech. "I'd like to thank the audience for being so charming," he said. "To show our appreciation, Mr. Sweeney will now pass among you with a ball bat and beat your brains back in."

When the booking office in New York heard this sample of Duffy's diplomacy, they canceled the act immediately.

But to get back to Detroit, where George and I were breaking in our new act. Not only were we sure we had what the big time needed, we were so elated about our leap from one hundred to two twenty-five a week it made us dizzy. We walked around in a gold-plated dream, while we mentally spent our loot. Russ Morgan and his band were a fixture at the State. The M. C. there was Fred Stritt. During one of our rehearsals with Russ and Fred, a stagehand told us about a gambling place just across the street. We perked up our ears like a couple of not overly bright mules.

"What happens there?" we asked.

"They've got the whole box of tricks," the stagehand said. "Anything you want to play, they've got it."

Between us, George and I lost our savings before we even opened at the State. After that, we did four shows a day with the zest and bounce of zombies. The audience couldn't understand why the management had hired two performers with no personalities at all. If we seemed preoccupied, it was because we spent all of our time on stage trying to invent "winning systems." Finally we had a lucky day, got even and quit.

We stayed in Detroit for a couple of months, playing different theaters. Then a Harrisburg, Pennsylvania, agent, Ed Fishman, booked us into the Stanley in Pittsburgh along with Tol Henry and his North Carolinians. It was the custom then for a theater to hire a favorite orchestra leader and keep him around indefinitely, like Paul Ash in Chicago and Phil Spitalny in Cleveland. We got three hundred dollars at the Stanley, so we were moving.

From there we went into New York, ready, cocked, and aimed at the big time. We had even bought a new theatrical trunk. We'd had to rope our old one together to keep it all in one piece. One month we almost went broke on rope. We finally bought an H. & M. trunk. To a vaudevillian, having an H. & M. was like having "sterling" engraved on your bottom—if you were a teapot.

We also flossied ourselves up in the costume department. We bought Eton jackets and big white collars and beautiful high-waisted pants and white spats and high hats and black canes with white tips. All solid class.

Our act opened with a soft-shoe dance. We wore the high hats and spats and carried canes for this. Then we changed into a fireman outfit by taking off our high hats and putting on small, papier-mâché fireman hats. George had a hatchet and I had a length of hose with a water bulb in it. We danced real fast to "If You Knew Susie," a rapid ta-da-da-da-da tempo, while the drum-

mer rang a fire bell. At the end of this routine we squirted water from the concealed bulb at the brass section of the orchestra in the pit. It not only made an attractive finish but it had the added advantage of drowning a few musicians.

We couldn't believe it at first, but the big time proved a shifty target and we had to scurry around auditioning our act and sniffing for bookings. Keith's gave us a few tryouts at places like Keith's Flushing—the kind of tryouts for which you were paid the minimum salary so they could see your act. Then we got a job dancing with Daisy and Violet Hilton, the Siamese twins. The biggest factor in our landing that job was our wardrobes. We actually sold the act on the basis of the photographs George and I had of us in our snazzy getups. When I asked the bookers for money, I'd get twenty-five or fifty dollars more by saying, "Just look at our pictures. Why those pictures alone are worth fifty dollars more in front of any theater."

Abe Lastfogel, now head of the William Morris Agency, saw our photos and booked us on those alone. Summoning us to his office, he told us, "If you're only half as good as your pictures, you'll do."

Our act was the second spot on the bill—known as the deuce spot—then we came back later to dance with the twins. At first it was a funny sensation to dance with a Siamese twin. They danced back to back, but they were wonderful girls and it got to be very enjoyable—in an unusual sort of way. The only thing wrong was we had to do too many shows a day. The twins' uncle —he was also their manager—wouldn't give us a raise, so we finally bounced that.

Between jobs, George and I stayed at a flea-bag hotel with a generous credit policy. We picked one near the Palace Theater, in case we got a hurry call to come over and save it from financial ruin. We lived on the hotel's thirteenth floor. I don't know why any hotel has a thirteenth floor, especially a hotel populated by people who're looking for work. Most hotels don't.

George and I slept in the smallest double-bed room in hotel history. It was impossible to squeeze two beds in, but the management did it. My bed had a big lump in it. I slept on that lump for weeks before I found out it was really my agent. Agent: that's an octopus with a derby.

Vaudeville eventually sickened. Its trouble was a creeping atrophy of the box-office muscles induced by the twin viruses, talking movies and radio. This no-customer disease reminds me of a story a pal of mine, Ukie Sherin, tells about a fellow who once owned a little night club out in the San Fernando Valley just across the mountains from Hollywood. You seldom saw any people there except on week ends. Everybody wondered how it stayed open. Sometimes week-night business was so bad that the owner bought everybody a drink, then closed.

One night when he walked in there were no customers at all, so he said, "Slam the door. I'm going home."

Reaching home earlier than usual, he walked in and found his wife necking with another man. "Oh, boy!" he said. "People!" and went into the pantry and shook up a round of welcoming drinks.

Ukie tells another story I'd like to work in here, although it has nothing to do with vaudeville. Ukie's always up to date and topical. Not long ago he stopped me and asked, "Have you heard about the rabbit and the reindeer?"

"No," I said.

Ukie brightened and said, "Well, the reindeer said to the rabbit, 'What are you running for?' The rabbit said, 'Senator McCarthy is investigating everybody.' So the deer said, 'What do you care? You're a rabbit.' 'I know,' the rabbit said, 'but can I prove it?' "

However when George and I were trying to get started, there was nothing weak about vaudeville. It was a rough, tough and rugged way to earn your cakes. At one time I thought of specializing in soft-shoe dancing. I couldn't afford soles. Even with the arrival of an occasional lemon pie, baked, boxed, and mailed by Mom from Cleveland, I was the thinnest man in vaudeville. I was down to one hundred thirty pounds. I was so thin I always made sure the dog act was over before I came on stage. I wore one of those short topcoats so popular at the time. I looked like a group of loud checks walking on stilts.

In vaudeville in those days, you came out battling and you protected yourself at all times. If you didn't, the other acts flattened you. When I played the Inter-State Time in Texas later on as M.C., the Cirillo Brothers were an act on my bill. The Cirillos were four Italian boys who sang and danced. They were hot-tempered, and one night in Dallas while I was introducing them, they had a terrific row backstage. They kicked up such a commotion I couldn't make myself heard. Asking the audience to excuse me, I went backstage and said, "Sh-h-h, I'm trying to tell those people out there how lovable and attractive you are."

They subsided and I went back on. When I finished my spiel they came out, bowing and smiling sweetly. But as I introduced the next act, the racket backstage started again. When I finished the introduction, I went back once more and asked, "What's eating you, anyway?"

They broke down and told me the reason for their wrangling. The night before, one of the brothers had taken one bow more than the others.

A boy called Matty King plays dates with some of our shows now and then. He used to be part of the team of King, King and King, one of the greatest tap-dancing acts in the world.

The three Kings were Italian boys from Philadelphia. Matty was the hot-tempered one. Many years ago they were opening at the Earle in Philadelphia. They'd been working too much and were tired and irritable. It was no time for an orchestra leader to play their first number too slowly, but the leader in the Earle pit did. The Kings hissed "Faster, faster" at him and made gestures which meant the same thing, but they couldn't speed him up. So Matty slipped off one shoe and, leaning over the footlights, hit the sluggard over the head with the tap end of his shoe, putting a small but attractive dimple in his skull.

After that the music went faster. But immediately after the show the manager walked up to the Kings and said, "You three are canceled."

"Why?" Matty asked.

"You hit the leader over the head," he was told.

"Why, that's part of our act," Matty replied, thinking quickly.

The manager thought even faster. "It'll be part of your act where you're going," he said. "You're through here."

The vaudeville I knew was full of extroverts, exhibitionists and "get-a-load-of-me-I'm-a-hell-of-a-guy" characters. If one of us were lucky enough to make the big time, we had JOE DOAKES NOW PLAYING THE ORPHEUM TIME painted on our spare tire. We didn't want to keep such important news from the world.

I had a thing I used to do to express my hatred for anonymity. I'd be driving my car in Omaha, where nobody knew who I was. I'd pull up at stop signs and stand up and say to everybody within earshot, "Have you folks been to the Orpheum this week and seen Hope? He's great!" Then I'd step on the gas and drive off, pleased with my wit and my gift for publicity getting.

"Vaudeville" and "headliners" are spelled with the same number of letters. But the team of Hope and Byrne gave little thought to the fact that "heartbreak" too used the same number. Before very long we were to find that out.

Chapter 6

ONE OF THE theatrical hotels where George Byrne and I put up in 1927 was the Somerset, just off Broadway. The Somerset would carry you even if you didn't have any dough. But George and I hadn't been reduced to cuffing it. We were just about making it. What with the various reverses we'd had, we'd become a very practical team. We could play club dates and were a nice-looking team as far as wardrobe went.

There was a lot of work around. We weren't getting much of it, but it was around. Pretty soon we got lucky and sliced off a piece of it. We auditioned for and were chosen for the cast of a musical show, *The Sidewalks of New York*. It was put on by Eddie Dowling and James Hanley. Eddie's wife, Ray Dooley, was its star.

Ray Dooley came of a famous theatrical family and she had quite a bit of money of her own. One day Eddie came to a pal of mine, Monty Brice, and said, "Ray's done a very foolish thing. She's put all her money into some silly new little company called Good Humor that makes a chocolate-covered ice cream on a stick. Can you imagine that? She didn't even ask my advice."

Also in *The Sidewalks* were Ruby Keeler; Smith and Dale; Jim Thornton, an old-time vaudeville monologist; and Dick Keene, who was half of the vaudeville team of Keene and Williams. It was quite a thing for Hope and Byrne to be in such high-toned company.

The routines of Joe Smith and Charlie Dale were famous.

60

"What kind of dishes are you eating?" one would ask the other. "Now I'm eating dishes? What am I, a crocodile?" the second one would say. They're veterans now, but they're still going strong. Smith and Dale were the nucleus of the Avon Comedy Four, one of vaudeville's real great acts.

Jim Thornton used to work in a high hat and a long coat, like a Senator. He was a preacher-type monologist, a burlesque Fourth of July orator.

The show had a nice run, but George and I had trouble getting our specialties in. After the opening night they never were in. The reviews the day after opening said, "Ray Dooley has something, Ruby Keeler has something, Bob Hope has something too, but you won't notice it if you sit back about five rows."

After that we just worked one singing and dancing number with Ruby, and did a few small parts. The number we did with Ruby was in a laundry. I forget its details, but it was a song-and-dance affair. However, we weren't important enough even for that, and after eight weeks in New York, the man who handled the salaries for Dowling gave us the stare with the ax hanging on it, and we were back on the Palace beach looking for jobs.

We killed time sitting around the Somerset lobby by exchanging vaudeville stories with other variety performers. Whenever I get together with other ex-vaudevillians I still trade anecdotes with them. One of my favorites is about the vaudeville artist whose act was wrestling an alligator in a tank. For a long time bookings had been thin for him but finally he got a date in Paterson, New Jersey. He did such a turn-away business there that the house manager called up the alligator wrestler's agent to ask if he could be held over for the last half of the week.

"Certainly," the agent said. "You can have him. I don't have him booked anywhere else."

Friday night the manager called the agent again. This time he said, "I'm sorry I held your boy over. He's not giving me the same act he gave me at first. Business is falling off."

"I'll come right over," the agent said. So he hotfooted it over to Paterson from New York and watched the act. Sure enough, it was dull. No action. He went backstage to talk to the alligator wrestler.

"Charlie," he said, "you had a chance to go places here. You were big enough for the manager to hold you over. Now he complains that you're not giving him the same excitement you did in the first half of the week. He's very disappointed."

"He's disappointed!" the alligator wrestler said. "How do you think I feel? The alligator died Wednesday night."

Another one I like is about the two hoofers who were playing in the deuce spot at the Palace. They put so much whammy into their stuff they almost killed themselves doing over-the-tops and slides. After taking their one bow, they collapsed in the wings and lay there puffing and gasping. There was a burst of music as Ethel Barrymore stepped over their bodies on her way to the stage. She was no sooner on than the audience gave her a cheer and tossed flowers at her. She read a couple of lines and the applause was deafening.

One of the bushed hoofers nudged the other and said, "Listen to that, will ya? Me for crap like hers next season."

The vaudeville historian, Joe Laurie, Jr., told me one about a bird act, and it kills me whenever I think about it. Bookings were so scarce for the bird artist he'd had to break up the cages for kindling. After that, the birds just flew around above his house out in Flushing, Long Island. They didn't leave, because every once in a while he'd put his head out of his attic window and say, "Don't fly away. Just be patient. We'll get work."

Finally he got a Cleveland booking. He rushed up to the attic, leaned from the window and said to his birds, "I don't have any cages. I don't have any money, but we've got a Cleveland date. I'll hitch-hike. You fly."

He thumbed a couple of rides while the birds flew along overhead. At last he was out around Albany and was two days ahead of schedule when he heard a bicycle bell. Turning around, he saw his agent, Sam, from New York, pedaling furiously behind him.

"I've got tough news for you," Sam said. "They decided to hold over the show in Cleveland that's already there. So you won't be playing there next week. They're switching you to Baltimore."

"After I've got this far too!" the bird man said. "Oh, well, that's life." He shrugged, looked up at the birds, waved his arms southward and yelled, "Baltimore, Baltimore!"

There's another story I like. It's about an actor who used to hang around the Somerset Hotel not getting anywhere. But he met a couple of writers with good material, and the first thing he knew he was on in No. 4 at the Palace. Everybody at the Somerset said, "Let's go over and catch the first show and help put old Charlie over because he's our buddy-buddy."

So they all went over and applauded until their hands blistered and Charlie took bows and encores and was a smash. At intermission the claque said, "Let's go backstage and see old Charlie." They all went back and waited for him at the stage door. When he came out, he said, "Oh, hello fellas. Sorry, I've got to go up and see my booking agent about a long tour on the Orpheum Time," and he brushed them.

On the Orpheum Time he took himself even larger, so large that he forgot to change his writers or his material, and he started slipping. He was down to No. 2 spot when all of a sudden he got wise to himself, went back to the Somerset and looked up his old pals.

"I don't know what happened to me," he said. "I've been a louse. I was such a hit that I got the big head and I forgot to change my material and I realize my mistake and I want you fellas to forget it. I just want you to be my buddies."

"That's all right, Charlie," they said. "We know how it is. That's show business. Forget it. You're still our old buddy-buddy."

They took him back into the fold and he hung around the

Somerset swapping stories and lying about his billings like old times. Presently he met a couple of new writers, and before long he got together a greater and bigger act. He played the nabe houses and finally he was booked into the Palace once more.

His pals said, "Let's go and see old Charlie, and case his new act."

They cheered the first show until they were hoarse and helped put him over. Charlie killed the customers. Afterward the Somerset claque rushed around backstage to see him and knocked on his door. He was wearing a beautiful new bathrobe and he opened the door about six inches and said, "I'm sorry, boys, I'm a louse again."

As tasty as such stories were when they flipped across the Somerset lobby, George Byrne and I couldn't eat them. I said to George, "We've got the wrong type of act. We ought to do more comedy and less dancing and singing. With all the dancing we're doing, we'll wind up wind-broken, and with varicose veins all over our bodies."

So we assembled a few japes like:

"Where do the bugs go in the wintertime?"

"I don't know, you can search me."

And others like, "You know George Riley?"

"What's his name?"

"What's whose name?"

"George Riley."

"Never heard of him."

It's a wonder we weren't tarred and feathered.

Milt Lewis, then my New York agent, got a date for us at B. S. Moss' Franklin, a big-time, eight-act house. George and I opened on No. 2. The headliners were Dooley—no relation to Ray Dooley —and Sales. This pair were famous for stealing bows. The management of the theaters where they played put up signs: NO ONE ALLOWED TO TAKE MORE THAN TWO BOWS IN THIS THEATER. When Dooley exited, he left one foot hanging out on stage in view of the audience to let them know he was still there, ready to come on again if they applauded. Naturally, they applauded, and Dooley and Sales came bounding back wearing surprised looks which asked, "Can you be making all that fuss for just little us?"

They'd hog the show and the management couldn't get the curtain down, which made it tough for the acts that followed. The trick is known as a "milking routine." Milking or no milking, I wish we'd had their talent. They were entertaining but they got drunk on applause. The rest of us liked it, too, but we didn't get stiff on it.

After our first show at the Franklin, we were sitting in our dressing room waiting to hear how the manager liked us, when we heard our names called. We rushed to the railing and yelled, "Yes?"

"You two could at least put on some make-up and look good," the manager shouted.

It was a low spot in our career. George and I had been hoping that a talent agency like the William Morris Agency would get interested in us and guide us to bigger and better things. I called the Morris office and asked Johnny Hyde, one of their top operatives, "Are you coming up to see our act?"

"No," Johnny said.

"Why not?" I asked.

"I heard about it," he told me.

"You did?" I asked weakly.

"You ought to go West, change your act and get a new start," Johnny said.

"Thanks, Johnny." I said. It was the only thing I could say. At the time I didn't know how valuable those words were to be.

I had a conference with George. "We've got to go to Chicago, get going all over again and break in a new and better comedy act," I told him. "That's where the money is. Big laughs, big money."

George nodded and we started. I'd wired Mike Shea, a Cleveland booker who specialized in breaking jumps for acts en route to Chicago from the East. He wired back that he could get us three days at New Castle, Pennsylvania, at fifty dollars. We were the third act on the bill. It only had three.

Before the show, the manager of the theater said to me, "When you finish, would you mind announcing the show playing here next week?"

So at the end of our act I said, "Ladies and gentlemen, next week Marshall Walker will be here with his 'Big Time Revue.' Marshall is a Scotchman. I know him. He got married in the backyard so the chickens could get the rice."

The audience laughed, and the next show I added another Scotch joke. That got a laugh too. For the next show I added two more. The manager came back and said, "Hey, that's good. Keep them in." The second night I told so many Scotch jokes to announce Marshall Walker's arrival that I found I was doing four or five minutes. One of the fellows in the orchestra took me aside and said, "You two guys are doing the wrong kind of thing. Your double act with that dancing and those corny jokes, that's nothing. You ought to be a master of ceremonies."

I thought it over, then called George in.

"I know what you're thinking," he said. "You're going to try a single. I don't blame you. I'll go back to Columbus and take it easy. I might even start a dancing school."

"I think I'll try it alone for a couple of weeks," I told him. "If it works, we'll break up the trunk."

I went to Cleveland, ate one of Mom's good meals; then, feeling brave on lemon pie, I went down to see Mike Shea in the Erie Building. "I want to do a single," I told him. "I've been fooling around with a single here and there. Try me, Mike. I can do it."

"What kind of an act?" he asked.

"Singing, dancing, talking," I told him, "and working in blackface." I threw in that "blackface" for no reason. I was just nervous, I guess. Aside from one time in McKeesport, when I couldn't get the black greasepaint out of my skin, I'd never worked in blackface.

"I've got a little rotary unit going around town," he said. (A rotary played a different theater every night.) "If you want to jump into it, it's yours."

"That's jake with me," I said.

I went out, bought a big red bow tie, white cotton gloves like Jolson's, a cigar, and a small derby which jiggled up and down when I bounced onstage. I'd picked up some new material here and there, plus a few things I'd thought up for myself and for an encore I did a song and a dance. I scored well, even if I was scoring in a minor league.

I ate and slept at home and took the streetcar to whatever theater I was playing. The fourth night I missed the streetcar and I reached the theater so late I didn't have time to put on the cork for my blackface act. I just ran out with the derby and the cigar and my bare face, but I scored better than ever.

Afterward Mike said, "Don't ever put that cork on again. Your face is funny the way it is."

I'd thought my profile handsome in a dark, smoldering way, and discovering somebody thought it amusing was a shock. But the more I thought about it, the more I figured Mike had something. So you might say missing that streetcar saved my career, although I didn't see it that way then.

Chapter 7

AFTER BREAKING IN my single act in Cleveland, I moved on to Chicago. But Chicago in 1928 wasn't ready for me. I couldn't get in anybody's door. I was living at a hotel on Dearborn Street and sharing a bathroom with a man who had a cleanliness complex. He only came out to eat. I couldn't get a date, and I owed four hundred bucks cuffo for coffee and doughnuts. I was so unfamiliar with steak I'd forgotten whether you ate it with a fork or drank it from a cup. And I was so desperate I'd changed my name from Leslie to Lester. I thought Lester sounded more masculine.

I was standing in front of the Woods Theater Building wondering whether to give up and hop a bus for Cleveland when

Charlie Cooly walked up. I'd gone to school with Charlie. He asked how I was doing. When I told him, he took me to see another Charlie, Charlie Hogan, who booked a lot of theaters around Chicago. "How'd you like to play the West Englewood Theater Decoration Day?" Hogan asked me. "Would twenty-five dollars be all right?"

I just managed to say, "I'll take it," without bursting into tears. The West Englewood had three shows daily. I emceed them and did my act.

After the second show, the manager said, "You're to open at the Stratford, Sunday."

"How do you know?" I asked.

"Charlie Hogan called me," he said. "He asked me how you were doing. I told him you were O.K., so he told me to tell you he's putting you in as master of ceremonies at the Stratford."

The Stratford had had an emcee who'd been such a local favorite that he'd been held over for two years. He had a wonderful personality and they hated to give him the heave-ho. But, unfortunately, he'd gotten to be hard to work with, and they'd had to wrap him up and cart him away. They'd tried a lot of emcees after that but nobody had caught on. I stuck my jaw even farther out than nature had stuck it, went on and did my stuff.

A little guy named Barney Dean was on the bill with me. Barney was a dancer and a favorite with the booking agents because he had a great sense of humor off stage. He had very little on stage. But off he was likable and lovable, and when there was a lot of work, they gave Barney a crack at it. After my first show at the Stratford, Charlie Hogan had called Barney too and had asked, "How is Hope doing?"

Barney said, "We're doing fine."

"I know how *you* did," Hogan told him. "*You* laid an egg. How did Hope do?"

"He did real good," Barney told him. "You'll be hearing about him."

That was one of the things that kept me at the Stratford. After the second day, Hogan told me they wanted me to stay two weeks. I stayed there six months. I went from twenty-five dollars a day to two hundred a week, then to two hundred and fifty. At the end of my stint I was getting three hundred, which was big for those days. It was like having a job in a mint with toting privileges.

The Stratford was a folksy place and I went down into the audience to sing. My hit number was "If You See Me Dancing in Some Cabaret, That's Just My Way of Forgetting You." I had to sing it every couple of weeks.

One of the acts I worked with was the Great Guilfoil. The Great Guilfoil juggled cannon balls. The Stratford was a converted movie house. They built an apron in front of the regular stage so the dancing acts could work there with a band on stage. The Great Guilfoil also juggled a cone of burning paper on his nose while he tossed his cannon balls. At one performance he forgot and walked right off the apron and went down in a heap behind the organ with the cannon balls on top of him.

I ran out and said, "Come up; joke over."

He came up. I never expected him to move; I thought he'd been killed, but he came up laughing and bowing to the audience. All he'd done was break one little finger. But I thought it a great display of ham and courage and everything else a trouper is supposed to have in his blood.

Since I had to come up with a fresh line of patter twice a week for six months, I got material anywhere and everywhere. If a new act played the house, I asked them if they had any fresh jokes I could use. Usually they gave me a few and I tried them out. And I clipped jokes out of *College Humor* and switched them around.

I simply can't tell a dialect joke. I tried, but the audience could see that I was bad at it. Finally I had an inspiration. I made it a bond between the audience and myself that I couldn't really tell dialect jokes, but I was going to tell them anyway so they might as well bear with me. They appreciated my honesty and we got along fine.

I learned a lot about getting laughs and about ways of handling jokes of different types at the Stratford. I'd lead off with a subtle joke, and after telling it, I'd say to the audience, "Go ahead; figure it out." Then I'd wait till they got it.

One of the things I learned at the Stratford was to have enough courage to wait. I'd stand there waiting for them to get it for a long time. Longer than any other comedian has enough guts to wait. My idea was to let them know who was running things.

One of my first jokes at the Stratford followed a loud crash off stage, that sounded like someone dropping a trunkful of glass. After the crash I walked on stage, dusted off my hands and adjusted my tie as if emerging from a physical struggle. Then I'd look back and say, "Lie there and bleed."

While I'm on the subject of how to get laughs, there's a line between being smart and too smart. People like a simple type of humor, too.

Sometimes I'd tell a bad joke, make a wry face at myself for telling it and say, "My brother writes my jokes. Someday I'm going to go up into the attic and loosen his straight jacket." Or I'd say, "I found that joke in my stocking. If it happens again, I'll change laundries."

I had another routine based on some of Frank Tinney's material. In it I used the orchestra leader as a straight man. I'd say, "Charlie, would you mind helping me with a joke? I'll say, 'I went to the dentist this morning, but I only had a dollar,' and you say, 'What happened?' Then I'll tell the funny answer which will convulse the audience and they'll roll in the aisles; then we'll have the audience put back in their seats and everybody will be real happy and ha-ha-ha; here we go." I'd walk off, come back and say, "Hello, Charlie!" and he'd say, "Hello, Les." I'd say, "I went to the dentist this morning. I only had a dollar." And he'd say, "Where'd you get the dollar?"

"Wait a minute!" I'd complain. "You're not supposed to say that. If you don't mind. Let me get the laughs. I'm the comedian around here. Just ask, 'What happened?' and I'll tell the joke. After all, they're paying me to be funny. You just wave your stick, Charlie. Understand?"

So I'd walk off again, come back on and say, "Here we go, Charlie. Hello, Charlie." He's say, "Hello, Les," and we were off. "I went to the dentist this morning," I said, "and I only had a dollar." Charlie said, "What happened?" and I said, "I had to get buck teeth."

It drew moans and catcalls from the audience, but it loosened them up. They thought, *This man has gall even if he doesn't have much talent*. It sounds corny, but it's the kind of buffoonery every audience likes. I can still loosen them up with it.

When I'd been at the Stratford six months I began to run out of material. Trying to get laughs with nothing to get them with was valuable but wearying. However, when I quit the Stratford, it was a cinch to put an act together, using material culled from my stay there.

As a partner, I'd sign up Louise Troxell, a girl I'd met around Chicago and had developed into a foil. She was quick and intelligent, but I'd trained her to hide that. All she had to do was to walk on and stand there looking beautiful while I told a story, then feed me lines. She'd come out holding a little bag in her hand and say, "How do you do." I'd say, "What do you have in your little bag?" and she'd say, "Mustard." And I'd say, "What's the idea?" And she'd say, "You can never tell when you're going to meet a ham."

As anyone can see, this started the routine off in sophisticated fashion.

Or she'd say, "I just came back from the doctor." "Well, what about that?" I'd ask. And she'd say, "Well, the doctor said I'd have to go to the mountains for my kidneys." "That's too bad," I said. "Yes," she said, "I didn't even know they were up there."

Believe it or not, we were paid for those jokes. After each of them, I'd look at the audience like a man in pain who was seeking relief. My eyebrows asked, "What can I do with a dumb broad like this?" That business of letting the audience in on my problem of being saddled with Troxell was the whole secret of the act.

I put a lot of such things together and the Keith-Western Time—a junior Orpheum circuit a little below the big time—signed us. We opened in St. Paul, then went to South Bend. I was still wearing the brown derby, and I had a big cigar stuck in my kisser. When I walked out on stage in South Bend, there was a roar of applause. When I told my first joke, they screamed. I couldn't figure it. Finally I got it. I had a Notre Dame audience; Al Smith was running for President. A brown derby and a cigar were his trademarks. Years later, I went back there. I wore the same wardrobe but I pulled only a ripple.

After that we played around the Western Vaudeville Circuit

for a while. We made such towns as Sioux City, Peoria and Bloomington. Then we opened on the Inter-State Time in Fort Worth, Texas. I did the same act I'd done in Chicago. I worked fast, snappy and impish. It was my idea to tell the audience, "You've got to get my stuff fast because that's the way I sell it." I'd been a show stopper with this tempo. In Fort Worth I was on next to shut. "Shut" is closing. "Next to shut" meant the featured spot on a vaudeville bill. It was usually reserved for a big comedy act.

But when I walked out before my first Fort Worth audience with my fast talk, I might as well have kept on walking to the Rio Grande. Nobody cared. I couldn't understand it. I came off-stage, threw my derby on the floor and told the unit manager, "Get me a ticket back to my country."

I went out and worked in the afterpiece anyhow. An afterpiece was a series of blackouts, sketches, and comedy bits thrown together and put on after the finish of the regular bill. It made use of the performers who had appeared during the first part of the proceedings. We all pitched in and worked in the different sketches.

When the afterpiece was over, a fellow walked into my dressing room and asked, "What seems to be the matter, fancy pants?"

"I'm not for these people," I said. "That's all that's the matter."

"Why don't you slow down and give them a chance?" this fellow asked. "These people aren't going anywhere. They came in here to be happy. It's summertime. It's hot. This is Texas. Let them understand you. Why make it a contest to keep up with your material? Relax and you'll be all right."

"Thanks too much," I said sarcastically. After he'd gone, I asked someone, "Who was that?"

"That's Bob O'Donnell," I was told. "He's head of the Inter-state Vaudeville Circuit."

Bob is now one of the ringmasters of the International Variety Clubs and one of the country's greatest all-round showmen. But all I thought then was, *How much nerve can one man have?*

However, I did slow down for the next show (as much as my stubbornness would let me) and the audience warmed up a little. I slowed down even more for the next show, and during the last show of the night, I was almost a hit. Before I moved on to Dallas I was a solid click—thanks to Bob O'Donnell. Bob did another thing for me. Without telling me he was doing it, he wired the B. F. Keith office in New York to tell them that when I hit that town they ought to look me over quick and sign me. In the meantime, I'd been corresponding with a firm of New York vaudeville agents named Morris and Feil. I'd sent them my photos and they'd sent me a series of form letters urging me to drop in and see them. The catch was I didn't know they were form letters. I thought they had me practically set for the Ziegfeld Follies. In 1929, when I got to New York, I dropped in all bright-eyed, eager and bushy-tailed to see them.

"Here I am," I announced.

"Who're you?" they asked.

"Who am I?" I said indignantly. "I'm Bob Hope!" (I'd changed it again, this time from Lester to Bob. I thought Bob had more "Hi ya, fellas" in it.) Drawing myself up I said, "I'm the Hope who's been writing to you."

"What do you do?" one of them asked.

"You don't know what I do? And you wrote me all those letters. Just give me my photos," I said. I took them and walked out.

After all of those wonderful form letters about how great things were going to be for me if they could handle me, and how they were the greatest agents in the business, I figured they'd at least have a limousine waiting to rush me up to Flo Ziegfeld. But while it was a low blow, I refused to let it bruise my ego.

I was even surer than Bob O'Donnell that I was "ready." At the B. F. Keith office, I met Lee Stewart, whose real name is Lee Muckinfuss.

"Keith wants you to show your act to us," he said. "Bob O'Donnell says you're good, and they want to see you."

"Where do they want me to show?" I asked.

"At the Jefferson," he said. The Jefferson was on 14th Street. It lacked class. Its audiences were tough and boisterous.

"You don't think I'm going to show there, do you?" I asked. "I'll show uptown at the Hamilton, or at the Riverside, or at the Coliseum. And," I added, "if you want me, don't fool around. Hurry."

"I'll have to talk it over with Keith's," he said. "You're sure you don't want the Jefferson?"

"No," I said, "I don't want any Jefferson."

In the meantime I'd been talking about my act to the William Morris Agency. The Publix Circuit was also toying with the idea of giving me a deal. So I said, "And don't call me with any con offer."

A few more days went by. Then Lee Stewart called again and said, "I've got you a spot."

"Where?" I asked.

"Proctor's Eighty-Sixth," he said.

"Who's on ahead of me?" I asked.

"Leatrice Joy, the movie star," Lee said. "She's doing a personal appearance."

I didn't know that the Eighty-Sixth Street was the size and shape of a barn. For some reason I took it that it was a small, intimate house. So I said, "O.K."

"There's not much money," Lee warned me.

"Tell your office I don't want any money," I announced.

"Are you crazy or something?" he asked.

"I just want them to see the act, that's all," I told him. "Publix is after me, but I'm willing to let Keith's see the act too. If they don't like me, O.K. But I don't need money."

What I was doing was throwing a bluff to give them the idea that trifling sums were of no interest to me. I thought this remark of mine was a sign of independence, although secretly I was wondering if I had enough talent to live up to it.

To make sure I was as great as I'd indicated, I called a friend,

Charlie Yates, who'd handled me for a few noncircuit independent vaudeville spots. "See if you can get me a little vaudeville date, Charlie," I said. "I'd like to break in a couple of ideas."

Charlie got me on at the Dyker in Brooklyn. It was only a three-day date, but I was willing to make it to break in my material. I was also willing to take the money, which was twenty-five dollars, or eight dollars and thirty-three cents a day. I didn't go over too well at the Dyker, but that didn't bother me. I told myself that the audience wasn't a quality audience, and that I was only warming up, like a golfer playing a practice round.

Lee Stewart came over to catch my last show. Coming back on the subway from Brooklyn, he was thoughtful. "Proctor's Eighty-Sixth Street is a pretty big theater, you know," he said.

I knew what he was thinking. He was thinking that he was just about to become a midwife at an egg-laying, but I asked, "Is that so?" as if the size of Proctor's was a piece of uninteresting information instead of a hazard.

"Look, Lee," I said, "I open there tomorrow, and if I don't score, we won't talk to each other again. O.K.?"

That seemed all right with him.

Just before I opened at Proctor's I asked the doorman, "How's the audience here?"

"The toughest in New York," he said.

My Adam's apple bounced against my shoes. I felt like a rat catcher trapped by his own cheese. I wasn't worried about the fact that the Proctor was as big as a barn. It was in the days before stages were equipped with microphones, but my lungs were young and I could bash them over the head with a gag in the back row. But a tough audience too, that was another thing.

I walked around the block twice to pull myself together.

I stood in the wings of Proctor's waiting to go on for the matinee with my cigar wobbling up and down the way a product named Jell-O (which I shilled for years later) shakes and quivers. I could see Louise Troxell looking at me as if mentally running over the names of other comedians who might give her a job. I watched Leatrice Joy walk up and down in the spotlight. And thinking about how she had been having marital difficulties with her husband, John Gilbert, and also remembering that what happened in the next few minutes would probably be the most important thing in my life, I had an idea. As Leatrice finished and the orchestra speeded up and went into my music, I walked out with my brown derby on my head. That derby always got a laugh. It indicated that something of a comedy nature was coming—anyhow, an attempt at something of a comedy nature.

I looked out into the audience and said, "No, lady, this is not John Gilbert." The Leatrice Joy-Gilbert heart problems were headlines in the papers; Gilbert was the country's biggest wheel in the great-lover and breast-heaving department, and I looked remarkably unlike him—so as it turned out it was just the right thing to say.

That got me started. I stopped the show.

For my exit I did two bows; then dropped my left hand as a signal to the electricians and orchestra leader. I'd arranged that signal in advance. It meant that the orchestra would stop playing my bow music while the applause was still at its peak, and the spotlight would go black, leaving the audience with nothing. It worked out the way I'd hoped it would. They couldn't switch off their applause that quickly, so they kept on clamoring. It also gave them that "they can't do this to us" feeling.

I didn't originate this gimmick for audience influencing. Other acts have used the notion. In fact, it had become almost standard technique if you ever got that much applause worked up.

I stood there in the wings for a full thirty-five or forty seconds and let them applaud. The stage manager said nervously, "Come on, boy; take your bow."

"Take your time, brother," I said. "I'm the one who's showing." And I let it roll for fifteen seconds more.

Then I said, "Spotlight," they put the spot back on, I came

out, did an encore dance, and walked off, the Mister Big of the Universe.

When I reached my dressing room, the door burst open and Lee Stewart rushed in. He wrung my hand and said, "I knew you had it. I could tell. This is it, isn't it? How about that audience?"

"What about the way I bombed at the Kyker?" I asked.

"That's no theater," he said.

I looked at him and remembered that dismal ride home from Brooklyn on the subway with him; then I thought, *I don't blame him. When you lay an egg in Brooklyn it has three yolks.*

A representative of the William Morris office had been out front. They had somebody catch first shows, especially if there was any new talent around they might want to sign. The Morris man came backstage and said, "Would you like to come down to the office after the next show?"

"I can't," I said.

"How about after the last show?" he asked. The last show went on at eleven o'clock. "Come down to the Bond Building. We'll be waiting there for you."

But after the second show, the Keith office offered me a three-year contract at four hundred dollars a week. I got them up to four hundred and fifty dollars and signed for three years, mainly because they booked the Palace Theater in New York, which was the dream of every vaudeville ham.

Chapter 8

FOR MY FIRST DATE on my new contract I opened at the Albee in Brooklyn. Out of my four hundred and fifty a week, I gave Louise Troxell a hundred. The first time I was paid, I was trying to figure out what I was going to do with the other three fifty. I was standing there in my dressing room, holding all of that money in my hot little hand when the door opened and Al Lloyd came in. I'd known Al when he was an agent working out of the Morris office and handling quite a few good acts. In fact, he'd tried to get the Hope and Byrne act set before it died. Afterward, he'd gone into the insurance business for the New York Life Insurance Company.

"How are you, Al?" I said. "I'm just trying to figure out what kind of a car to buy. I don't know whether to get a Packard or a Pierce-Arrow with those twin headlights."

"Let's not worry about that," he said. "Just give me two hundred and fifty dollars and I'll slap it into a policy for you."

"It's a little early for that," I said. "I'm not planning to kick off."

But he was persistent and before he was through he'd talked me into giving up some of my dough for annuities and life insurance. Once he had me hooked, I formed the habit.

To leap ahead a few years, in 1948, on Al's twentieth anniversary with the New York Life Insurance Company, I was invited to a luncheon given in his honor. It was held at the Hotel

Martinique at 32nd and Broadway where they have a lot of rooms for such parties. I got in the elevator, went upstairs and walked into a roomful of people. When I stood up to do my stuff, there was applause, but it subsided quickly. I did about three minutes and was going over like a wet meatball.

"I'm very thrilled to be here for good ol' Al Lloyd," I said. "He's been my insurance agent for lo these many years."

There was an even thicker silence. I was in the wrong room. Al and his party were down the hall. I'd been talking about insurance to a bunch of cattle herders. I slunk out of there like a rustler caught eyeing a dogie.

Another of my first Keith bookings was a date in Chicago. I had a little trouble because of a joke I did there with Louise Troxell. She walked on and said, "You're very attractive," and I said, "Yes, I came from a very brave family. My brother slapped Al Capone in the face." This was during the time when Capone reigned as the czar of Cicero, a Chicago suburb.

"Your brother slapped Al Capone in the face?" Louise asked in surprised tones.

"Yes," I said.

"I'd like to shake his hand," she said.

This cued my punch line: "We're not going to dig him up just for that."

I did it during my first show and it got a boff. But the manager, Frank Smith, came up to me afterward and said, "If you're wise you'll take that joke out."

"Why?" I asked.

"The boys come down here from Cicero on Saturday nights," he said. "They're liable not to like it and if they don't like it I feel sorry for you."

"I don't think they'll mind," I said. So I kept it in that Saturday night.

I was living at the Bismarck Hotel, and on Sunday morning the phone rang.

A low, gruff-type voice asked, "Is this Bob Hope?"

I said, "Yes."

This voice—it's the only voice I've ever heard with a flat nose—asked, "Are you the one who's doing that joke about Al Capone?"

"Yes," I said. "Why?"

"Do us a favor," the voice said. "Take it out."

"Who's this?" I asked.

"Just one of the boys," the voice said. "Take it out. We'll be around to thank you for it."

"Yes *sir*," I said; "it'll be out."

I never did find out who called me, but to reach the Palace stage entrance I had to walk through a long dark alley. A couple of actors had been held up in it and it was a lonely place—especially if you were having a little difference of opinion with the mob. I didn't want to make that walk with that on my mind.

Having taken the joke out, I was stuck for a substitute. Finally I remembered an old one I'd done at the Stratford. It was one in which I said to a girl foil, "I'd like to see more of you. Why don't you let me take you out tonight." And she said, "No, I'm busy. I'm taking my little dog to the hospital."

"You're taking the little dog to the hospital?" I said. "You must think a lot of that dog."

"I do," she said.

"I wish I could take its place," I said.

"So do I," she said. "I'm taking it to the hospital to have its ears shortened."

We got a fair boff with that and we didn't miss the Capone gag. Some years later I replaced Al Capone with Joe Louis—"Slap Joe Louis in the face . . . we're not going to dig him up just for that." It scored just as well.

After Chicago we played Cleveland. My brothers had been a little doubtful about the money they'd read I was making. When the subject came up they'd give me the arched, sceptical eyebrow. But when I got back to Cleveland and the manager of the theater handed me my check for one week's work, they got a look at it. From then on, they corresponded with me more regularly.

I'd been signed by Keith's, but I hadn't played the Palace in New York. I kept telling myself that it was only a question of time, but while waiting I played some New York neighborhood theaters, including a three-day booking at the Coliseum. Sid Fabello and his orchestra were in the pit there. Sid and his boys didn't play the overture before the vaudeville portion of the bill, as they usually did. The deeply moving film, *All Quiet on the Western Front,* was playing the house, so Sid and his boys did a musical finale which blended into the end of the picture. When the picture and the musical finale ended, the curtain went up on me.

The situation couldn't have been better calculated to ruin my act if it had been planned that way. *All Quiet* wound up with a young soldier being blown up. At the finish, all you saw were his hands reaching for a butterfly on the barbed wire in no man's land. It affected people so strongly that they didn't want to talk to anybody or have anybody talk to them afterward. Then, whammo, up struck my jazzy music, and out walked a fresh, bouncy, overbearing so-and-so named Hope.

The audience couldn't have wanted me less.

I know now that I should have walked out and said quietly, "Ladies and gentlemen, trying to follow a dramatic and wonderful film like that is the toughest thing in the world. But the vaudeville part of our show has to go on sometime. They tell me I'm funny. At least, they're paying me to be funny, so I hope you'll try to imagine I *am* funny."

If I'd used that, it might have helped. But I didn't have enough sense. I just ran out, fresh as paint, went into my act and laid such a blockbuster stink bomb that they had to take the seats out and air them.

At first I couldn't figure it. But finally I got it. Then I got mad.

I began to scream about the injustice of the thing and how I was dying out there and how they couldn't do this to me, when the phone rang backstage. It was Arthur Willis, the booker for the theater. "What are you doing?" Arthur asked. "Laying down on me out there? They tell me you aren't trying."

I was so mad I spluttered. Then I heard him laugh. He knew what I was up against and he was ribbing me. It took some of the edge off the situation. I said a few unprintable words to Arthur, went on for the last few shows, and died peacefully without fighting.

After all, I told myself, *this will only last three days. After that I'm going to Proctor's 58th Street. Then I'll be back in vaudeville and out of the backwash of a movie.*

But when I got to Proctor's 58th and looked up at the marquee, it said: ALL QUIET ON THE WESTERN FRONT. I was to have it with me for four more days. I called Arthur Willis up and said, "Fun's fun! I quit!"

"You're getting paid, aren't you?" he asked. "Shut up and do it."

I shut up and took the money. But it was a long four days.

Those old-time vaudeville jumps were brutal. But when I made my second trip on the Inter-State Time I had bought a car. It was classy if secondhand. This shiny monster ate gas and oil like a dragon eats people, but I'd convinced myself that I could save money with it on some of the jumps instead of using a train. This particular trip we were going from Houston to New Orleans, which is quite a jump. Along the way we picked up a small Negro boy who was hitchhiking. He assured us that he knew the way and could direct us. We drove a hundred miles farther and I looked questioningly at this kid who was sitting in back. He just nodded.

We drove another hundred miles. Finally we pulled into a gas station and got out. I asked the gas pumper, "Are we on the right road to New Orleans?"

"Well, no," he said; "you're seventy miles out of your way."

I turned to ask the colored boy about it, but he was running down the street. I yelled after him, "Where are you going?" "I live over here!" he yelled back. I gave him a look, but it bounced off his back. After that we had to ride as if we were trying to qualify on the Indianapolis Speedway to make our New Orleans matinee.

In the fall of 1929 when I went around the Orpheum Time with Louise Troxell, we traveled as far north as Vancouver and as far south as San Diego. We were with a stage unit built around Harry Webb and his orchestra. Before I came along, Ken Murray had worked with Web. I had taken Ken's place. I did my own act and also worked the afterpiece.

I've already described what an afterpiece is, but maybe it will do no harm to add to that description. The afterpiece was thought up as vaudeville's answer to the talkies. It was a pocket-edition comedy revue featuring a comedian and a string of black-out sketches. It was played full stage. It involved a lot of slapstick and comedy bits, and it went on after the regular acts. The big wheel of the afterpiece was the principal comedian, and the band was on the stage instead of in the pit. In short, all of us who'd had anything to do with the regular show spread out and did a revue-type thing. There were many afterpieces in vaudeville in those days and they were very successful.

About this time I picked up a writer named Al Boasberg, and he began to turn out material for me. Boasberg had written many of the top acts of vaudeville. He'd whipped up the one called "Lamb Chops," which made Burns and Allen famous—a Dumb-Dora act which set the trend of Burns-and-Allen's routines from then on. He also wrote for Jack Benny. I remember a joke he wrote for Jack when Benny was stopping at the Waldorf: "The Waldorf is so swanky you have to shave before they'll let you into its barber shop."

I don't know how I met Al. That's not important. But it was important that he started to work for me, for he was a great joke mechanic. He could remember jokes, fix jokes, switch jokes around, improvise on jokes. He could even originate jokes. When I was in New York I'd take him to a Chinese restaurant, Lum Fong's, and sit there with him until three or four o'clock in the morning while the waiters wearily poured tea for us. I'd ply Al with questions and conversation, and during the course of our talk when he came up with a nifty I'd jot it down on the back of a menu.

For example, I'd say, "I'm afraid our show is going to close," and he'd say, "I guess you'd better recast the backers."

It might not sound like much, but there'd be a time when I'd find it a useful crack to have on tap.

One joke we made up at Lum Fong's was very successful, so successful that it was stolen by every other comedian who was working around New York those days. This must have been around 1932, as anyone who reads the joke will realize. I came on stage and said, "You have a nice show here. I was just standing out in front watching the other acts when a lady walked up to me in the lobby and said, 'Pardon me, young man, could you tell me where I could find the rest room?' and I said, 'It's just around the corner.'

" 'Don't give me that Hoover talk,' she said. 'I'm serious.' "

It pulled one of the biggest boffs I ever got in vaudeville.

If you're too young to remember, Hoover was using the slogan, "Prosperity is just around the corner." We were still waiting for it then. Vaudeville's been waiting for it ever since.

Boasberg was responsible for my first movie test. He wrote to a Hollywood agent, Bill Perlberg, about me. Perlberg is a successful producer nowadays. Then he was a ten-percenter, a flesh peddler. "Take a look at Bob Hope if he happens to be out your way," Boasberg suggested. So, when I hit Los Angeles to play the Hill Street Theater, Bill called me to ask, "How'd you like to make a movie test?"

I was large about it. I said that we had a few open days before playing San Diego, after our Hill Street closing, and I thought I could work a test in. Bill didn't seem too impressed by my willingness to give the cinema a chance. "Get out to the Pathé lot next Thursday," he said.

At Pathé, when the camera began to turn, I did my stuff. Then Louise Troxell came on and worked with me. The stagehands and crew laughed, and I went away convinced that all the movie industry needed to put it on a firm basis was me.

When I went down to San Diego with Louise, my head was filled with such happy thoughts. Our first Sunday there, I went to Agua Caliente and left six hundred dollars in a gambling joint. I was philosophical about it. I knew I'd recoup that loss many times over in the movie racket. It was only a question of time before every studio would be sending their talent heads panting to get my signature on a contract.

When I got back to L. A., I called Perlberg and asked, "When do I see the test?"

"Do you want to see it?" he inquired.

"Of course," I said.

"Go out to Pathé," he told me. "They'll show it to you."

"What do you think of it?" I asked.

All he said was, "Go and see it."

When I walked in at Pathé, they said, "Projection Room 12-Z."

I had to find 12-Z myself. No one bothered to escort me to it. I smiled grimly and told myself, *There'll be a few changes made here when I'm on salary.* I sat there waiting for me to appear on the screen and leave me speechless with my talent. Then the screening began.

I'd never seen anything so awful. I looked like a cross between a mongoose and a turtle. I couldn't wait to get out. I wanted to run all the way to Salt Lake, our next booking, clasp vaudeville to my bosom, and say, "Honest, Honey, nothing happened. That movie wench didn't touch this precious thing we have."

I've found out since that the way I felt when I saw myself on the screen for the first time is the way most people feel. You simply can't believe it. Your efforts to be funny make you actu-

ally nauseated. It's more a stomach test than a screen test. You think you're going to look like a cross between Tyrone Power and Robert Taylor, and you can't understand why the camerman didn't give you that Taylor lighting.

There's a story about a great movie actress who came back to Hollywood to make a film after an absence of eight years. She looked awful in the rushes and she blamed it on the camerman. She wanted to have him fired. The director said a subtle thing to her, "If you don't look as young and glamorous as you did when you made your last picture, don't forget your camerman is eight years older." It wasn't too subtle for her to get the point. She calmed down and stuck to acting instead of beefing about the way she photographed.

When I came to work for Paramount seven years later I had the same head, but by that time I had made a few movie shorts and was used to looking at it. However that floppo screen test at

Pathé stands out in my memory. It's burned on the inside of my skull.

The things I thought terrific in the late 1920's and early 1930's don't look so much so now. They seemed earth-shaking when they occurred, though. Some of them even got into the public prints and I pasted them into my scrapbooks so future historians can find them easily. Once in a while I riffle through those scrapbooks. The last time I did one of the clipping hit me in the eye. It was dated Kansas City, 1928. It said: "Hope's gags are new and the wrist watch thing is a wow." That review was written by Goodman Ace, who later went to glory as half of the Easy Aces and is now one of the best TV writers of them all. He was then a critic.

"The wrist watch thing" he mentioned, went like this: I'd begin to sing a song and as I sang I looked at my wrist watch every few bars. Finally I took a bottle of medicine from my pocket, said, "Pardon me," took two spoonfuls of the stuff, and finished my song. Then I'd shake my whole body and say, "I forgot to shake the bottle."

I've been doing this bit since 1928. Last season when one of my favorite clowns, Sid Caesar, did it on TV, I sent him a letter to tell him that if he ever sees me doing it, I'm not stealing it from him. For that matter, I wonder if I was the first to use it twenty-six years ago?

There are clippings in my scrapbooks about an ambitious, skinny youngster sometimes listed as Bill Hope, sometimes Bobby Hope, sometimes Ben Hope. I was a household word in those days, but each house had a different word for me. Looking over those scrapbooks makes me think of the time when I was playing Evansville, Indiana. I walked into a coffee-and-cakes palace, bought the Evansville paper and sat down to gloat over my billing. Under: ORPHEUM THEATER, EVANSVILLE, I read: THE AMAZING TRAINED GOLDEN BIRD, and under this, in smaller type: BEN HOPE, COMEDIAN. Not only did I resent being under a bird—certainly a precarious position—but I didn't like the misspelling of my name. I went to the manager and complained. "You put me under a bird," I said. "In addition, you mangle a name that will mean something someday."

"You can't lose," he said. "Nobody here ever heard of either Ben Hope or Bob Hope. In fact, it's a break for you. If you stink out the joint, the next time you play here you can be Bob."

Tucked in between those clippings is one of the professional cards George Byrne and I had printed to send out to agents. In one corner of the card is a diamond-shaped picture of me. In another corner is a diamond-shaped picture of George. Printed below is: THE DANCEMEDIANS. TWO DIAMONDS IN THE ROUGH. A COMEDY ACT IN ONE. We thought that word "Dancemedians" the greatest ever coined.

Nobody ever stole it, that's how great it was.

There's an accidental quip embalmed in those scrapbooks too. I was asked to name my three favorite books. I wrote: ANTHONY ADVERSE. There was an interruption and I didn't have a chance to jot down the next two. It was such a thick book that the studio publicity people thought I was wise-cracking about it being three times as long as one book. They planted it in the papers as an example of my wit.

Then there's a one-sentence clipping from the New York *Telegram*. It was written by Robert Garland: "Mr. Hope was said to have come out of the West by airplane, and I am pleased he took the trouble." I like that. And under that it says: "Hope's walk-on line, 'Now that the amateurs are finished—' killed the critics."

Chapter 9

BUT TO GET BACK to that omelette I laid in my first screen test. After the verdict was in, Louise and I flapped on to Salt Lake like a couple of homing pigeons, victimized by a fit of over-confidence in a windmill.

When we got to New York I decided to put on my own after-piece. My youngest brother, George, wasn't working. Later he developed into a script writer of some talent, but at that time I figured I could use him and also a friend of mine, Toots Murdock, from Toledo. The Murdock family was famous in show business. Two of Toots' brothers, Lou and Tech, were great vaudeville dancers. Toots himself was a youngster with a fine talent for rambunctious comedy.

I had an idea which would involve stooges in the boxes on

each side of the stage. Not one stooge, two. If one stooge was good—and acts with one stooge had gathered a bumper crop of yuks and boffs—two stooges ought to be better, I thought. And so it worked out. The only trouble was that at times it was a close decision who was stooging for whom.

In my scrapbooks it also says that a reviewer wrote, "Some of Hope's stuff is so new that the audience didn't quite catch on for a minute or two." This clipping has to do with my whole philosophy of how to get going with an audience. I've gone into it and over it before, but I'm bringing it up now because it was a tie-in with my stooge idea. I'd discovered that I was a success if I could lead with a joke the audience didn't grab right away— a good, solid, big joke with a certain amount of subtlety to it, one that would challenge the audience and let them know right away that they had a fight on their hands. They rose to that. It's real good. I'd stand there and look at them as if to say, "Are you going to get it or not?" With that kind of start I had the upper hand.

A part of my new idea was for my stooges to come out and start whipping at me, and saying, "What's going on behind the curtain?" and I'd say, "Nothing," and they'd say, "Well, there's nothing going on in front of it either." I figured it would be a great device for them to tear down this character on the stage who'd been so cocky, brash and bumptious. I was right about that too.

When I got back to New York in 1931, I went into a huddle with Boasberg, who wrote *The Antics of 1931* as a showcase for my new idea. The *Antics* opened on a fellow named Johnny Peters, who looked like Rudy Vallee. Rudy was a smash in those days. I introduced my Vallee imitator and he sat there playing a saxophone. Then he got up and mooed Rudy's theme song, "My Time Is Your Time," into a megaphone. I had my brother, George, parked in one upper box, and he leaned out and yelled across the theater to my other stooge, Toots Murdock, "Hey, Herman!"

I looked up at him and glared, and he pulled his noggin back in. As soon as I took my eyes away, he poked his head up again and yelled, "Hey, Herman!" once more.

Toots called back, "What do you want?" and George asked, "What time does the show start?"

I cut in then and said, "Just a minute. Do you realize you're upsetting our act?"

This was George's cue to ask, "This is an act?"

A variation on this was when the guy who looked like Vallee began to sing, a stooge in one box would whisper hoarsely to the stooge in the other box, "How do you like it?"

"It sounds just as bad over here," the second stooge would say.

I'd interrupt. "Just a minute," I'd say. "Don't you boys know you can be arrested for annoying an audience?"

Both of them said in unison, "You should know."

Big laugh.

After that we went into the jokes. I had a hotel bit in which I called up one of the hotel guests and said, "I'm the room clerk. Did you leave a call for nine o'clock? Well it's five now. You have four more hours to sleep."

We also did a Mata Hari scene in which we shot a lady spy. I

played the captain of the execution squad and gave commands in my own brand of auto-backfiring German. I'd leave the girl who played Mata standing there and we'd all walk away from her, my firing squad with their guns and me with a sword. Then I'd goosestep up to her again and ask, "Madame, have you anything to say before you die?"

"Nothing," she'd say, and I'd whisper, "Remember, not a word about last night."

Then in a loud voice I'd say, "Ready, aim. . . ."

She'd drop her cloak so that her brassiere was uncovered, and I'd say, "At ease men."

I started for her once more and the soldiers followed me. I'd tell them, "Back, pigs. What do you want?"

And they'd say, "The same as you, only you're captain."

Finally, when I said "Fire!" she threw off her cloak. In addition to the bra she only wore scanties and the firing squad threw down their guns and started for her. Black out! Obviously we'd stolen the whole thing from a kindergarten play.

Then we'd do some more jokes, a dance and a finale.

No story of vaudeville would be complete without some mention of Louis Guttenberg. When we put on the *Antics* we needed a few Army coats, a few old muskets, a few hats and other assorted costumes for our acts. It was natural to us to go to Louis Guttenberg's for them. Louis rented old theatrical costumes from his shop on New York's East Side.

You'd drop in to see Louis and he'd ask, "What do you want?" When you told him, he got it all together and piled it in the middle of the floor. You'd ask, "How much?" He'd says, "Twenty-two dollars," and you'd say, "I'll give you six." He'd faint and when he came out of his dizzy spell, he'd go into a heartbreaking speech that made Paul Muni or Spencer Tracy seem like sphinxes.

Louis told us that he couldn't possibly let us have what we wanted for a sum we could afford because he was practically bankrupt. "O.K.," we said, "if that's the way you feel about it," and we stalked out.

He called us back. We finally settled for twelve dollars for ten old costumes and we parted good friends.

We had a big bag into which we fitted our costumes and props. When we took the subway around New York to play dates, one of us had to carry the bag. Between shows the stooges played cards to see who would lug it.

When we weren't toting it around, we ate in the B-E sandwich shop, next door to the Palace Theater. Many a lie about what a smash your act was was told between mouthfuls of hot pastrami in the B-E. It was a great place, the old B-E. You could get a full breakfast there for thirty-five cents, and pile on the McGoo about your act. The fact that all the waitresses knew how you were *really* doing didn't slow you down at all.

Not long after this I was booked into the New York Palace. While I was waiting for the opening—and trying on larger hats —I walked into the Palace lobby. There was a sign: BOB HOPE, THE COMIC FIND OF THE WEST. Also as a silly publicity stunt, there were fellows walking up and down in front of the Palace carrying signs which read: BOB HOPE IS UNFAIR TO DISORGANIZED STOOGES. REFUSES TO PAY FOR THEIR LUMPS, BUMPS, DOCTORS' AND HOSPITAL BILLS.

I'm not a shrinker, a toer-inner, a button-twister or an "aw-shuckser," but I must admit I was momentarily abashed. I thought, *This is too much.*

That hoopla must have given me a complex, for when I opened the following Saturday I was numb. Not just scarced, numb. I did my act mechanically. The newspapers were kind, except one assassin, who drew his blood money—so much for each actor's scalp—from the *Daily Graphic*. This character with the triple bile duct wrote, "They say that Bob Hope is the sensation of the Midwest. If that's so, why doesn't he go back there?"

Sunday night was "celebrity night" at the Palace. Sunday night I had the shakes so badly that I began to do my poorest show of the week.

It was a lucky thing for me that Ted Healy was sitting in the first row. Ted had always been a Hope plugger. When he was playing in *A Night in Venice*, he'd come over to catch me at the Albee. After the show he came backstage, put out his hand and said, "Brother, you've got it." Coming from him, it was an ele-phant-size compliment.

Ken Murray was also a member of my first Celebrity Night Palace audience. When I introduced him to the crowd, he climbed up over the orchestra pit onto the stage and said: "I'm going to tell a joke."

Healy jumped up and said, "I've already heard it." They had quite an exchange of banter and it helped ease the strain. It ended up by being a great night for me.

Toots Murdock was a great boy with one very human failing— the same failing my father had. Once in a while he would get into a contest with a bottle, overestimate his strength and lose. Aside from that, he was a clever performer with real talent, and uni-versally beloved.

One night when I began my bit with him, I noticed that he was leaning too far out over the railing, and doing his part real happy. Certainly he was happier than the audience. I tried cool-ing him by quipping to the crowd, "You can tell that my friend in the box is destined for greatness. Nothing can stop him, not even his talent." But it didn't work. We were doing four shows a day, and after the first show I called him backstage and said, "O.K., Toots, you're having lots of fun, but for the next show,

how about doing your lines the way they're written instead of giving them your own interpretation."

But next show he was even more free-wheeling. After that I tried a threat. "If you don't pull yourself together," I said, "I'm going to have to fire you and get somebody else. Buy yourself a couple of mugs of black coffee and calm yourself."

He must have cut his coffee with something stronger than cream, for when he appeared for the next show there was no improvement. To my surprise, it went over very large that way. At first the audience had thought that I was using a stooge who was pretending that he'd had one too many as a part of the act, but finally they got wise. And after that they howled at his every movement.

There were four acts in the *Antics,* before I went on with my afterpiece. These acts were Mady and Bay, a brother-and-sister roping act; Nell Kelly, a madcap singer with a Cass Daley style (Cass Daley's singing style is the frantic, eccentric kind of chirping, something like the way Betty Hutton sings) my own act and a monkey act called Joe Peanuts. The monkey act was owned and trained by a fellow named Everest. He had acrobat monkeys and a monkey orchestra on a little bandstand.

There were about twenty monkeys in all, and I fell into the habit of playing with them on their bandstand before they went on. I fed them candy mints and got to know their different personalities and moods. One nasty, antisocial monk played the bass horn. I wasn't too chummy with him. One day in Omaha I got too close to him. He scratched my face, leaving five raw, red marks. I sent out for a styptic pencil, dried some of the gore and powdered my face, but when I walked on, I looked as if I'd run into a safety razor with fangs.

It was Everest's custom to take his Thespians into the alley behind the stage door for an airing. But he did this money-curbing routine once too often. When we were playing Minneapolis, they got loose, ran back into the theater and under the seats through the audience. I can't think of words to describe what a pack of monkeys frisking about under ladies' skirts can do in the way of creating hysteria in a crowded theater.

There was screeching and leaping upon seats and the flutter of hoisted skirts. Finally, all the monkeys were retrieved except Tommy, the leader of the troupe. Everest spotted Tommy on the roof of the theater. The trick was to get him down without scaring him. If he was startled he might leap to the roof of the next building. He sat there taking a census of his fleas, while Everest and a posse of stagehands and ushers stood at the bottom of the fire escape, begging him to come down. Then one of the girl ushers had an idea, and Everest sent one of his lady monkeys up to see Tommy. After they'd necked awhile, they came down, went into the theater and did their show. Which proves that monkeys are no crazier than people.

Since I had my kid brother, George, with me, I tried to make him learn to dance. I knew it would be valuable for him to learn. Finally he did. But I had to pound his eardrums to get him to do it. Sometimes we got into such arguments that he walked out and went home to Cleveland. I'd wait a while, then call Mom long distance and ask, "Is George there?" If she said, "No," I'd say, "Well, he'll be there soon. We had a fight about his learning to dance."

Sure enough, Mom had hardly hung up when George walked in. She'd wait a day or two, and then, instead of saying, "Why don't you get back there and do what Les wants you to do?" she'd say, "Les needs you, George. You're important to him." Mom was a diplomat. She made each of her sons feel he was her favorite. Probably all mothers with seven boys have that gift.

As a result of my appearance at the Palace with *The Antics of 1931*. I was tagged for a musical, called *Ballyhoo of 1932*. Bobby Connelly, Norman Anthony, Lewis Gensler and Russell Patterson were putting it on. Billy Grady, Al Jolson's manager, brought them into the Palace to see me. They looked my act over and decided I'd do. The name "Ballyhoo" was borrowed from a magazine edited by Anthony. This magazine featured burlesque versions of advertising. It had been a six-month sensation.

Keith's gave me a leave of absence to do the show and I signed for it at six hundred dollars a week. Keith's were wonderful about giving me such leaves. At the same time, they knew that I'd be more valuable to them afterward if I made good in a Broadway show. After each show I went back on the road to work out my three-year contract with them.

A big cast had been assembled for *Ballyhoo*. It included Willie and Eugene Howard, Lulu McConnell, Vera Marsh, Paul and Grace Hartman, plus a plentiful supply of beautiful girls. This last item interested me a lot at the time.

Ballyhoo featured more blackouts than an air raid. One of them was a nudist sketch written by Norman Anthony. I appeared in it with Vera Marsh. We opened in Atlantic City. After that, it was decided to go into Newark for an extra week of polishing and pruning. Bobby Connelly thought up some new dance numbers, and the ticket brokers and the Broadway wise boys came over to catch it. The Newark curtain was late. The girls weren't ready for the opening number, so the orchestra played the overture again. The girls were still running around in circles and little else. The Brothers Shubert had a small investment in the project, and Lee Shubert came backstage and said, "Somebody ought to do something." Eying me, he said, "Go out there and ad lib."

"Not me," I said. "If I go on now they'll be tired of me before they see my first number."

"Don't be hard to work with," Shubert said. "Get out there and say something."

By this time the audience was applauding sarcastically, so I ran out and said, "Ladies and gentlemen, this is the first time I've ever been on before the acrobats, but we're doing a new number for you tonight and we had a little late rehearsal, and things aren't set up, and this is a new show."

I looked up in the balcony and said, "Hello, Sam."

"That's one of our backers up there," I told the audience in confidential tones. "He says he's not nervous, but I notice that he's buckled his safety belt." It was a stage-wise audience. They knew I was on the spot, so they bought my ad libbing.

I stayed out there for about six minutes. Then the show went on. Afterward Lee Shubert said to the production staff, "Why don't you have Hope open the show that way every perform-ance?"

When they came to me with this notion, I said, "I don't want to do it that way again. But I've got an idea. I'll open it in a box. I'll be the complaint department."

"How do you mean, complaint department?" they asked.

"I'll show you tomorrow," I said.

The next day I popped up in a box before the overture, with the spotlight focused on me, and I said, "Ladies and gentlemen, we're inaugurating a new policy called the Complaint Depart-ment. If you don't like this show, come to me and whisper your beefs to me. If you tell others, it might prejudice them against our production. Also, we could use a few really funny skits. So bring your ideas to me, I'll help you to rewrite them. Maybe be-tween us we can hold the management up for some important dough."

I kept on like that for a while. Then I said, "Well, I guess I've killed about four minutes. Let's go, orchestra!"

I clapped my hands. Nothing happened. I pointed to the or-chestra and said, "Take it away," but they were sleeping in the pit. I yelled, "Men . . . boys, let's go! Boys? Fellas?" Snores. I took out a pistol and shot it. Still they didn't wake up, so I held up a little cash register, pushed a lever, made a bell ring, and the orchestra jumped up and went into the opening number. This became a permanent part of the performance. Before long I was asked to put my stooge act in, too, and Hope and Co. wound up doing quite a lot of the show.

About a third of the way through *Ballyhoo,* I did a few jokes and a little monologue-single. While I was doing it a guy came down the aisle calling out, "Peanuts! Popcorn!"

"Just a minute," I said. "What's the idea selling peanuts and popcorn during my act?"

"I have to do this to make a living," he said. "I only make a hundred dollars a week."

I walked down into the aisle and said, "How much did you say?"

"A hundred dollars a week," he said.

"Give me that basket," I said. "*You* get up there on the stage." I had dozens like that.

We opened in New York at the 44th Street but our notices were only lukewarm. The amount of gold the Shuberts had in the show wasn't large. The other backers were mostly anteing up talent instead of cash. One Saturday night (after a run of about sixteen weeks) our pay was slow in reaching the theater.

"Don't let your blood pressure get out of hand," we were told. "It'll be here Monday."

On Monday a fellow walked down the aisle and announced, "Ladies and gentlemen, there is no money."

There were no more feathers in our angels' wings. I still have about eight hundred dollars in heavenly eiderdown coming to me from *Ballyhoo*.

Chapter 10

I'D MET a young vaudeville comedian named Richie Craig, Jr.,
with an original turn of wit. He began to write some of my
material for me. But before long he contracted T. B. and went
to Saranac Lake for a while. He came back when I was in *Ballyhoo*. When he came over to see me I said, "I'm going out to
Hackensack tonight to play a benefit. Why don't you come
along?"

On the way out I said, "Why don't we do a double Master of
Ceremonies act. I'll open it and introduce you and you can do
your stuff."

Having T. B. had made him blue, despondent and unsure of
himself. I wanted to get him started again, and I knew if he got
out there in front of an audience he'd like it and he'd feel good.
He promised to take a crack at it so I opened the show, did a few
acts, then introduced Richie.

His lines were just beautiful, just great. But they were a mite
subtle for the kind of consumers we were playing to. They didn't
get him and one fellow began in heckle him brutally. I knew that
Richie had "the feel" back again and his belief in himself when
he put that heckler away.

"They took a fellow to the hospital in this town just last week,"
Richie said. "Had a brain operation. They took out his brain
and examined it, and while his brain was out he jumped out of
the window. They found him later in a theater heckling the
actors."

We finished the show with a parody about Milton Berle, who was the outstanding thief of bad gags in the history of show business. He kids himself about it now. But for all I know he's stealing gags from others about him stealing gags. In those day he was operating like the James Brothers. He'd steal anything he thought would get him a laugh if it wasn't nailed down. He was delightfully unabashed.

Richie died while I was in *Roberta* a year later. We held a benefit for him at the New Amsterdam Theater and almost every performer in New York turned out for it: Eddie Cantor, Pat Rooney, Ted Lewis—everybody who was in town. There must have been forty acts. It was tremendous. Richie willed me some of his comedy books. I still have them. Some day I hope to have enough time to study them. If they can hone my wit to a razor edge the way they sharpened Richie's, I could use them.

After *Ballyhoo,* I went back into vaudeville once more, dovetailing it with picture-house work. Then, in 1932, I met God's gift to the other Crosbys. Just before I opened at the Capitol I saw Bing for the first time. It was near The Friars club on 48th street. He was on the Cremo radio program then. Two months later we were both booked into the Capitol with Abe Lyman and his orchestra.

The big electric sign hanging before the Capitol spelled out BING CROSBY AND BOB HOPE, just as it has spelled it out many times since on the marquee of the Paramount and on other theaters. I was emcee, and after Bing sang his songs, we clowned together. We did our impression of two orchestra leaders meeting in the street. Each of us pulled out a baton and led the other while we talked as if we were leading an orchestra. Next we did our impression of two farmers meeting. One of us asked, "How are things down on the farm?" The other said, "It's pretty cold in the reading room." Real Noel Coward! Then we milked each other's thumbs. It was the beginning of a long, pleasant and profitable association.

The second time I played the Capitol, Major Bowes asked me to be on his radio program. The Major's original "Amateur Hour" was one of radio's all-time high spots. But he also had a show called the "Capitol Family Hour." It went on every Sunday morning. Every time I appeared on the Bowes show I built up a bigger following of radio listeners, and since such Loew executives as Louis K. Sidney and Marvin Schenck figured that a lot of my radio listeners would come to see me in person, they'd book me back into the Capitol. It wasn't that Loew's brass loved my big brown eyes. I did the kind of act they wanted, and I knew how to handle a Capitol audience.

I liked doing my stuff for the Major because his shows had prestige. Being on them was great publicity for me. Bess Mack, the Major's publicity woman, would ask me, "What do you plan to do on the air?"

"I'll get some stuff together and send it over," I told her. Then on Friday I'd send over a script which included the jokes I thought I'd like to do with the Major on Sunday. When I got there on Sunday he'd hand me back my script. By that time he'd have changed it and have taken a lot of the jokes himself. He was real cute, the Major. He was the comedian. He had me playing straight man for him. But he was such a great showman and such a nice guy that I didn't really care. With the exception of his orchestra he had no live audience, but his orchestra did as much laughing as they did playing instrumental music.

The Major must have auditioned them with a joke book in his hand.

A typical Capitol audience was made up of older folks and family types. They liked their comedy slow-starting. You had to be chummy and folksy until you had them warmed up. Richie wrote some of my Capitol material for me. I still remember one of Richie's jests: "My grandfather got caught cheating at chess. He was using loaded bishops."

The Capitol was an exciting theater to play because the stage manager, a man named Lala, could really handle that stage, and it had one of the greatest sound systems anywhere in the world at the time. The place was miked so you could stand on the stage and talked in a natural voice and be heard instantly all over the huge auditorium.

I came into the Capitol one day with what I thought was a clever bit. It led out of a song called "My Mom." I started out by saying: "Ladies and gentlemen, I want to sing about a little lady I know is dear to all of us, 'My Mom.' I don't sing serious songs very often but for once I'd like to wax serious."

The orchestra would play an introduction, and I'd sing "My Mom, I love her, my Mom, you'd love her, who wouldn't love her, my Mom; that sweet somebody thinks I'm somebody. I love her, I love her, my Mom," and so on.

It was a popular song at the time, and smart guy that I was,

105

I thought it would be amusing to satirize it. I employed a little old lady to walk out from the wings while I was singing. She'd come up to the microphone and say, "Son, I need food."

I'd flag the orchestra down and say, "How many times have I told you not to bother me while I'm working, Mom."

"But son," she'd say, "I haven't eaten for three days."

I'd go back to my singing and she'd interrupt with "Son, please, I need food."

"How'd you get over the wall, Mom?" I'd ask. "I thought you'd be happy out there. Remember, I sent you a shawl."

It wound up with two stage hands heading her off stage and me finishing the song with a big finale of "She's my madonna, my Mom."

Looking back at it, I have a feeling that I was a fellow with no particular taste or sensitiveness at that point. Strangely enough there were others who felt that way about me, too. After the second show, Louis K. Sidney of Loew's, Inc., called me up and said, "Do me a favor, Bob. Take that 'My Mom' number out of the show."

"Why?" I asked.

"Maybe you don't know it," he said, "but a lot of old ladies come in to see this show. Afterward they go out into the lobby and cry because you're treating your own mother like that."

"Stop it!" I said. "They understand that it's all in fun."

I was stubborn and didn't take it out. After the next show Major Bowes called me and said, "Bob, I think you ought to take that Mom bit out."

"Look," I said, "you don't have to tell me anything about mothers. I have one myself."

Then I stopped. After a little interval, I said, "Thanks Major. It'll be out."

Anybody can have a moment of temporary blindness.

Appearing at the Capitol got me into *Roberta*, a show Jerome Kern and Max Gordon were planning. *Roberta* ran from No-

vember, 1933 through July 14, 1934. It meant that I could watch
a genius, Jerome Kern, close up.

I'd have worked that show for nothing (almost) to stand in
the wings and listen to his music. I also enjoyed the artistry of
Otto Harbach, who did the lyrics and the book. And I got a boot
out of being associated with Fay Templeton, Tamara, George
Murphy, Fred MacMurray—he played sax as one of the bands-
men in the show—the California Collegians, and Sidney Green-
street.

Also on the female side of the talent jamboree was Lyda
Roberti, the original blonde bombshell. The bombshell went off
at every performance. Lyda may be gone, but she's in my book
for good.

The girls in *Roberta* were beautiful and I was young and looking for detours. Once I got a load of them, I went out and bought
a bottle of an after-shave lotion which was supposed to make a
man smell like old leather.

My role in *Roberta* was Huck Haines; I led the band in the
show. George Murphy was cast as my manager. Ray Middleton
played a football player who owned a women's dress shop. I was
his pal.

Because it's such a stand-out in the memory of all theatergoers
old enough to remember it, it's hard to realize now that *Roberta*
had rough going when it opened in Philadelphia; that it was decided that it needed more comedy and extra staging. Hazard
Short was brought down from New York to relight the show.
When he was through, it was beautiful enough to eat with a
spoon. I myself suggested a few jokes and an idea or two to
Otto. One of those ideas was for me to get together with the
California Collegians and do "the organ bit" they'd done in
vaudeville. The Collegians wore gloves which looked like organ
keys. I played those keys. Each time I touched a glove it brought
forth a different note.

Since the plot had to do with my football player pal who
owned a women's dress shop, it gave me a chance to talk about

different dresses and colors and things like that. I had a joke that went, "Long dresses don't bother me. I've got a good memory."

Otto let me use all of the jokes I suggested, with one exception. When Tamara sang "Smoke Gets in Your Eyes" to me, I lit a cigarette, sat there, watched her and listened. It was her musical way of telling me that she was in love with my football-player pal, but that she wasn't going any good with him.

She led into the song by saying, "There's an old Russian proverb, 'When your heart's on fire, smoke gets in your eyes.'"

At that point I wanted to say, "We have a proverb over here in America too. 'Love is like hash. You have to have confidence in it to enjoy it.'"

When I asked Otto if I could insert this, he said, "I don't think it'll go."

I still thought it would slay them. So one night, just before we went on for the second act in which Tamara sang "Smoke," Jerome Kern joined me in the wings.

"I have a joke I'd like to use," I told him. And I told him about it. "Try it," he said. So I put it in and it pulled one of the biggest laughs, if not the biggest, in the show. After the last curtain, Otto said to me, "That joke was successful. Keep it in. I was wrong about it."

During one scene, I wore a silk hat and carried an ebony cane with an ivory knob. Fred MacMurray asked me, "Could I borrow your hat and cane tomorrow? I'm making a test for Paramount." A couple of weeks later he said, "I'd like to borrow the hat and cane once more. They want me to do an extra test. I'm testing for *The Gilded Lily*, with Claudette Colbert."

Not long after that he told me he was going to Hollywood. I remember thinking, *They'll kick his brains out out there. That's not for me.* At that time most people in the "thittuh" made a point of saying Hollywood stank. It was the smart thing to say that they got you out there, gave you a run-around, then sent you back East with calluses on your sitz platz.

Three or four months later, while I was walking down Broadway, I looked up at the Paramount Theater and flipped. A big sign said: CLAUDETTE COLBERT IN *THE GILDED LILY*, WITH FRED MACMURRAY. I couldn't wait to run in and catch him. There was Mac just floating through his part like an old master. He'd skipped the usual drudgery of playing bits and was a star from the start.

I'd had a couple of offers myself while I was in *Roberta*. One from RKO, who wanted me for a picture with Jack Haley. But I couldn't see it. I was doing radio guest shots and I liked them. I figured that radio was coming fast as a medium and that it deserved me.

Nor would it have been profitable for me to take a chance on going out to California to do a picture for seven hundred fifty dollars. I didn't think they would have had too much respect for me at those prices. So I decided not to take the offers. At the time I was earning dough by doing radio, movie shorts, and working in *Roberta*. (Although the way I was getting rid of it, I was thinking of working at a gas station on the side to get up enough money for the laundry.) But seriously, I was doing very well. And Al Lloyd, my insurance agent, was still collecting part of my take and socking it into annuities.

It hadn't always been that way between radio and me. During *Ballyhoo*, I'd been on the Rudy Vallee show for Fleischmann's Yeast. I got a rise out of nobody. Then I'd been on the RKO "Theater of the Air" a couple of times without making *Variety* get out an extra. I think it must have been this failure of mine to set the airwaves on fire that inspired a joke I thought up later when I could afford to jest about flopping. "The first program I did was so bad," I'd say, "that I got an envelope from my sponsor. But there wasn't any letter in it. Just a handful of his hair."

In addition Willie Howard, Lulu McConnell and I had done one of the first experimental TV shows for CBS. I don't recall the exact date, but it must have been before February, 1933, for the station stopped TV operation then. Those early TV days were rough going. The electricians threw oceans of light on you, but if the viewers could decide which sex you were, it was a technical triumph. Watching some of those prehistoric TV shows, all I saw were a lot of dots trying to look like people. I didn't think it was going anywhere. Nobody thought so in those days. Otherwise, we'd all own nineteen TV stations apiece now—over the FCC's dead bodies, of course.

For that matter, if Willie Howard had been even partly right in his selection of horses, I would be independently wealthy to-day and I wouldn't need TV. He was a great man for the ponies, and I was his constant companion in such ventures.

About this time I remember being in Atlantic City helping Jack Benny celebrate a new radio contract he'd just landed.

Canada Dry had promised to give him six thousand, six hundred dollars a show, so we had all had a drink on him. To me, that's a stickout because I used to think: *Wouldn't it be amazing to make a thousand dollars a week! If I ever made a thousand a week I don't think I'd talk to anybody. How could you make a thousand dollars a week! If I'd told them back home that I was making four hundred a week they'd think I'd been robbing a bank and was hiding out.*

But to get back to *Roberta* and the flood of memories it brings. While I was in it I had a little Scottie dog called Huck. He was named after the character I played in the show. I had Marilyn Miller's old dressing room at the New Amsterdam, and Huck sat at the top of the stairs. He was a great come-on, great bait. When the girls went by they stopped and petted him. As a result, I did a nice business with those beauties. My dresser, Frank Rockwell, said to me, "Don't ever get married. You're doing fine the way it is."

"Don't worry," I said, "The way I figure it, marriage will only dull things up."

I'd also bought a long, sleek Pierce-Arrow and had hired a chauffeur. My reason for this flashy turnout was my feeling that now that I was in a Broadway hit, I ought to stop using anything as plebeian as a taxi. I thought I ought to drive up to the theater, get out, throw copies of my photographs to the populace like confetti, then dash into the stage door, calling over my shoulder, "Wait, Meadows."

One night while I was in *Roberta*, my pal George Murphy invited me to the Lambs Club. We downed a couple of beers and he said, "I want you to hear a girl sing. Her name is Dolores Reade. She sings at the Vogue Club."

We went over to the Vogue on 57th Street. It was a little club Bea Lillie had opened. She didn't own it but she'd opened it. And I heard this girl sing. She had a low, husky voice. She sang somewhat in the style of Marian Harris, soft and sweet, not a shouter. Dinah Shore comes close to being like Dolores.

She sang, "It's Only a Paper Moon" and "Did You Ever See a Dream Walking?" That did it. I asked if I could take her out. Once we were alone she asked, "You're in *Roberta?*"

"Yes," I said. "Why don't you catch me in the matinee tomorrow?"

When she didn't come backstage to see me next day after the matinee I couldn't understand it. A couple of days later when I saw her I asked, "What happened?"

"I didn't come back to say hello because I didn't know you had such a big part in the show," she said. "I thought you were in the chorus and I was embarrassed at my stupidity."

From then on I was at the Vogue every night, waiting to take Dolores home. I must have given the doorman at her apartment hundreds of dollars in tips to let me park in front of the joint and sit there with her. I dismissed the chauffeur and we talked. It was our inspiration point, our Flirtation Walk, our moonlight canoe trip all rolled into one—there in front of the Delmonico on Ninth Avenue. It wasn't long before Dolores' mother took her to Florida to play a night club date in Miami. While she was gone, I lived on long distance from morning till night. I was in love. Dolores said she was, too.

She must have meant it because she broke her Florida contract and came back to New York. About that time I went back to Cleveland to see my mother, who was desperately ill. While I was gone Dolores saw a statement in a gossip column which said: "A certain chorus girl says she's going to marry Bob Hope." I hadn't seen that particular girl for six months, but it almost broke up our romance. It would have finished it if I hadn't convinced Dolores that the whole thing was a columnist's blooper.

After that we went back to sitting in front of the Delmonico and making plans to get married. We picked Erie, Pennsylvania, for our wedding. I can't remember why. I was in a thick, pink fog anyway.

Once we were married, I put Dolores into my vaudeville act. *Roberta* had closed so we went around the big-time circuits together. Our act went like this: I did my regular act, then I introduced her. She came out dressed in a lovely gown, looking very beautiful, and sang a song. After her first song I came back out and when she started her second number, I didn't leave the stage. I just stayed there, stood close to her and looked at her. Then I looked at the audience, my expression asking, "Ain't she beautiful? Ain't she something? How about it. Just how about it!"

I stroked her arm and pretended it looked good enough to eat, which wasn't hard to do. Then I nibbled it gently. This brought a roar from the audience. Then I hugged her; she broke up and stopped singing and I said, "Don't let me bother you. Just keep right on."

She did another half chorus and I lay down before the footlights, rolled over on my back looked at her adoringly. If she hadn't been so beautiful and if it hadn't been so obvious to the onlookers that we were really in love, the act would have fallen flat. As it was, it played very well indeed.

Chapter 11

AFTER I'D BEEN on the road with Dolores a while, Jack Mc-Gowan, the librettist, and Ray Henderson, the composer, asked me to be in a show called *Say When*. It was produced by A. L. Berman. It starred Harry Richman and it featured Linda Watkins and Prince Mike Romanoff. The only trouble was Dolores didn't like working as a single any more. *Say When* was set for a Boston tryout so the Loew office told Dolores, "Why don't you do an act at Loew's State in Boston? That way you'll be there while Bob's there."

She thought that fine and dandy, so she put an act together and went up to work alone as Dolores Reade, a singing act.

I stayed at the theater each night, rehearsing, and the morning Dolores opened at Loew's State I was sleeping late in the Ritz-Carlton Hotel. If I'd been gallant, I'd have been up and in the theater, cheering. I tried to salve my conscience by telling myself it was good experience for her to get in there and pitch by herself.

While I was lying there the phone rang. It was Dolores. She was crying. "Come right over," she sobbed. "I'm going to quit. They didn't like me. The band played too loud and the lights were wrong. Everything was wrong."

I went over for her next show. I discovered that she hadn't known what to tell the people at the State. She'd just walked on and sung. Period.

"Get the lights down," I told the manager. "Let's give her some better lighting. A magenta spot for her dress. A white pin spot for her head. Have the orchestra keep it down a little."

They gave her a little more production and her act pulled together beautifully. Give her any kind of decent staging and my girl was good.

Before we'd shoved off for Boston, Dolores and I had been eating at an Italian restaurant on 46th Street. We'd gone in there three times a week to wind a little spaghetti. The same fellow was always seated by the door and he smiled at me as I came in.

He'd say, "Hello, Bob. How are you?"

I'd say, "I'm fine. How are you?"

One day during a rehearsal at the Imperial, I saw this same man sitting out front, and I asked Harry Richman, "Who is he?"

"That's Lucky Luciano," Harry told me.

"Why is he watching rehearsals?" I asked.

"They say he's got a piece of the show," Harry said.

After that, my collar felt as if it were a tourniquet. I was on a spot. If I didn't get laughs the "boys" might come up and see me. As a result, my jokes were a little on the frantic side and I speeded up my timing until I was whizzing.

But the tension created by Signor Luciano's participation in our enterprise didn't bother one member of our cast, Prince Mike Romanoff. A number had been written for Mike about how he was on his way out to crash a party on Long Island. He worked in shorts and a Tryrolean hat and he did the act with a bunch of girls who were all hitch-hiking out to the same party.

In those days, it wasn't quite clear whether he was Harry Gurgesen of Brooklyn or one of the legitimate Romanoffs. Either way he was an interesting and stimulating personality. Every night after the show he dressed in tails and top hat and went out on the town—after coming to me first and asking me if I had a ten spot I wasn't using. He always paid me. He came back on Saturday and laid it right on the table. When he got up into the chips with his Beverly Hills restaurant, he went back to New York, looked up all the waiters he'd cuffed for so many years, and gave each of them a hundred-dollar bill.

Say When was supposed to be a starring vehicle for Harry Richman, but the way it worked out, my comedy part was the fat one. Harry was one of Broadway's greatest stars, but he was playing an unsympathetic lover and his part was thin. If he'd had a good score, he'd have been all right, but he had no big songs. I was shortsighted and hamola enough to enjoy the situation.

Coming back on the train from Boston for the New York opening, Harry asked me into his drawing room, opened a bottle of champagne and said, "I'm thrilled about your success in the show. You've got a great part and you handle it well. I wish I were half as good. It's unfortunate for the show that I'm not. I'm the star, and if I'm weak, it won't help any of us."

I thought it mighty white of him to be so big about it. He could have gone behind my back and beefed, and tried to take away some of my lines.

He was right. The show played sixteen weeks, then folded. A horse from Cain's Warehouse passed me one day and winked at me. It was as if he was saying, "It won't be long now." Cain's in the place where old scenery, props and costumes go when they die. Sure enough, pretty soon a crew from Cain's added our scenery and costumes to their stock.

Say When's year, 1934, was a pretty tough year along the street of dreams. Roosevelt was doing the best he could, but the Blue Eagle was laying an egg. In 1934, I remember seeing an actor in front of the Palace tighten his belt. I said, "What are you doing?" and he said, "Just having breakfast."

Nevertheless, when the show closed, Dolores and I went on a trip to Bermuda. A fellow came up to me and said, "If you and Mrs. Hope would like to go on a Bermuda tour, with all expenses paid, all you'll have to do is do a show on the boat coming back."

"That," I said, "sounds great. I need a little rest. But I don't want to be announced as a working guest. They can ask me if I'd care to get up and do a show, but I don't want the people on the boat to think that I'm singing for my trip."

We went bucketing and rolling and pitching and tossing across the Gulf Stream, stayed at a luxury hotel and played all the Bermuda golf courses. On the way back when they had the ship's concert, one of the ship's officers announced, "We're fortunate to have a gentleman on board from Broadway. He's a comedian. I'd like to have you meet him. Take a bow, Bob Hope."

I stood up and said, "I'd like to do a little something to entertain you but I have a sore throat."

It was supposed to be a gag. But nobody laughed. I looked at the captain and he looked at me and I could see that he was thinking in terms of a long swim. So I hurriedly went into a twenty-minute show.

In the last few weeks of 1935, I landed in the Bromo-Seltzer radio show on NBC, with Al Goodman, James Melton and Jane Frohman. Which brings me to a girl called Honey Chile Wilder. Her real name was Patricia. I'd met her in Louis Shurr's office. Louis is Broadway's "Doctor" Shurr, one of the most colorful theatrical agents who ever worked that stem. He's famous for his ermine-coat routine. He had an ermine coat which he'd lend to a girl when he took her out. Then when he took her home, he repossessed the coat. The doctor is a little on the short side, but he likes to go out with statuesque blondes who tower above him.

His title "Doctor" stems from the fact that theatrical producers who're in trouble call him in to doctor their sick shows. He doesn't prescribe new material, but he knows whom to approach for a medicinal bank roll and how to give a cast a transfusion of new blood. Doctor Shurr has been my agent for shows ever since *Roberta*. He also handles me for pictures.

I could do a whole play about the Doctor. I'd like to get that on the record before Tennessee Williams or Rodgers and Ham-

117

merstein get inspired about him. He's been out in California of late, but before that he had an office in the Paramount Building in New York. That office was the Broadway equivalent of Hollywood's Central Casting Agency. If you were looking for any kind of act, comic or tragic, you dropped in and the Doctor wrapped it up for you to take out. He was like a king in that office—Otto Soglow's Little King. It was a treat to watch him operate.

But to get back to Honey Chile. She was from Macon, Georgia, and she had a thick, spoonbread Southern accent. I was looking for a "different" personality and when she said, "Ha you, Mistah Hope?" I knew I had one. I took her on for a couple of tryout shows. I was worried about the possibility of her having stage fright—until she walked out before her first Capitol audience and said, "Pahdon me, Mistah Hope. Does the Greyhound bus stop heah?" then instead of looking at me, she looked at the audience and smiled. I knew then that Honey Chile had been born unembarrassed. In fact, she had so much poise I began to worry about whether anyone would notice me on the stage.

Honey Chile was an unusual doll. You rarely find a girl who's pretty and funny at the same time. Usually if a girl's funny, it's because she's unattractive and being witty is a way of attracting attention. But Honey Chile was naturally funny. She became a Broadway celebrity and people wanted to see her and listen to her. I once asked some prominent folks to meet her and catch her show. I'd told them about her deep-South accent, but unknown to me, she'd been out with an English lord the night before and she'd absorbed his "what-what" way of talking. She did that one performance with an English accent. She must have had chameleon blood.

Later, after a screen test, RKO signed her. Her first morning in Hollywood, she rented an apartment, paid a one hundred dollar deposit, and reported to the studio. At the end of the day she couldn't remember where the apartment was. She never did remember. She just found another one.

118

It was also on her first day in Hollywood that she waited a long time to see the head of RKO, Sam Briskin. When she was finally admitted to his office, she said, "I've been waiting to see you for two hours. Who do you think you are, Darryl Zanuck?"

With some movie moguls that could have been the end of her contract. Not Sam. He had a sense of humor. He kept her working for him.

Honey Chile and I were on the Bromo Seltzer show for fifteen weeks. Radio contracts usually run in units of thirteen weeks. I forget why this particular one ran two weeks longer. Our Hooper never soared above two and a quarter. As a result, our sponsors took so much of their own product they finally shucked the whole deal. When Bromo-Seltzer fizzed out of my life, I went back into vaudeville with Dolores and we tootled around the Loew Circuit together once more.

In 1936 I landed in the *Ziegfeld Follies* with Fanny Brice, Josephine Baker, Gertrude Neisen and Hugh McConnell. Fanny and I did an English number called "Fawncy-Fawncy"; and I played Daddy to her Baby Snooks. But for me, the big thing was that I introduced a song written by Vernon Duke and Ira Gershwin. It was called "I Can't Get Started With You." I picked out a big, beautiful, redheaded show gal in the show to sing it to. Her name was Eve Arden. She wore a crimson cape. I wore a dinner jacket and a Homburg. The idea was to look as if we'd just come from the theater.

When I began to warble this ditty to Eve, she walked away from me and I followed her, sang another eight bars, leaned over her shoulder and breathed deeply with unrequited passion. When I looked into Eve's eyes and sang, "I can't get started," the people didn't believe it. The first four rows could hear my motor running.

The doorman at the Winter Garden studied this scene for a while, then said to me, "When you lean over her shoulder and

puff like that, why don't you have her look around and ask, 'What's the matter? Have you been running?' "

Eve adopted his line and she got big mileage with it. It just goes to show that humor, like gold or oil, is where you find it.

"I Can't Get Started With You" put me in pictures. Mitchell Leisen and Harlan Thompson (two Hollywood workers who were preparing a script for *The Big Broadcast of 1936* for Paramount) saw me do the number with Eve, and they hired me. However the hiring was a sort of delayed reaction. They did nothing about it right away. They really wanted Jack Benny for the picture, but when the time came, he couldn't do it. So since they'd thought me Bennyish they eventually hired me. But as I've said, that was to come later.

The *Follies* opened in Philadelphia. About the middle of our second week there Fanny had a bad cold. She'd seen a doctor, who'd given her some pills, but one night she got her pill boxes mixed and at intermission she took some sleeping pills by mistake. The two kinds of pills collided in her insides and did strange things. During her last-act specialty, she forgot where she was in the number and kept starting it all over again. The rest of us stood there in the wings dying for her, for we loved her not only because she was a great star but because she was a great woman. The orchestra leader tried to lead her out of her fog and finally the stage manager rang down the curtain and got her offstage. She didn't go on for the rest of the show. I've never forgotten that moment of frozen horror when we saw her floundering, confused, and could do nothing to help her.

Later on, the *Follies* was shuttered for two days while Fanny had some dental work done. For this ordeal, she flew to California to see Charlie Pincus in Beverly Hills. Charlie is my dentist now. He's one of the greatest and most expensive dentists in the world. It costs about fifty dollars just to walk through his door. He's so much a Hollywood dentist that you feel that you ought to get up early and drop in at a make-up department before you check in at the Pincus office. I think he's working up to have specially piped-in music come through his tools.

But Charlie's worth it. He's a genius with his hammers and drills. A lot of the stars go to him to have their teeth whitened and to ask him to make portable caps for them. These caps make their smiles attractive when they're before a camera, but at other times they can be discarded. Charlie's so exclusive I sometimes think he checks both your Hooper and your Dun-and-Bradstreet rating before taking you on as a patient. He's mighty useful, though. If your teeth need him, he'll fly to London for your opening.

Another reason why I loved being in the *Follies* was because it was put on at the Winter Garden, and the Winter Garden was in the middle of all Broadway activity. My favorite barber, Teddy Lopez, was in the Taft Hotel across the street from the stage door. I'd gone to him off and on for ten years when I was in New York. If you went to Teddy you didn't have to buy a paper; Teddy gave you all the Broadway scoop. He knew whose options were being picked up and whose were being dropped, and the latest word about what romances were budding or withering.

He shaved Winchell five times a week and also took care of a lot of other Broadway personalities, so you really got the news from him. He insisted on good tickets for opening nights—for free. He was my guest on such occasions. I didn't want to find a small fire breaking out on top of my head the next time I had a trim.

I hiked to the theater and back from 65 Central Park West, where I lived. It was just the right distance for an after-dinner stroll. It was a kick, whipping down to the theater and saying "Hi" to the traffic cops and to people on the Avenue and to the people in the show when you got there. That was really living. There was always something going on.

A lot of things happened to me while I was in the *Follies*. For one thing I got a radio job with Atlantic Refining. Then, when the *Follies* began to show signs of petering out, I was asked to go and see Vinton Freedley, who was putting on a show called *Red, Hot and Blue*, with Ethel Merman and Jimmy Durante. Doc Shurr went along with me to quibble about money, and he quibbled me into one thousand dollars a week. Then the doctor took up the matter of my billing. He didn't want me lost among the stars. Ethel and Jimmy also had their eyes on the billing, and a crisscross arrangement of names was worked out so nobody would be top dog.

The plot of the show had to do with a girl who'd sat on a hot waffle iron and had been branded by it. It was an intriguing thought, but the thing that intrigued me most was the fact that

I had a Cole Porter song or two to sing. One of them—a number I did with Ethel Merman—was called "D'Lovely."

I had fun with Merman and Durante at rehearsals, but the fun didn't really bubble and become riotous until our opening in October, 1936, in Boston. I had a specialty act with Jimmy. In it we were dressed as hunters. We aimed up into the stage loft, pulled the triggers of our shotguns, there was a loud bang, bang, and ducks fell around us. The gag was that once when we *didn't* shoot, a duck fell just the same.

We rehearsed it until Jimmy had it letter-perfect, but when he came to this routine on opening night in Boston, he went blank. He walked to the edge of the orchestra pit, said, "Ha-cha-cha" to the orchestra, as if he'd gone up in his lines. Then he came back to me, gave me a frustrated look and slapped his hips. Next he walked over to the wings and said in a loud voice to the prompter, "Trow me da book." No one can blow lines louder and funnier than Jimmy and it broke the audience up.

Later, I realized that this forgetfulness on Jimmy's part was framed. He'd worked it out down to the last frustrated motion, knowing that it would wow that first-night audience. Lou Clayton, a brilliant guy and a big help to Jimmy, was still alive. Jimmy and Lou worked out such "extemporaneous" stuff together.

In the same show, Jimmy and I had a scene in which we leaned out over the orchestra pit at an impossible angle without falling. This gimmick is especially effective for drunk acts. You wear a cleat in your heel with a slot in it. There's a screw in the stage, you slip the slot over the head of the screw, and after that you can lean at any angle you like. Our second night in Boston, Jimmy didn't do it the way it was supposed to be done. He fell into the pit among the trombone players, flailed around, broke three or four instruments, and had himself a ball. The audience loved it too. Jimmy is never satisfied with the laughs the script writers put in for him. He's always after the extra-hysterical laugh that's not in the book.

Imagine both of our noses on the same stage. We used to fence with our snoots for the spotlight!

A man named Harry Donnelley played piano for Jimmy. At intermission, Donnelley went out and wandered around. If he saw anybody out front Jimmy knew, he said, "Come on back and see Jimmy." Then he'd stop at the end of the dressing room hallway and say, "Wait. I'll see if Jimmy's dressed."

The visitor waited while Harry went to Jimmy's dressing room, three doors away. My own dressing room was next to Jimmy's and I could hear the conversation. Jimmy would be reading a racing form to see if he still owned his home, and Donnelley would say to him, "You've met the guy who's waiting outside. He's so and so from Punxatawney. He did a story on you back in 1941." Then Jimmy'd get up, go out and say, "How are ya? How's Punxatawney?"

Ethel Merman and I had to hold our hands over our mouths when old Schnoz said those things because we'd heard him being cued in advance by Donnelley. Comical as it seemed, being cued into good public relations made a lot of friends for Jimmy.

If you meet thousands of people, a memory-man like Donnelley is a useful thing to have around.

Myself, I have no particular system for remembering the names of old friends. I just try to keep lucky. Once when I got back to Cleveland, I was told that a fellow was coming up to see me, but he wouldn't give his name, and I thought, *So he's going to make a quiz show out of it.*

As he came up the steps, backstage at the Palace in Cleveland, I took a look at him and I remembered that he was the father of Wilbur Zink, a boy I'd gone to school with who's now a Cleveland attorney. I also remembered that he used to be a fire chief at the 105th Street Station. I'd walked by that station doing my Charlie Chaplin imitations.

When I asked, "How's the fire department, Mr. Zink?" he stopped halfway up the steps, broke into a big smile, and we were home.

You like to remember names because your old friends get a complex about you and begin to ask themselves, "I wonder if he'll remember me?" They think "you've gone Hollywood," or maybe "gone Beverly Hills," or even "gone Bel Air." So you like to give them no reason for suspecting such a thing.

When I first came to Paramount and walked around a corner of one of the stages, I met Fred MacMurray. I hadn't seen him since I'd loaned him a hat and cane in *Roberta.* Now he was a big shot, an important star in pictures and I wondered what his reaction would be. I didn't have to wonder long. He rushed up to me and gave me that old college reunion bear hug. If I needed anything to tell me how important it is to stay human, that was it.

There's another side to the picture. People I've never known claim to be my long-lost friends. It's no secret that I used to play pool at the Alhambra Billiard Palace in Cleveland and I meet a lot of people who open with, "We used to play pool together."

I played with many people, but not *that* many.

I get a different reception from my real poolroom cronies. I could walk into the Alhambra and say, "Hey fellers. I'm Bob Hope. I went outta here several years ago." And they'd ask, "How far didja follow that blonde?"

To go back to Durante, though, my pet story about him is this: He has always been a soft touch for a benefit, and during the run of *Red, Hot and Blue*, he came into my dressing room and said, "I want you to play a benefit with me in a couple of weeks over in Hackensack, New Jersey."

"What kind of a benefit?" I asked.

"It's for a bunch of the boys over there. I'd like to do a favor for them," he said. "If you'll do it for me, I'll appreciate it."

The benefit rolled around and we were in Jimmy's car with Harry Donnelley at the wheel. We reached Hackensack, went into a hotel, walked up to the second floor and down a big hallway to a banquet room. When we appeared, everybody yelled, "Hey, Schnozzola! Hey, Jimmy! Hi, Schnozzola!"

They all knew him. None of them knew me. After all, I'd only been in a couple of shows. Jimmy went into his "I was walking down Broadway de odder day" patter, then after one number, he introduced me. He said, "I want you to meet a good friend of mine, Bob Hope. He's in the show with me."

There were only men there. They were a tough-looking group. They had granite faces. As I recall it, their reason for getting together was a common interest: the manufacture and sale of beer. I got up and did five or six minutes.

I went over with a hush and I thought, *I've done my part. I'll get Jimmy back.*

So I said, "Let's bring our friend, Jimmy Durante, back for another number."

Everybody applauded, but Jimmy wasn't there. I looked toward the door. The doorman shrugged and said, "He went down the hall."

I said, "Get him, will you?" and to kill time plunged into a golf routine. I did this routine for four or five minutes, then said, "Now for Jimmy Durante."

The hard-faced citizens out front applauded again. I looked at the door once more and the guy said, "I told ya. He went down the hall."

I said, "Fellas, it's been wonderful. You've been kind, but I think I'll go and get Jimmy."

I ducked out into the hall, but I couldn't find him. Running to the hotel desk, I asked, "Where's Mr. Durante?"

The man there said, "He went downstairs to the street."

I rushed down to the street level, and there was Jimmy in his car, just sitting there and laughing. "How'd you do?" he asked.

"How did I do?" I said. "I thought this was your benefit. What's the idea of doing one number and running out on me and leaving me holding the bag?"

He said, "What were you staying on all night for? I didn't know you'd be so hammy."

He was laughing so hard he had trouble asking me even that. To him, it was the big gag of the year. Me, I was speechless.

In the summer of 1937 our show, *Red, Hot and Blue*, moved to Chicago. One night Jimmy and I were driving to the Lake Shore Athletic Club for the annual charity show. We'd promised to do our stuff after our last curtain. The same thing happened that had happened in Hackensack. Everybody yelled, "Hi ya, Jimmy! Hi ya, Schnozzola." He grabbed the mike, did one number, then introduced me.

It wasn't the same kind of audience we'd had in Hackensack, but it was tough in another way. They'd had a few snootfuls; they were real happy. Everybody wore paper hats and rattled noisemakers. I'd done a few jokes, when I looked from the corner of my eye and saw Durante trying to sneak out of the door. Unfortunately for his plans, he'd been stopped by five or six fellows who wanted to talk to him. I put all the strength I could muster into my voice and screamed into the microphone, "Let's bring old Jimmy Durante back here for his favorite number!"

When he heard me he turned and heeled like a sick beagle. By this time I had built him up until he was a bigger attraction than Stalin would have been riding Churchill piggyback. The crowd applauded riotously and he *had* to come back.

As he passed me I said, "Hackensack, you double-crosser."

Then I ran outside, got into a cab and left him there. The next day he wrote, "You are a louse," on my dressing-room mirror with lipstick, and threw powder all over the place.

But with all of his violent ideas of humor, he's bighearted and he lives to be nice to people. I don't think he has an enemy. I've never heard of one.

Ethel Merman is one of the greatest feminine clowns the theater has known. She's a genius if there ever was one. And could she sing? What a power house! One day her high note threw every Hoboken ferry off schedule. I love that Merman. With all her clowning, she never abuses her material. She knows how to clown and still make the audience enjoy it and also make the cast feel that they're having fun, but she never hurts a laugh.

The way some performers clown, they hurt jokes to a point where the audience doesn't enjoy them. But Merman has the ability to clown and let the audience get in on it too, and the whole thing is a big ball. I'm afraid I used to go a little too far clowning with her and kidding with her in the show. I used a lot of ad libs and tomfoolery not in the script. Every three or four days the stage manager came to me and said, "Mr. Hope, I wish you'd use more discretion. The clowning you're doing with Miss Merman is hurting the number."

In May, 1937, while I was still in *Red, Hot and Blue,* I began twenty-six weeks on radio for Woodbury Soap, with Shep Fields and his Rippling Rhythm. It was also when I was in *Red, Hot and Blue* that I finally closed a deal with Paramount to go to Hollywood in *The Big Broadcast of 1938.* I finally went for a seven-year deal with options, starting at twenty thousand dollars a picture. The deal called for me to make three pictures a year.

In the meantime, I'd had a couple of brushes with film making, but I hadn't fallen in love with it. During the run of *Roberta*

I signed a contract with Educational Pictures to make one short, plus five more if Educational still wanted me after seeing my first one. I went over to Astoria, where Educational had a studio, and a famous director, Al Christie, directed Leah Ray and me in a short called "Going Spanish." You can still see it on television, which proves that TV must be stronger than some people think.

It was the second time I'd seen myself on the screen—the first was that test at Pathé. Once more I thought I was terrible. In the picture Leah Ray and I had a hokey, Mexican-jumping-bean scene. I ate some of the beans and they made me jump around. Leah was good in the picture, but I didn't like myself, the comedy or the script.

After the short was wrapped up, I dropped into the Rialto one night where it was showing. Walter Winchell was there. As we came out of the theater, he asked, "How do you like your picture?" I must have been pretty bitter about it, for the next day Winchell's column carried this item: "When Bob Hope saw his picture at the Rialto, he said, 'When they catch John Dillinger, the current Public Enemy No. 1, they're going to make him sit through it twice.' "

The column had no sooner hit the streets than Doc Shurr called me. I could hear big drops of sweat splashing at his end of the wire. "I've just had a call from Jack Skirball at Educational," he said. "That was a very funny crack of yours in Winchell's column, but Educational doesn't think it's funny and they're dropping your option."

In spite of my parting with Educational, Sam Sax, of Warner Brothers, decided to take a chance on me. He gave me a contract to make six pictures at Warner Brothers' Eastern Studio on Avenue M. They made quite a number of shorts and trailers down there.

There was a desperate situation there one day because I couldn't get a certain scene right, and we were two or three hours behind schedule. Lionel Stander was working in the picture with me, and I was supposed to come out of a phone booth and run into him. The public might not be aware of it, but Lionel has one brown eye and one blue eye. I didn't know about this color mixture until I saw him for the first time in that phone-booth scene. It struck me as so funny that it broke me up and I couldn't deliver my lines. Each time I tried it got worse and worse, until finally Sam Sax came out of his office, hit me with a look that meant, "You are in danger of joining the faceless army of the unemployed." That sobered me.

Sax could turn out a short in three days. If we fell behind schedule, we got a three-minute lunch period. If we really fell behind, Sam put a lunch scene in the picture, and we ate while the cameras rolled. When I went to Hollywood to make *The Big Broadcast of 1938* for Paramount, I was prepared to find things there done the same way, only on a much bigger scale. If they put a meal in a picture, I figured it would be a seven-course dinner.

Chapter 12

I ARRIVED in Hollywood in September of 1937 carrying a log-size chip on my shoulder. I had the feeling a lot of Broadway people had then. I've already said that we were convinced that we'd be pushed around in the movies and that we wouldn't be given a square shuffle. The truth is that while the movie makers try to produce critical successes, they also have to make money. And popular names with star value are a help at the box office. The studios' brass can't be blamed if they don't give an unknown the same break they give a Gary Cooper, a Jimmy Stewart or a Clark Gable. A newcomer has to prove himself before he gets the big buildup.

I didn't know this when I got off the train in Pasadena to begin work at Paramount. I was still on the muscle, still belligerent. I said a very hammy thing to my agent, Doctor Shurr, who was with me. "Doctor, this town isn't going to shove me around. I've saved a little money, you know. If I don't like it here, I can always go back East. My part in this film had better be good, that's all."

At Paramount I met Billy Selwyn, the assistant producer assigned to the film. He greeted me with, "You're a lucky fellow. Wait until you hear the number Leo Robin and Ralph Ranger have written for you to sing with Shirley Ross in this picture."

He took me over to the studio music department and played a recording of "Thanks for the Memory." It sounded so beautiful that I asked if I could borrow it to play for my wife at the hotel, where we were staying.

I played it for her. She listened and said, "I don't think it's so much."

"It's a terrific number," I protested.

"Not to me," she said.

Dolores is a wonderful girl; she's both the salt and the pepper of the earth. But she's only human, and being human, she makes human mistakes. (When I tell her this she stares at her wedding ring, then looks at me. I know what she's thinking.) "Thanks for the Memory" was only the number that kept me in pictures when I finished work in my first film. For that matter, it was only the most important song in my life.

When I was in *Ballyhoo* in New York, I'd gone to a little speakeasy in Greenwich Village after the show. Beatrice Kay was singing there, gratis. For fun. She was also working clubs.

On my way, I used to stop in at One Fifth Avenue, where they had a lovely cocktail dinner room. There I saw this beautiful gal named Dorothy Lamour. She leaned against a wall with her head back, à la Libby Holman in the *Little Shows*, and she sang wonderfully. The next time I saw her she was at the Navarre Hotel on 59th Street. I used to drop in there and look at her too. In fact, she looked so good my car stopped there if I didn't. We got to be friends, and when I came to California and found out that I was playing opposite her in *The Big Broadcast of 1938*, it was a nice reunion.

My option was picked up when the public saw the finished film, but I don't think I'd have stayed around long enough to finish my first picture if it hadn't been for "Thanks for the

Memory," as Mitch Leisen directed it and the way Shirley Ross helped put it over.

Before we began, Mitch said, "I want to have lunch with you and talk about the picture." We went over to Lucy's, an eating place near Paramount, and sat in a booth. "I'm not going to play the heavy director with you," Mitch said. "You've been on the stage long enough to know what it's all about. I saw you in New York, and you'll do. But I want to tell you one thing, and I hope you remember it. In pictures, everything comes through the eyes. Try to think through your eyes."

That tip from Mitch was a mighty useful lesson in movie dramatics. It's the works. He didn't mean that people see a lot of actors' eyes because they're so big on a screen. Even when they're projected, my eyes aren't big. Bing calls me Button Eyes. What Mitch meant was that if a man's happy, you can see it on the screen in his eyes. You can't have happy eyes and a sad face. It doesn't work that way.

In spite of Mitch's advice and "Thanks for the Memory," Paramount almost lost me. During the first day of shooting I was walking down an alley near the executive offices with Ted Lesser, who was then Paramount's casting agent. Someone had erected a scaffolding against a building. Suddenly Ted grabbed my arm and yanked at me. The scaffolding chose that particular second to fall. If Ted hadn't pulled me, I'd have been crushed.

Paramount seemed a chancy place to be. Martha Raye was in *The Big Broadcast*, too. On one set a mirror about seventy-five feet wide and six feet high had been set up behind a bar as part of a gag. Martha was to take a long look into the mirror and as she did it, it would crack. The special effects department had worked it out so that they could apply air pressure behind the mirror at the crucial moment.

This gimmick was O. K. in theory, but when it was time for special effects to do their stuff, they put on too much pressure and the glass shattered. Pieces of it a quarter of an inch thick blew all over. Jagged knives of it shot at us. It was a miracle that

133

none of us were hurt or killed. Slivers could have jabbed us in the brain or sliced our eyeballs. I still wake up at night in a cold sweat remembering it.

One night after we finished *The Big Broadcast,* Mitchell Leisen, Shirley Ross and I dropped in at the Biltmore Bowl to see Shirley receive the Forestry Award. I'm still not sure who gave it, or what it was given for. Could have been a reward for being kind to trees. Publicity workers are always asking you to make a public appearance for reasons you don't understand, but they tell you that it'll get your picture on the A.P., U.P., and I.N.S. wires.

Shirley had been in a couple of pictures, including *Waikiki Wedding,* with Bing. Mitch Leisen had made quite a few good films and was well known. I hadn't and wasn't. Jimmy Greer was master of ceremonies at the Biltmore Bowl, so, after the floor show, he said, "Here's Mitchell Leisen, a director who's directed some great pictures," and so on and so on. "And this lovely leading lady of the films is Shirley Ross." Shirley stood up, took a bow and received her award.

"Now," he said, and he read from a card he pulled from his pocket, "here's a young comedian from Broadway who has just finished his first picture for Paramount." He looked at the card once more, then said, "Bob Hoke."

It made no difference to that audience. Most of them didn't know my real name. Hoke was fine with them. They applauded anyhow. Jimmy was probably right at that. He could have been thinking of some of the pictures I was to make.

I was better known in radio circles back East than I was in the Biltmore Bowl. Before coming to Hollywood, I'd been on the Woodbury radio show. The others in the show had stayed on in New York. The announcer in New York would say, "And now we take you to Hollywood for Bob Hope," and I'd do my portion by leased wire.

In that first crosscountry hook-up I ran head-on into a crisis. Two nights before the show I said to NBC's program man in Hollywood, "You've given out the tickets, haven't you?"

"What tickets?" he asked.

"You know, for the audience," I told him.

"I didn't know you wanted one," he said.

"I've got to have an audience to bounce my comedy off of," I said, "or I'm dead."

Sunday came around and with it my two spots on the Woodbury show—a monologue and a comedy spot—and still no prospect of a live audience. Nobody even bothered to tell the people who were roaming around the broadcasting studio that I was there.

Remembering that Edgar Bergen was broadcasting in the next room, I had an idea. I said to an usher, "Why don't you arrange the ropes you put up to handle the crowds so when the people walk out of the Bergen Hour they'll walk straight into mine?"

He looked doubtful. "They wouldn't do it," he said.

The way he said it, I could see that he meant, "What makes you think they'll welcome such a fate?"

"Leave that to me," I told him.

The Bergen show ended just as the Woodbury hour began, but the New York part of the Woodbury show used up about five minutes before I went on. I'd have that much time in which to trap the unsuspecting. I'd already talked it over with Edgar. "I don't do any aftershow," he said, "and I'll chase them out quick so you can snaffle them." When they streamed out of the Bergen show between the ropes which led them into my studio, they stopped short when all that they saw was me on the stage.

I was hearty, jovial and winning. "Come right in and sit down," I said. "I'm Bob Hope and I'm going to do a show for New York in a minute. It's a very funny show and I think you'll enjoy it."

I suctioned in a house about three-quarters full—counting ushers, newspaper boys and the shoeshine kid from across the street I'd bribed to show up. So I stole my first California radio audience. But it worked. Without the laughter and the feeling that comes from a live audience, I'd have been stone cold dead in the market. By the time I got around to my second Sunday night show from Hollywood, NBC had had tickets printed and distributed and I was okay.

I closed out that radio season with Woodbury. Then I signed with Lucky Strike for a revue originating in Hollywood. Dick Powell was its emcee. He sang a few songs and introduced the guest stars. My share of the goings on was a ten-minute monologue.

Lewis Gensler—he had put on *Ballyhoo* with Bobby Connelly, Norman Anthony and Russell Patterson back in my two-stooge days—produced my next picture, *College Swing*. When I sneaked a look at the script I could see that there was no chance for me to do anything in it. My part was a tiny one. I wasn't well enough established to be that skimpy in a picture and survive. So I put on quite a moving scene in Lew's office. "Lew," I said, "you can't do this to me. I'm new out here and you've got to give me a chance." He came through like a friend. Maybe he remembered the money they still owed me for my work in *Ballyhoo* and maybe he was just a good guy. Anyhow, he built up my part. As a result, once more I looked good enough to stay on at Paramount.

We'd begun to shoot *College Swing* when *The Big Broadcast of 1938* was previewed and Damon Runyon heard me sing "Thanks for the Memory." He wrote a column about it. I remember one sentence if no one else does: "What a delivery, what a song, what an audience reception!"

I saw to it that clippings of Damon's review floated around the Paramount lot by the hundreds. To make sure that they were read, I even dropped them from a balloon over the front office. But seriously, Damon's boost and the fact that I was beginning to be seen by people who counted, at such places as the Turf Club, and doing a show or two for Bing down at his Del Mar race track, was another help to me in surviving in the Hollywood elimination race.

Shirley Ross and I did a recording of "Thanks for the Memory" and it sold quite a few copies, but it wasn't what's called a record smash, like the song "Buttons and Bows," a tremendous hit which I afterward sang with Jane Russell in *Paleface*. In fact, it was Number One for seven or eight months. I've never been terrific with records. I mean I make records, but I'm not known as a Platter King. I just make them and they're played here and there, and everybody has a little fun.

In my next picture, *Give Me a Sailor*, I was with Martha Raye, Betty Grable, Andy Devine and Jack Whiting. By this time I was a combo light comedian-leading man. I could look reasonably presentable or I could throw a pun—whichever was needed.

Martha and I were doing a scene with Andy Devine, and between shots, Andy turned to me and asked, "Would you like to play a little golf this afternoon?"

It was a beautiful day, so I said, "Sure, but we can't escape from this chain gang."

"Maybe we can," he said. "Watch me."

He walked up to Martha Raye and asked, "How do you feel?"

"Wonderful," she said. "Just fine."

"You look good, too," he said, "but you've been working too hard."

"What do you mean?" she asked.

"You know pictures," Andy told her. "These producers get all they can out of you while you're hot. They don't care what happens to you. You're working all the time and you're beating your brains out and they're getting the money. It drains your energy and you ought to watch yourself."

"I guess you're right," Martha said thoughtfully.

We shot another scene and Andy gave her another dose of his patented treatment. When the director, Elliott Nugent, called the lunch break, Andy sat with Martha and gave her some more of the same. In addition to being one of the great comediennes, Martha is a very sensitive person. And when she came back to do the first scene of the afternoon, she fell over in a faint.

"That's all for today, boys," Elliott said.

"It's simple," Andy told me. "It's called the power of suggestion."

He tried to use it on me on the golf course all that afternoon but with small success.

I found out that it was also possible to get an afternoon off from the movie jute mills—by accident. During the making of *Ghost Breakers,* with Dorothy Lamour and Paulette Goddard, somebody gave Paulette a motor scooter. Some people use them to ride around a golf course. Put to this purpose, they're called the arthritis special. They're built like the one-legged jobs kids used to use, only the modern version has a motor and a little seat. In my next scene, I was supposed to walk down a flight of steps. While they were setting it up, I went outside and tried out Paulette's scooter.

I whipped around the lot until I grew careless. Rounding a curve at thirty-five m.p.h., I fell off, skinned my hand, tore holes in my suit, skinned my knees and generally mangled myself. I was so embarrassed at my clumsiness that I didn't want to walk back on the set and admit that I'd fallen from a souped-up kiddie car. I went in through a back door without anyone seeing me and climbed to the top of the steps I was supposed to walk down. When the director called "Lights, action, camera!" I tripped, made a fake fall and when I got up I said, "A fine thing. Slippery steps." The carpenter apologized and the director called off work for the afternoon. The only catch was I felt too tattered and torn for a golf course.

My 1939 picture, *The Cat and the Canary,* with Paulette Goddard, really broke the ice of audience acceptance for me. Paramount has always treated me fairly. When I became a greater draw, they paid me more. All I had to do was ask for it in a threatening way. And it didn't tucker me out to ask.

After *The Cat and the Canary*, I went into the first *Road* picture, *The Road to Singapore*, with Bing. The *Road* pictures grew out of a typical Hollywood switch, one of those it-starts-out-to-be-this-then-somebody-gets-a-brighter-idea things. Originally there was a projected picture called *The Road to Mandalay*. Harlan Thompson was set to be its producer. Who it was who wrote the original version of *The Road to Mandalay* I don't know, but two Paramount contract writers, Frank Butler and Don Hartman, did a rewrite job on it. They changed it from serious to funny—they had George Burns and Gracie Allen in mind for it—and retitled it *The Road to Singapore*. Burns and Allen proved unavailable and the next notion was to star Fred MacMurray and Jack Oakie in it. When MacMurray and Oakie were lost because of a previous commitment, Bing and I were tapped for the assignment.

The name "Singapore" was used because Don and Frank didn't think "Mandalay" sounded treacherous enough. As Don put it, "You take a piece of used chewing gum and flip it at a map. Wherever it sticks you can lay a *Road* picture, so long as the people there are jokers who cook and eat strangers. If they're nasty and menacing, it'll be a good *Road* picture. The key to the thing is menace offsetting the humor."

Nobody thought that that first *Road* picture would develop into a series. It became a series when a writer named Sy Bartlett brought in a story about two fellows who were trekking through the Madagascar jungles. The catch was a movie named *Stanley and Livingston* had just been released and it was so similar to Bartlett's that it ruined it. Bartlett's story was a highly dramatic one, and Don Hartman took it, gagged it up, and named it *The Road to Zanzibar*.

Bing is the greatest singer of popular songs who ever lived.

This is not just my opinion. Ask anybody. But not everyone knows how shrewd he is when it comes to the entertainment business. He instantly recognized the value of the *Road* picture as a way of getting a spontaneous, ad-libby type of humor. There were doubters in the studio who shook their heads and said, "Well . . . I don't know." But Bing was an important star. They listened to him. He was right.

Every *Road* picture has made large juicy chunks of money—including our last *Road* film, *The Road to Bali*—in spite of the softness at the box office when it was released.

Most of the *Road* pictures have the same plot: Crosby chasing Lamour, me chasing Crosby, and the public behind us—gaining all the time. Dorothy is my nomination for one of the bravest gals in pictures. She stands there before the camera and ad-libs with Crosby and me, knowing that the way script is written she'll come up second or third best. But she fears nothing. Sometimes she adds to the fun by coming on the set with a couple of teeth blacked out, and she should be decorated for patience because, when Bing and I are working out our lines for the next take, she just stands there and listens.

Once in a while she'll say, "How about a line for me?" This usually brings a fast "Quiet, honey," from us. "All we want you to do is to look beautiful and twirl your sarong!"

I've made several pictures with Dottie other than the *Road* pictures; among them *Caught in the Draft, The Big Broadcast of 1938* and *My Favorite Brunette*. And we had a lot of fun, especially doing the love scenes. It seems a dream that I was lucky enough to have her as my leading lady. But that's America for you, the land of opportunity.

The Road to Singapore was directed by Victor Schertzinger. He was an ideal director for us. He didn't try to hold us down. "I'm not worrying about directing you boys," he told us. "All I have to do is start the camera. You'll take it from there."

He was right. There was no stress and no strain of trying to remember we were actors. And before the shooting was over, everybody connected with the picture had the same feeling. That's why the customers had fun watching it. Some of the fun we had making it rubbed off on them.

The public knows that there's going to be a lot of clowning in a *Road* picture, that nothing is premeditated, that anything can happen. And everything does happen. Even the animals in a *Road* picture get into a nutsy mood. In one scene in *The Road to Morocco* we were working with a camel. As I walked up to the camel's head, he turned and spat in my eye.

Dave Butler, the director, said, "Print that. We'll leave it in." So it was in the finished film. There may have been those who thought that spitting sequence was faked. It wasn't.

In *The Road to Rio*, there was a big scene on a South American set. One day in addition to the two hundred extras hired for the picture there was three hundred visitors on the set. The electricians spent hours lighting the scene, but when the director called, "Camera!" the whole place had to be relit. What with all those people milling around, things were so confusing that the electricians had lit the visitors too. Bing and I were partners with Paramount in financing the picture so we put up quite a squawk about the expensive delay. We piped down when it was pointed out to us that two hundred ninety-eight of the visitors were our friends or relatives—mostly the latter.

I'll never forget Bing clinging to his hat in *The Road to Singapore*. After much persuasion, he had been cajoled into wearing a skull doily when he uncovered his head before a camera. That doesn't mean he liked it. We had one scene in bed and I said, "We're going to take off our hats when we're in the sack, aren't we?"

"No," he said firmly. "We'll sleep with our hats on."

When we crawled into bed, the director took one look at us and yelled, "What goes? Take your hats off!"

"Bing won't let me," I said.

The director said, "Cut!" Then he summoned the producer to talk Bing into removing his hat and putting on his skull doily. I lay back on my pillow and enjoyed it. After two hours of gentlemanly discussion, a compromise was reached. We kept our hats on.

Before we made *Road to Rio*, Bing and I had a little talk with a group of businessmen who were planning to market a lime-flavored soft drink. We got interested in the company. We bought a lot of its stock—that was before Bing started going steady with a frozen orange juice—and had an option to buy still more. We decided to plug this concoction in *The Road to Rio*, and we put a big sign in one of the scenes advertising it. An emissary from Paramount's front office called upon us to tell us, "You can't plug a real commercial product in a movie."

Bing gave him a long, cold look and said, "I own a third of the picture, Bob owns a third of the picture, and Paramount owns a third. We'll vote."

Strangely enough, the balloting resulted in a two-to-one vote for keeping the sign in.

There are other pleasant things about owning part of a picture. In *The Road to Bali* there was a beach scene for which tons of beautiful white sand had been trucked in from Pebble Beach. I had just put in a one-hole golf course at my house on Moorpart Street in North Hollywood. I had four sand traps standing empty, with nothing in them in which my friends could leave hoof-prints. When I saw that sand a light switched on in my head.

"We own two thirds of this sand, don't we?" I asked.

"Sure," Bing said. "Why?"

"Well," I replied, "I'd like some of it for my course at home." He said, "Why not?"

I called the prop man and said, "Take ten truckloads of this sand out to my house when we're done with it."

"No dice," he said. "This is Paramount's sand."

Bing and I had another little talk with the boys in the front office. As a result, part of *The Road to Bali* is in my backyard.

Those routines in which Bing and I rib each other began as a peg upon which we could hang our jokes. We started to give each other the needle when we rehearsed our radio shows to-gether. When he called me "Clabber" and I called him "Lard Belly" or "Blubber" or "Dad," it drew laughs from the bystanders and the crew. It occurred to us that that kind of ribbing might amuse a wide audience, and gradually we worked our verbal jabs into the show itself.

As an extra refinement upon this technique, we developed a kind of boring-from-within trick, an infiltration-behind-the-lines stunt. Our writers would say to Bing, "When he calls you 'Fatty' you say to him, 'That's not exactly baby fat you've got there yourself. I happen to know that Sophie Tucker lends you her cast-off girdles.' "

Then they'd come to me, tell me what Bing was going to say, and suggest, "Right ahead of his line you say, 'And don't pull that ancient wheeze about Sophie Tucker's girdle. There's no bounce left in the joke or the girdles.' "

This piece of skullduggery left Bing standing there with his script in his hand, wondering just how he'd been double-crossed.

He got even for that in a scene I did with him in *The Road to Rio*. The action was superdramatic with me down on knees clutching his coat and saying, "Don't leave me! Don't leave me!"

When I finished the first take, Bing pulled the Oscar he'd won for *Going My Way* from under his coat and presented it to me. It amused the visitors on the set. I think he'd arranged for an extra number of them to be there.

Although he goes to great pains to conceal them, Bing has his sentimental moments. In 1944 we were playing a charity golf match together in Indianapolis. Afterward I was to appear at a bond rally in South Bend in the Notre Dame stadium before fifty-five thousand people. Those of us who were entertaining at the rally were scheduled to enter the stadium in jeeps, then drive around the circle. While I was playing with Bing in Indianapolis, I asked, "Why don't you come over to South Bend with me and appear in this show?"

"I think I'll just do that," he said.

When we entered the stadium, Bing was in the jeep behind me. The crowd didn't know he was going to be there, and when they saw him they went crazy. It was a nice thing for him to do.

Next day he went to Chicago while I stayed in South Bend to do a show at the Navy installation there. It was my birthday, and just before the finish of my show, Bing walked out from the wings with a birthday cake in his hands. He'd flown all the way back to South Bend from Chicago to give it to me.

Chapter 13

THINKING OF BING and our *Road* pictures makes me think of
my make-up man, Charlie Berner. He has been with me
fourteen years. He is a veteran of the picture business, having
started in Fort Lee, New Jersey, when pictures were in diapers.
He came to Hollywood as an assistant director, but eventually
went into make-up. I drew him in 1939. He is one of the braver
fellows in his line of work. He was once a used-car dealer and
he figured that if he could face-lift a rusted and dented jalopy,
he could handle my problems.

In 1939 there was need for a lot of corrective work on my nose
as well as other places. They were putting shading on each side
of my snoot and a white line on top of it to straighten it and make

me look leading-mannish. Charlie was nominated for the job because he proved that he could work on me without first bracing himself by pinching a pinch bottle.

But occasionally Charlie showed the white feather. He'd run to his boss, Wally Westmore, head of all Paramount make-up, and say, "I can't stand it! I can't stand it!"

When that happened, Paramount bolstered him with more dollars in his pay envelope and he came back. For the most part, the make-up men at Paramount were very glad to see me. They could use the overtime.

Charlie has given up on my nose now. He's decided to just let the customers have the regular face.

They used to use a lot of shading on my chin too, but now that people have seen me on TV the way I actually am, they've given up on that too. There's not much they can do about make-up on television. There you are with your face hanging out in a glare of flat lighting. Which reminds me of a thing Joe Frisco, the stuttering comedian, said to me on the phone one day. Joe is brash but honest. "How about p-p-p-putting me in your next TV s-s-s-show?" he asked. "I s-s-s-saw it. I can't h-h-h-hurt it."

Joe Frisco and Charlie Berner are not the only stimulating characters I've met along my particular Road to Laughter. There are scores of them. Among them are Bert Lahr and Dave Butler. Bert is one of my good friends. He's very nervous about bookings and he's very conscientious. He's one of the real workmen of the theater, but he always worries. He was playing a Broadway show called *Hold Everything*. It had been at the Selwyn Theater for about fifteen months, and it had a year on the road to look forward to, but Bert was worried about what was going to happen the season afterwards. He kept calling Doctor Shurr, who's also his agent, for reassurance. Anyhow, he'd been working in town all that time when he walked into the Lambs Club as Bugs Baer was coming out.

Bert said, "How are you, Bugs?"

Bugs said, "Hi ya, Bert. When did you get in town?"

Bert worried so much about the fact that Bugs didn't know he'd been there that he didn't eat for a whole day.

When he came to Hollywood to play the Cowardly Lion in *The Wizard of Oz,* he worried about that part too. As it happened, a girl singer, June Knight, got married at that time. There was a big Beverly Hills wedding. Everybody was invited. I was out of town but Doctor Shurr, who had gotten Bert the *Oz* role, was also handling June Knight. The Doctor is quite an operator. He was probably handling the rice at the wedding and the preacher, too.

Bert was sitting in the middle of the church and the Doctor was up front, taking bows for the way he'd handled things. As the bride and groom marched down the aisle after the marriage, the Doctor was right behind them, marching too. As he passed Bert he said, "Doesn't she look beautiful!"

"I read that *Oz* part yesterday," Bert said. "It's wonderful."

That was the important thing to him.

To me this is a great story. I love it. It's so honest and so show business. It wraps up being an actor into one neat package.

There's also a story I like about Dave Butler directing on the first day of *Caught in the Draft.* Dave was very anxious to do well with the picture and wanted to start the thing off with a bang.

He gave us a big, booming, "All right, now, let's get going. Lots of pepper now," and we launched into the first scene, which involved No-Man's Land, trenches and a lot of big mud holes. Dave weighed about three hundred, but nevertheless he was running here and yelling directions there when he fell into one of those mud holes up to his head. When he came up sputtering the rest of us almost fell into mud holes ourselves laughing. We left him there for fifteen minutes, while we sent for a derrick to haul him out. Mack Sennett, in his best days, never came up with a funnier bit of action.

Somehow we hit a clinker in trying to finish *Caught in the Draft.* We had it all done with exception of one location shot, but we were stymied by bad weather on that one. In California I could be tried for treason for saying this, but we had to wait around for two or three weeks until we got the right kind of weather to go out and grab that one day's location work. Having crews wait around and a skeleton crew remaining on duty had cost the studio a lot of money, but finally we got a good day and we all dashed out into the San Fernando Valley around Chatsworth for this scene. We were to shoot at Chatsworth, then join another outfit at the Paramount Ranch, in Malibu Canyon, for the last shot. That meant that we had to go six or seven miles between shots.

We broke up our Chatsworth camp about mid-afternoon and were told, "See you over at the Paramount Ranch."

I thought that we'd have at least an hour and a half between shots while they were setting up the cameras. I didn't know they already had another camera crew ready and waiting at the other place. So I said to the make-up man, Harry Ray, "Let's stop off at Hidden Valley. I want to show you my idea of Shangri-la. There's a little spot in the valley I'd like to buy. It would be a good place to hide after a bad picture or a bad radio program."

It took us about thirty minutes to find this place. Luckily, the gate was locked, otherwise I would have driven in and spent another hour looking it over. But as it was we turned around and drove to the Paramount Ranch.

There stood Mr. Butler as mad as one human being could get. I thought David was going to knife me. He gave me a blistering. Then he turned to Harry Ray, the make-up man and said, "I thought that at least *you* would have some sense."

By that time it was getting dark and we were fighting for light. They had to set up booster lights to help the sunlight which was disappearing rapidly. We finally made it. But I picked up so much suntan from the rays of the boosters that I looked a little dark in the film.

The business of milking what light there is out of a smog-bound California sun reminds me of a thing that happened on one location to Joe Lefert, an assistant director. About four-thirty at night when they'd lost what little light they had Joe dismissed the crew and assigned everybody to different cars. "You two take this car," he said. "You guys take this one."

He sent all the stars away and packed all of the extras into a bus. Finally he heaved a sigh of relief and looked around. He was standing there alone. He'd kept no car for himself. He had to walk to the nearest bus station.

While I'm on unusual characters, the greatest one-man audience I've ever known was Buddy DeSylva. Buddy was brought into Paramount at one time to run the production end. I loved to drop in on him because no matter what I said—if I just said, "Good morning—" he practically fell behind his desk laughing. People ran to him with jokes because anything they said to him made him collapse. Laughter rolled, bubbled and gushed out of him.

After the scenes I did with Bing we used to add little things to amuse Buddy since we knew he'd be seeing the rushes. Buddy had started to play a ukelele so Bing and I would finish a scene, persuade the director to keep it rolling until we told him to cut and say, "Now let's try the same thing over again with a ukelele."

I remember another one-man audience, a synthetic or self-made one. Along about 1939 I was doing a personal appearance at the Paramount Theater in New York. (The Paramount's picture that week was the *Magnificent Fraud* with Akim Tamiroff. Outside, the lights on the marquee said: THE MAGNIFICENT FRAUD, BOB HOPE. I liked that "Magnificent" anyhow.) After my third or fourth day there, when I walked out of the stage door and headed down 44th Street, there was a fellow standing there who said, "Hi, Mr. Hope. I was the fellow who was laughing."

That stopped me. "You did what?" I asked.

"I was the fellow who was laughing up your show."

I remembered that there had been a fellow laughing out of

turn louder than anybody and getting quite a bit of the attention from the audience I should have been getting.

"I do a lot of laughing," he said. "Last week I laughed up Ben Bernie."

"Is that so?" I asked.

"Yup," he said, "I've got all kinds of laughs. I can laugh high on. I can laugh deep. And I sing and whistle and recite poetry."

He had a wonderful face with apple cheeks. He was a real happy looking fellow.

"This is very interesting," I said. "I've never run into a laugher like you before. I mean a fellow who goes around laughing up shows for kicks. Let me hear your poetry." He recited a very stale poem about down in the mine and a fellow drinking wine and so on and so on. Then he did a song.

"I can use you," I told him. "But we'll need signals. When I hold up one finger it means laugh, then I'll cut you off. Then I'll give you three fingers and you go into your poetry."

We rehearsed it for a while, and I took him back into the theater with me to test it out. We walked up to Johnny Perkins, who was on the show with us, but who was kind of nervous that week, and who would have shaken hands with anybody because he was jumpy and unsteady.

"This is Mr. Perkins," I said.

"Nice to see you," Johnny said.

I gave the signal and the professional yukker laughed in Johnny's face. I watched Johnny as the laughter soared and thought: *If the audience reacts like this we're in.*

However when I took the laugher on for the second show of the day nobody laughed at him but the musicians in the pit. The audience didn't get him at all. But when I came off he grabbed me by the hand and said, "Thanks, I've done it."

I asked, "What do you mean?"

"All my life," he said, "I've wanted to go on the stage."

I was conscience-stricken. For all I knew he'd never settle for ordinary work again, and he certainly wasn't going anywhere in show business. I gave him a little money and told him everything was fine but I was afraid I couldn't use him. "The other actors are jealous of you," I said.

But he'd tasted the heady wine of backstage life. Next week when I opened at the Brooklyn Paramount he was standing right outside the stage door, waiting. Finally I explained that I was a little jealous of him myself, that I couldn't stand his competition as a laugh getter and that he'd be better off laughing up somebody who was less self-centered. That did it.

I mentioned the fact that Buddy DeSylva was one of Paramount's long line of guiding geniuses. I've also given another Paramount wheel, Don Hartman, some footage. Y. Frank Freeman is now chief of Operation Paramount.

Freeman is from Georgia. He's also head of the Motion Picture Producers' Association. He does some very fine things. For instance, along with Harry Joe Brown, he headed the show Hollywood put on last year to entertain the Boy Scouts who attended the Jamboree in Los Angeles.

That Scout Jamboree was something. There were fifty thousand Scouts here from every nation in the world. It was an immense thing and I was lucky enough to be one of those who was

asked to talk to them. I told them that I liked Boy Scouts, but I wished they would stop helping me across the street. And I commented upon how much food they'd eaten at the Jamboree: ninety thousand hot dogs, eighty thousand hamburgers, thousands of gallons of beef stew—and twelve Scoutmasters were also missing. I told them that a lot of great men still stick to Scout ideas. In fact, Eisenhower can make a fire by rubbing one Democrat the wrong way. He doesn't even need two.

If the notion is put to him persuasively, Y. Frank is capable of doing a good turn for adults too. When I started in the Pepsodent radio show, I saw Madeleine Carroll in a picture called *The Thirty-Nine Steps*, and I began to talk about her to anyone who would listen. I thought her a vision of loveliness, an all-time champion blonde doll. I said as much on the air, and I kept saying it until I built it up to a point where I got laughs by just saying, "Madeleine Carroll," making wolf noises and growling a little.

There I was giving this girl I'd never met so much publicity that finally she called my agent and said, "I want to go on the air with Bob, because I appreciate what he's doing for me." So we did a show together.

I kept drooling about her in public and finally I said to Y. Frank, "If you'd let me do a picture with Madeleine Carroll and call it *My Favorite Blonde*, I think it would clean up."

Y. Frank latched onto the notion. Panama and Frank, two boys who were writing for me then, turned out a great script and Don Hartman and Dave Butler did the screen treatment.

Madeleine must have been much impressed with me, so much so that she married Sterling Hayden right in the middle of the picture. However, she was thoughtful enough to marry him secretly, which cut down on the mass suicides which would otherwise have followed.

Among other people who fascinate me are the two Sams, Goldwyn and Bagley. Although I'd joked about Sam Goldwyn in some of my comedy routines, I didn't meet him until 1940.

One of my routines went like this: "Naturally I'm interested in Sam Goldwyn. Our lives have been parallel. He was born poor. So was I. Then our lives began to differ. He became a producer and I went straight."

Bagley is a Hollywood extra. Hollywood has some fabulous extras, but Bagley can hold his own with any of them. Sam's always saying, "I don't know why some studio doesn't do *The Bagley Story*. We could open *The Bagley Story* with my birth. I'm picking the doctor's pockets, and my mother is proud and happy because she knows that that means some day I'll be a politician."

Bagley is always on the rib. When I was making *The Son of Paleface*, Roy Rogers brought his radio sponsor to the Paramount lot on a sight-seeing tour. Roy was trying to happy it up with everybody and show his sponsor a good time. As he walked through the stage door, he saw Bagley with a couple of other extras playing poker. Roy said, "Hello, Sam."

Sam looked back, took in the sponsor and Roy's nervous, mother-hen attitude, and said coldly, "Who are you?"

When last seen, Roy was explaining that to his sponsor.

In one of my pictures Bagley had a line and fluffed it. When I asked, "What's the matter? Can't you read even one little line of dialogue?" he looked at me and, after a long pause, said, "If I was any good I'd have an agent handling such questions."

After one big mob scene, the director said, "Cut!" Sam, who was in back, lost in the mob, called out, "I'd like another try. I didn't feel that one."

The director, Norman McLeod, also has a sense of humor which appeals to me. Norman's an improbable blend of Cal Coolidge and Fred Allen. One day in 1953, when we were working on *Mister Casanova*, he said, "All right, let's shoot this scene. Everybody ready. Let's go." Then he said, "H'm'm. I can't think of my next line. . . . Oh, yes. Camera!"

We shot another scene for *Mr. Casanova* and I looked at Norman and asked him, "How was it?"

153

"It damn near made sense," he said.

It was also while we were making *Mr. Casanova* that Norman told me, "I wish you'd give me another version of that scene, Bob."

"I don't know what you mean," I said. "I'm trying so hard now my eyeballs are dancing on my cheeks. But I'll give you something different if you want it."

"Let's try one without the animation and the dancing eyeballs," he said. "Just give me your George Raft mood."

Norman is a quiet-type director. He doesn't yell at people. Bing and I call him The Mumbler. Half of the time we have to say, "Speak up, Norman. We can't hear your direction." This sets the key for a McLeod picture. After a couple of days of shooting, even the fellows who fix the lights whisper.

A few years ago Norman was making a picture at M-G-M. The company had broken for lunch when somebody got the sound stage on the phone and asked, "Is Mr. McLeod there?"

The cleaning man who took the call was all alone, but when he replied, "Everybody's out at lunch," he found himself whispering, too.

I crept up on my meeting with Sam Goldwyn in Hollywood by way of Chicago. In 1940 I took my radio troupe East on a personal-appearance tour. We'd been on the air for two and a half years, and we'd jumped into the top circle of radio shows. We had developed a lot of sayings, like "Who's Yehudi?"—one of Jerry Colonna's sayings—which had caught on with the public, but I had no idea how popular our show had really become. So we were surprised on the Super Chief that at every stop along the way a crowd was waiting to see us. I'd announced on the radio that I was going East with my troupe and I had given the date. For the first time, looking at those crowds, I began to realize that when I said something on the air it was being heard.

We stopped at Joliet for one day to break in our show before taking it into Chicago. In Joliet we packed the auditorium. We were only supposed to do two shows, but the management asked us to do three to take care of those who wanted to see us, and we wound up doing four.

From Joliet we went into the Chicago Theater at a twelve thousand five hundred dollar weekly guarantee for the unit and fifty percent over a fifty-five thousand dollar take. We broke the house record. It was so crowded the management posted an hourly list of survivors. The take went to seventy-three thousand dollars a week, of which my share was around twenty thousand dollars. When the man gave me that check, I went over to Henrici's Restaurant across the street from the Woods Building. I wanted to sit in the window at Henrici's and look over to where I'd stood on the sidewalk twelve years before, starving and thrilled to get one date at twenty-five bucks.

That first day in Chicago was our second indication that we were a national hit. People lined up all the way around the block in the rain. There was a peephole in the Lake Street door of the theater. I looked through it and saw them there. After looking for a long time, I got my agent, Doctor Shurr, on long distance and said, "Get here, Doctor."

He was in Philadelphia taking the pulse of an important show bound for Broadway and he said, "I can't leave now."

"Is there anybody there who's more important to you than I am?" I asked.

"Well—" he said.

"If there is," I said, "maybe Abe Lastfogel will come out and talk to me." Abe was with the William Morris office which was one of the biggest and most successful theatrical agencies.

"What's the matter?" Doc asked.

"Just get here, that's all!" I said.

The Doctor took the night plane. The next day he walked into the Chicago Theater. By that time we were doing six and seven shows daily to accommodate the people who wanted in, and we were eating our meals in the theater. We didn't have time to go out. It would have been dangerous anyhow. The crowds around the theater and at the stage door would have torn our clothes off.

When the doctor came in, I pretended I didn't know why he was there. "What are you doing in Chicago?" I asked.

He was stunned, but he pulled himself together and asked, "What's so important?"

"I'll show you what's so important," I said. "Follow me."

I led him across the stage to the peephole in the door. "Look through there," I said. "Do you see those people lined up?"

He nodded.

"They don't do that very often, do they?" I asked.

"No," he said.

"I want you to go back to the Coast," I told him, "and tell Paramount we want fifty thousand dollars a picture."

"I have an idea," the doctor said. "I saw Sam Goldwyn in Philadelphia and he said, 'You've got to get Bob Hope for me for a picture,' and I told him, 'That's going to be difficult. He's signed exclusive for Paramount.' 'You can do it,' Sam told me. 'I just loaned them Gary Cooper for a picture.' That may be a solution. We'll ask Paramount for the right to do an outside picture. And we'll ask for more than Paramount pays you."

When we got back to the Coast, we talked it over with Paramount. They said "Okay."

Then the Doctor called Sam and said, "Mr. Goldwyn, Paramount has O.K.'d the deal."

"That's great," Goldwyn said. "I want to be fair with Bob. I don't want to take advantage of him. I'll pay him what Paramount pays him."

"That," the doctor said, "is not the idea."

We had a series of dinners, luncheons and cocktails at the Goldwyn home. Nothing happened.

Finally I said, "Mr. Goldwyn, I like your home, I like your food, I like your charming wife, but I don't like your idea of doing right by me."

"We don't seem to be getting anywhere," Doctor Shurr added. "I'll have my partner, Al Melnick, close the deal."

We had another session—this time a four-man one, with Al talking to Goldwyn.

Finally Sam said, "I'll give you a percentage of the profits."

"Gross?" Al asked.

"Net," Goldwyn said.

We stalked out. Half an hour later, Goldwyn called the doctor and said, "You know, Louis, I think you and I are going to have trouble with that Melnick. He doesn't understand me."

In some fashion known only to him, Sam had worked it out in his mind that the Doctor and he were now trying to get the best of the Doctor's partner. Even the Doctor was confused, and had to give it some thought before he untangled it and remembered whose partner he was.

While the negotiations were hanging fire I was invited to go on a junket to Fort Worth as part of a promotion stunt to promote the picture Gary Cooper had made for Paramount on his Goldwyn loan-out. I emceed the whole thing. There was a big parade and four premieres in four different theaters, plus a tremendous show in the Will Rogers Colosseum. Goldwyn was with us, and at the last theater he said, "I'd like you to introduce me."

So I announced, "And now, one of our great men in Hollywood, Mr. Sam Goldwyn."

Sam walked onstage and said, "Ladies and gentlemen, I hope you've enjoyed Gary Cooper. I haven't made a comedy since Eddie Cantor left me. I haven't found a comedian I want to work with, but I think I've finally found one in Bob Hope."

Before he could continue, I grabbed the mike. "Wait a minute," I said. "That's all very fine, but we've got to talk money."

"Later," he whispered. "We'll talk later."

"No, Sam," I said. "We're going to talk right here in front of all these witnesses. There's no better place to talk money, Sam. Why don't we just lie down and talk things over?"

I took the microphone, lay down on the stage and pulled Sam down beside me. The audience was in stitches. I mumbled a few words into Sam's ear.

Then we got up, and I said, "It's going to be a great pleasure to make a picture with Mr. Goldwyn."

We finally worked out a deal for me to make a film for Goldwyn for one hundred thousand dollars. That picture was *They've Got Me Covered*. When I went back to Paramount, they upped my pay to match the sum Goldwyn had paid me. So that momentary grappling with Sam was one of the most profitable wrestling bouts ever staged.

While we're on Goldwyn, Dave Butler told me a story about something that happened while Bing and I were making a picture for Dave. One scene involved a big village with four hundred extras. Dave had had a phone installed at the end of a street in the village under a low shed. It was so low you had to stoop to get under it. He thought that would cut down my trips to the telephone while the picture was shooting. Dave was crotchety about my taking more than twenty or thirty calls a day. He was small enough to think that it held up production.

Ironically, the first call to come through was from Sam Goldwyn to Dave himself. The day was so hot eggs could have been poached on Butler's neck, and, as I've said, he weighed three hundred pounds tubside. Nevertheless, he had to walk all the way to the shed, squeeze under it, and squat over, while Sam told him about a picture he wanted me for.

Dave listened, sweated, and said, "It would be all right for Cary Grant, but it's got to have more gags in it for Bob."

"We'll get the gags," said Sam.

The conversation went on and on and finally Sam ended by saying, "Well, thanks for calling me, Dave."

Somehow he'd gotten the idea Dave was calling him. That's Sam. He's fabulous, just fabulous.

Sam carries his search for perfection to fantastic extremes.

He's a great one for asking other people to pass judgment on his product. If he doesn't like a scene or if he's worried about it, he talks it over with anyone whose opinion he respects. He discusses scenes with Darryl Zanuck or Mervyn LeRoy or he'll send them a few reels of his product and ask them, "How do you like it?" In that way he gets a lot of expert appraisals for free. Then if he still doesn't like it, he'll redo it or even scrap it. He wants his product to have a high finish.

Chapter 14

S PEAKING OF a high finish, I have a nice, shiny high finish of scar tissue on my carcass to remind me of some of the films I've made. I've had a number of close calls. When I remember them I get an uneasy feeling that I'm living on borrowed time. Especially when I recall the close calls I had flying a million miles or so for the USO in World War II.

Once while I was making a film with the gay and carefree title of *Fancy Pants,* I was thrown from a prop horse seven feet high and landed on my back on a cement floor. Lucille Ball was supposed to be giving me riding lessons, and George Marshall, the director, wanted more action and more jiggle for the close-ups. So he'd ordered the restraining straps removed from the prop steed. When it started its mechanical jouncing it went faster and faster. Then it tossed me off.

I was still conscious when they carried me out, and I was sure I had broken something important. Still, once a ham always a ham, so, as I passed the doorman, I said in a confidential tone, "Straight to the Lakeside Country Club, please. Maybe I can break seventy too."

Instead they took me to Hollywood Presbyterian Hospital and put me under the X-ray machine. Aside from a sore back and a sorer head, I was all right. But my head was so sore that I wrote a letter to Henry Ginsberg, who was then head of the studio. As I cast an eye backward, Paramount had as many heads as Hydra, a monster I remember vaguely and unpleasantly from Fairmount

Junior High. Henry is now teamed with Edna Ferber and George Stevens, who made *Shane* and *A Place in the Sun,* to film the Ferber story, *Giant,* as an independent venture. Anyhow I wrote:

Dear Henry:

I want to thank you for your kindness during my recent illness and tell you that you did not have to do it, I wasn't going to sue. . . . Inasmuch as you are going to have to explain my $4,500 doctor bills at the next stockholders' meeting (assuming you are still with the company), I think I should explain that they are not out of line.

You and I know that in the old days when a man fell on his back, he got up, tightened his belt and walked back into the bar. . . . But medicine has made great strides during our generation. When I woke up in the hospital, four nurses were standing over me, a doctor was feeling my pulse, and a specialist was busy on the phone checking with the bank to see how much we would go for.

Then they started the tests which you find on Page Three of the bill. . . . Meantime, no one would tell me how I was doing. Finally I picked up the phone, got an outside wire, called the hospital and asked how Bob Hope was doing. I'd taken a turn for the worse. . . . We've sure come a long ways from sulphur and molasses.

That kind of wear and tear didn't start with the prop horse. Paramount has been out to get me for years. In *The Road to Utopia,* a bear was supposed to sniff Bing and me while we were sleeping in a cabin. I gave my reluctant consent. I didn't like that bear's personality or the way he sniffed. My instinct was right. We made our shot on Wednesday. The next day the bear tore off his trainer's arm.

I've often asked myself what would have happened if Wednesday had been bruin's day for arms.

A burned child shuns the fire. Not Hope, the Brain. When I was making *The Great Lover* I was supposed to dive from a ship and see strange and frightening things underwater. The director wanted it "realistic," so no one mentioned a double. I didn't mention one either. I had my pride. I wouldn't be that proud

today. They connected me to a contraption which was, in turn, attached to a wire so the jokers up above could guide me with ·it. Then I took off.

The wire caught on a hook underwater. I had quite a fight, but I finally got away. The assistant director, Harry Kaplan, dived in and helped untangle me. After that they called the fire department and pumped the herring out of the lungs. After all, they had to return those herring to Central Casting when the day was done.

Speaking of sea food, in the past ten years I've flown well over a million miles, often in weather so soupy I could reach out and dig clams from it. Sometimes a motor got tired and quit. With all that winging back and forth, the trip I made to the South Pacific in 1944 stands out as being "the stickiest," as my British cousins would say.

Patty Thomas, Frances Langford, Tony Romano and Jerry Colonna were along with me. Also, a little peewee named Barney Dean. Bing and I had persuaded Paramount to put Barney under contract as a writer, but his main value to us is the fact that he is an amusing companion who helps keep life light.

Barney puts on an act of being afraid of airplanes. He swears it isn't an act, but he can't help going into a comedy role, which is why he pretends to be a coward. The rest of us cooperated by feeding him lines. I'd wait until Barney was within earshot, then say to Jerry Colonna, "I hope the pilot makes a tight landing at our next stop. It's one of our Air Force's shorter runways, you know."

"What do you mean, short runway?" Barney asked anxiously. "How long is it? It'll be all right, won't it?"

A few days later we'd toss him another line. I'd say, "But grease on the wheels doesn't mean anything."

Jerry would come back with, "No, I guess not. These fellows are all experienced men."

This was Barney's cue to ask frantically, "What do you mean, grease on the wheels? What's that do?"

"The mechanic was working on the landing gear and he forgot to wipe the grease off the wheels," I'd say. "However, if we're lucky and we come in at the right angle, it won't mean a crash landing." Barney was very amusing in such scenes and in our quieter moments they were a lot of fun.

About the eighth week of our trip, we left Moumea, New Caledonia, in a Navy Catalina, bound for Sydney. We were flying across a mountain range when the left motor began to spit. Our pilot, Lieutenant Ferguson, grabbed the wheel and feathered the prop. His problems was now a double one. He had to balance the ship and keep her from losing altitude until he could find enough water to sit her down.

He yelled to us, "Jettison everything in the plane."

I flung out all the loose gear I could find—luggage, oxygen tanks, a case of cigarettes, three sacks of liquor. They went out through the blister Navy Cats have in the rear of their fuselage.

When we first noticed the failing prop we were fifty miles from water. By this time Lieutenant Ferguson had worked us closer to the coast. After nursing us over several mountain ranges, he sighted a little bay. "This is it!" he said. "Everybody brace! Lie flat on the floor!"

Frances Langford strapped herself into a seat. Those of us who were on the floor braced ourselves. Patty Thomas lay next to me with her tap shoes tied around her neck. We came down on one motor, hit and skipped one hundred feet. On our second bounce we skipped fifty more feet. Then we thudded into a sand bar. When we crawled out on the wings, Colonna let out a Colonna-type yell of relief. After that we thanked God that we were safe.

In the distance we saw a fisherman rowing in our direction. When he reached us, he looked at us standing on the wings and said, "Have you any Ameddican cigarettes?" We almost hit him with Barney Dean. Restraining ourselves, we asked, "Where are we?"

"Laurieton," he told us.

Laurieton is an east-coast Australian resort town. Its population is roughly seven hundred fifty. We went to the post office, and met the postmaster, Mr. Plunkett, and his wife. They took us to the hotel. Before dinner one of the Laurietonians came up to me and asked, "Would you do a Victory show for us tonight? We put one on whenever we get a chance to raise money for the troops."

"For dear old Laurieton," I said, "we will do anything."

We trooped over to a little dance hall and two or three hundred people showed up. They stood there looking at us, solemn as owls.

A local chap announced, "We have an unexpected visitor with us." Then he went whimsical. "He arrived today in a big bird and landed in our pond. Mr. Bob Hope."

I could see that the Laurietonians weren't exactly inflammable, so I went into a routine past experience had proved sure-fire. But that was only past experience. The Laurietonians stood there with their mouths open, looking at me as if I were talking a foreign language. I was so happy to be alive that it didn't depress me—much. Still, I was enough of a ham to want to get them started. I figured that something broad was indicated, so I tried a rewrite of an ancient jest.

"I was standing on a corner in Brisbane," I said. "It was raining and a lady was standing there holding her skirts up over her hat. And I said to her, 'Lady, you're getting your legs wet.' And she said, 'That's all right. My legs are fifty years old. The hat's brand-new.'"

That got 'em. They laughed. I didn't press my luck. Quickly I said, "Here's Miss Frances Langford." Frances sang a few songs. Tony Romano did his bit and everything was ginger-peachy.

Speaking of landings, I've had my share of overshooting a runway, then having to take off again. That kind of thing really tests a plane, the motors—and the passengers. The whole fuselage shudders. You feel the terrific strain and you wind up bushed from trying to hold the crate up in the air through sheer will power.

I drew one of those approach-too-long-for-the-runway jobs on a trip to England in 1943. I'd flown to a Lockheed base at Belfast, Ireland, with our USO troupe. In London we'd picked up Bob Considine, the columnist and feature writer, who was going to Ireland to do a feature story. Before we took off, we had to sign a statement that if anything happened to us, it wasn't the fault of the Air Force. Another question was: "Whom do we notify in case of an emergency?"

I wrote: "Louella Parsons." The query was a whimsical way of asking, "Where do we send the body?" I didn't want the Air Force to think that they had a corner on grisly humor.

When we flew to London from Belfast, the pilot of our C-47 made a "long" approach at Henden Field. Realizing he wouldn't be able to stop in time, he gunned his motors and I held my own hand while our aluminum boxcar fluttered over a hangar at the end of the field before zooming up again.

A lot of clever things were said by others on board while I was using the paraffin-coated container. I don't remember them, but they were awfully clever.

I see that I'm not too clever at keeping this thing in its right order. I should have started with the first show I did during World War II. It was one of the first shows anybody did anywhere during that fracas. In 1939 I had taken Dolores to England. We went over on the *Normandie*. George Raft, Eddie Robinson, Madeleine Carroll, Charles Boyer, Pat Patterson, and Mack Gray were fellow passengers. I had just closed at the Paramount in New York and the second night out, when the captain asked me to do a ship's concert, I said, "I'm not anxious to do anything. I'd just as soon relax and rest." But Eddie Robinson said, "I think you ought to do a ship's concert for the Seaman's Fund. It would be a nice thing to do." So I said, "Well, I'll do something. Maybe we can get some people together and can have some fun."

I worked out a bit for Eddie to do with George Raft. I introduced them as "two killers from Hollywood who happen to be with us on this trip. I won't vouch for what's going to happen." With that they started to walk toward each other from different side of the stage. As they got to the center they glared at each other slit-eyed and both said, "Yeah?"

Then Eddie said, "This boat isn't big enough for both of us." George said, "Yeah?" and Eddie said, "Yeah!"

"What are you going to do about it?" George asked. Whereupon they embraced and started to dance together.

It doesn't read like much but in that ship's concert it was a hit.

Dolores and I kicked around England and Europe for a while. We were in Paris at the George V Hotel when a fellow came up to me in the lobby and said, "Better get back to London right away."

"Why?" I asked.

"Didn't you hear Chamberlain's speech?" he wanted to know. "All American tourists are to get back to America immediately. Looks like trouble brewing."

Dolores and I rushed upstairs, got our bags together, scrammed out, got across the Channel and made it to the *Queen Mary* in time for her last run. The ship's brass asked me to do a concert on Sunday night and on Sunday morning I was sleeping when Dolores walked into the cabin—she had come down from Mass, so you can tell who's the good member of the family—and said, "You were wrong."

"What happened?" I asked.

"England has just declared war," she said.

She meant that I'd said there would be no war. "I wish you could see the scene in the salon," she went on.

I got dressed and went up there. Many of the British people were in tears; women and men too. Nobody was saying anything. They just sat around thinking. I guess they knew that a lot of their people and their relatives were going to be killed before things were better again. I thought about this for a while. Then I went to the captain and said, "I don't think I ought to do a concert tonight. This is no time for comedy."

He said, "Just as you wish, Mr. Hope."

Two hours later Harry Warner of the brothers Warner came to me and said, "I had lunch with the Captain. He says that he wishes you would do the concert tonight anyhow. He thinks that would be a good thing if you could get this crowd to laugh a little."

So I did the show. I opened by telling them the truth. I said that, since that tragic situation had arisen, I'd tried to beg off doing the concert, that I still didn't know whether it was right to do it or not, but maybe it might help if we all got together and tried to forget the tragedy which faced the world and had some fun.

I did a routine about the trip. In it I mentioned that my steward had told me when I got on board, "If anything happens it's women and children first, but the Captain said in your case you can have your choice."

I got a few laughs, then I went into my regular vaudeville act. I finished by doing a parody on "Thanks for the Memory." I had written it that afternoon. It went something like this:

> Thanks for the memory
> Of this great ocean trip
> On England's finest ship.
> Tho' they packed them to the rafters,
> They never made a slip.
> Ah! Thank you so much.
>
> Thanks for the memory
> Some folks slept on the floor,
> Some in the corridor;
> But I was more exclusive,
> My room had "Gentlemen" above the door.
> Ah! Thank you so much.

These lines won't make Robert Frost or even Irving Berlin lose any sleep. A few passengers on the *Queen Mary* even snored through it, but most of them cheered the parody. The Captain sent for me and said, "Could I have a copy of it?"

I said, "Of course," and the next morning I gave it to him. He had it printed and when we docked, he handed it to the passengers as they left the ship. It was afterward reprinted in *Variety*. Anyhow, it was appropriate. The *Queen Mary* had everybody on board she could crowd on. She was carrying the maximum. People actually were sleeping in the passageways.

Chapter 15

M Y AERIAL MARATHON to put on shows for servicemen during World War II began in 1942, when I was at the Goldwyn Studio. I'd played some shows at nearby camps and had gotten a taste of it, and when I heard that Joe E. Brown and Edgar Bergen had been to Alaska to entertain the troops, I said, "I'd like some of that."

Frances Langford, who was on my radio show, said, "I'd like some of it too."

There was a brief delay—but only a brief one—while her husband, Jon Hall, told her, "You can't go. You have symptoms of acute appendicitis."

Frances said, "They have doctors in Alaska too."

End of argument.

So I got a unit together and off we went. The members of my unit promised each other that we wouldn't fly in Alaska at night, unless we had to. That way we'd have daylight on our side in case of a forced landing or if a storm came up. But the city of Anchorage, Alaska, was having a street dance and Lieutenant General Simon Bolívar Buckner, who was our No. 1 man up there, asked us to be on hand for it. We took off from Cordova, Alaska, for Anchorage at seven-thirty, thinking we'd make it before it got too dark. No sooner were we aloft than we ran into a combination lightning and rain storm and began to bounce around. We felt as if we were flopping back and forth between two giants who'd somehow gotten the notion that we were a badminton bird.

We buffeted along that way for forty-five minutes. We could hear the pilots having an argument in the cockpit. Then they slammed the door. That didn't help our peace of mind. The storm was bad enough, but to have our pilots arguing worried us even more. Our pilots were a twenty-one-year old second lieutenant and a twenty-two-year old first lieutenant. I'd nicknamed one of them Junior, the other Growing Pains. We liked them but they did seem kind of young to be juggling our lives.

We flew in that mess for about twenty minutes more. Then we could tell that we were circling. I asked the plane's staff sergeant, "What goes?"

"They're having trouble with the radio," he said.

Finally the flight mechanic came back, told Frances to stand up, and put a parachute on her. He put a Mae West on her, too. Then he said, "That's in case we land in water."

"We might have to jump," he said to me. "You put on a parachute and a Mae West too."

I thought, *This is it.* I felt chilly. I looked out of a window, but I could see nothing. So I said my prayers. I knew that if you jumped in Alaska—especially in a storm—the odds against you were fantastic. I'd heard that the water was so cold you lived only forty-five seconds in it.

"What do you think?" Frances asked.

"I guess when we land this time the station wagon won't be there either," I said.

In our show I told a joke about how my brother had gotten into the paratroopers, and his first day in, some joker in his outfit told him, "When you're up there, count ten; then pull the ring. When you land, the station wagon will be there to pick you up and bring you back to camp."

The way I told it, the chute didn't open when my brother pulled the parachute ring, and he looked down and said in an annoyed voice, "And I'll bet that station wagon won't be there either."

In saying that to Langford, I was trying to be funny. But my teeth were chattering and my delivery was bad. It was an unhappy a moment as I've had. Then a light broke through the clouds and we followed it down. We came into the runway crosswise instead of parallel, but we landed. This was what had happened: General Buckner, who was waiting for us down there had been told that we were in trouble by the pilot of a United Airlines ferrying plane. This pilot had landed and had reported that he'd felt our backwash—he'd come that close to us!—and that we were off the beam and were lost. We'd gone off the beam when our radio conked out. Since then, our pilots had been trying to keep us from losing altitude because the mountains around us were thirteen thousand feet high.

General Buckner had ordered every antiaircraft searchlight in the place to throw up its finger of light—there were thirty of them. One of those fingers had broken through the cloud blanket. We saw it and dived for it. With our radio out, they couldn't have "talked" us down. Anyway, it was too early for Ground Controlled Approach, the device which was afterward developed to enable those at a landing field to lead a fog-bound pilot in by the hand.

People have told me, "I couldn't have gotten on another plane after an experience like that. From then on I'd have done my traveling underground by mole team." I didn't affect me like that. I've flown a million and a half miles since. It's like falling off a horse (and I don't mean a studio prop horse). If you get right back on you're all right. However, I admit that I didn't sleep much that night.

You don't have to fly over Alaska in a storm to remember that you're heavier than air. I was once going East on a commercial airliner with Barney Dean. We were sitting there laughing when we noticed that we were circling over Albuquerque. One of the pilots came out of the pilots' compartment, lifted the covering from the floor and crawled into a hole with a wrench. The landing gear was stuck and he was cranking it down by hand.

Barney asked me, "Do you think I can get a cab here?" and I said, "You'll have to wait until you get down." Neither of us was making much sense.

But to get back to the Air Force. In 1945 we did a show in Kassel, Germany, for our guys who were stationed there at a fighter base. The next day we went on to Berlin in a C-47. Ours was the first entertainment unit to reach the German capital. After doing a show in Berlin for the 82nd Airborne, we did a show in Potsdam; then went on to Nuremberg, where we did a show for twenty thousand boys.

We lived in a hotel with only three sides. One side had been bombed off, so that when we walked down the hallway on the second floor, we looked into the street. In that hotel I met Billy Conn, the Pittsburgh prize fighter. Billy was attached to a sports unit under golfer Horton Smith, who is now president of the Professional Golfers' Association.

When I ran into Billy, he told me, "I think this unit is about through and I'd like to get on your show."

I had an idea. "I've just thought of a routine I can do with you," I said. I remembered the joke I'd substituted for an Al Capone joke back in my vaudeville days in Chicago. "I could ask you about how hard Joe Louis hits—stuff like that," I went on.

"If you could, it would be wonderful," Billy said.

I headed for the dining room. When I walked in the head of

United States Army Special Services, Major General Ben M. Sawbridge, was there. "I'd like to thank you and your unit for coming over," he said. "If I can do anything for you, just let me know. We want you to be happy."

"Your timing couldn't be better, General," I said. "Billy Conn is here. He's about through with Horton Smith's unit. If you'll let me have him, I think I could use him in my show and do some good with him."

General Sawbridge called a colonel and said a few words to him. The colonel called a major and said a few words to him, and so on. Before I'd finished my meal, the General told me, "Billy Conn is now with your unit."

I went out into the lobby, found Billy and said, "Pack boy. You're with me."

"Stop it," he said. "I don't feel like kidding about it."

"I've fixed it," I told him. "You're speaking to a man who goes to the top. You're with me. Pack."

He didn't believe it, until a man with shiny things on his shoulders came along and gave him his new orders. Then Billy looked at me and said, "We'd better get out of here because when my brother, Jackie, finds out that I'm ditching him like this, he'll beat hell out of both of us." His brother was with the Horton Smith unit too. He had more rocks in his knuckles than Billy.

Billy made his first trip with us around the Alps and down to Marseilles. We flew through very mucky weather. For a while I was busy checking with the pilots to see how we were doing, then I got tired and lay down to catch some sack time. I'd been asleep for about twenty minutes when the plane gave a jerk. I woke up and looked at Jack Pepper, an old vaudevillian member of our unit. He was sitting on a box on the other side of the plane.

"How's everything?" I asked.

"It doesn't look good," he said. He pointed at Billy. He was on his back with his rosary in his hand, praying.

I leaned over and said seriously, "I hope you'll make it a package deal and include all of us."

"Don't worry," Billy said, "I've included everybody, especially the pilot."

Maybe it was because of Conn's package deal and maybe it wasn't, but we ran out of the storm, reached Marseilles safely and did a flock of shows there.

Not all of the things that happened to me while I was flapping around the world were scary. At times we got more laughs than we gave. Also, things happened that were interesting because they were so revealing. In this last category is a story that's never been told, so far as I know. I want to tell it myself before someone else gets it fouled up. Our entertainment group went into Palermo three days after our boys took it. We played for the 1st Division, the 82nd Airborne, and other outfits.

Then we paid a courtesy call on General Patton, whose divisions had gone snorting across Sicily like a herd of fire-breathing mountain goats. We shook hands with him and left to do more shows. That night we were scheduled to do an outdoor performance. But before we took off we arranged to have a late supper of spaghetti and meat balls at the Excelsior Hotel, where we were staying. Tony Romano had worked the whole thing out. He'd done the ordering and was to supervise the meal and visions of spaghetti and meat balls danced through our heads.

While we were doing our show, a captain came up to me and said, "I'm from General Patton's headquarters. The general wants you to have dinner with him after the show."

"Tell the General that's very nice," I said, "but we've arranged to have spaghetti and meat balls at the hotel."

"I think you'd better go to General Patton's," the captain said.

"I'm afraid we can't," I said.

"Look," he said, "if you don't show up at the General's it'll be your scalp and mine too."

A lot of my hair had been scared off by German air raids and

I didn't have any to spare. "That's different," I said. "We'll go."

"No spaghetti and meat balls," I told the others. "We *have* to dine with General Patton."

When we left the field, the soldiers were standing behind ropes and a little fellow in the mob yelled, "Hi ya, Bob!"

I hollered back, "Nice to see you."

He could tell from my voice that I didn't recognize him, for he said, "Ernie Pyle."

I rushed over and asked, "How long have you been here?"

"Ever since the invasion," he said. "Where are you staying?"

"The Excelsior," I said.

"I'm at the Excelsior, too," he told me. "Let's have dinner there."

"Can't," I said. "I have to go to General Patton's for dinner."

"See you after," he said.

The general served us pot roast, and we sat around while he told us stories about the Sicilian campaign. To us it was thrilling, being that close to a great American military hero.

I said to our group, "Why don't we do a little show for the General?"

When we finished, the General put his arm around me and said, "I want to ask you a favor."

"Certainly, General," I said.

"You can do me lots of good when you go back home," he said. I was puzzled. Why should he need a helping hand? I didn't get it.

"Tell all the people who listen to you on the radio that I'm crazy about my men," he said. "That I think they're great; that I'm very proud of them."

"You don't have to worry about that, General," I said. "The whole country gets a wallop out of you."

"I know," he said, "but there're press people here who're out to get me." *What this man needs is rest,* I thought. *He's been going so hard he's beginning to snap his cap.*

So I said to the others, "Let's let the General have a little sleep." When I got back to the Excelsior, Ernie Pyle was sitting in the lobby, and I asked, "How've you been, Ernie?"

Instead of answering, he said, "How'd you enjoy your visit with the General?"

"It was wonderful," I said.

"How do you like that heel?" he asked.

It rocked me back on my own heels. "Don't you know what happened in the hospital?" Ernie said. "He slapped a wounded soldier." Then he told me the story and for the first time I understood the reason for the General's request.

But for every serious thing that happened to me, like being around when a General lost his head, there were ten comical things. When we reached Tarawa in 1944, we did a few shows. They had a wire stretched across the stage—an electrical wire—because they used this amphitheatre for pictures. During the show while I was on a mouse started across the wire. He stole my audience. Three or four thousand marines stopped looking at me and watched this little mouse walk across that wire. I stopped trying to get them back and watched it myself. When the mouse finally made it across, we went on with the show.

To detour for a moment, that reminds me of a thing which happened during my first trip around the Orpheum Time. Everybody told me, "You think you're good, brother. Wait until you hit St. Louis." Louise Troxell and I approached St. Louis by way of Kansas City. As I have said Goodman Ace was a critic on a Kansas City paper. My act got a good notice from him. But he, too, said, "Wait until next week when you play St. Louis. They have a big barn of a theater there. It seats forty-five hundred."

"I'll kill 'em," I said. "They don't scare me. I'm loud. I don't need a mike. I've got lungs, haven't I?"

In St. Louis I walked out on the stage ready to go. I slam-banged into my routine and I was going good. After five minutes I was asking myself "What's so tough about it here?" when a

woman in the front row had an epileptic fit and the ushers came tramping down the aisle to carry her out. I never did get that audience back. After they'd watched the ushers carrying that poor woman away, not knowing whether she was alive or dead, I couldn't dig myself out.

When at last the heads all turned and looked back at me, I said, "You folks remember me, don't you?" I could look at their faces and tell they weren't sure they did.

In 1949 I did a personal appearance tour with Doris Day and Les Brown. When we hit Little Rock, Arkansas, one of my advance publicity men was waiting for us. "I've arranged a show for you at a hospital up on the hill," he told us. So Doris Day and

I went up there. We didn't find out until we reached it that it was a mental hospital. The patients were very moody, very sunk in depression. You've got to lift such an audience, and to lift them you have to do something broad. Usually physical comedy will get through the shell they live in. Edgar Bergen and Charlie McCarthy are wonderful in such a situation. A ventriloquist's dummy intrigues a P.N. audience. It's a little out of this world, a little fantastic and they buy that.

I started by saying to these boys, "Who won the ball game today between Cleveland and New York?" I got a couple of 'em yelling answers at me. Then I started to ad lib and I opened them up pretty good. But I thought, "I'd better not stay here too long. I'd better bring out Doris Day because a girl may open these fellows up even more."

Doris came out and they liked her. She did a couple of songs, without a piano, then I went back on and said, "I'd like to sing a little song for you, but I need music. Is there anybody in the audience who can play 'Buttons and Bows'?"

"Yes," the crowd said. "Charlie can do it."

They yelled for Charlie and he came up and I shook hands with him. He sat down at the piano and played "Buttons and Bows" with one finger. Also he lagged behind me, following me with the notes instead of keeping up with me. This made it difficult, but I went through with it. When I finished, the crowd applauded, I thanked Charlie and shook his hand again.

A month later, when we were back in Hollywood, a Paramount publicity man brought me a letter from a doctor at that hospital. The letter said, "I thought you'd like to know that the fellow you brought up on the stage to play piano was one of the worst cases we've ever had in this hospital. But from the day you brought him up on the stage and made him smile, he has improved. We think now that he'll eventually lead a normal life."

My nomination for the top comedy spot of my travels is a series of events which happened at Crestview, Florida. In 1944

I was at Brookley Field, near Mobile, Alabama, with an entertainment troupe on our way to the Officer Candidate School in
Miami. When we played in that area we usually used Brookley
as our headquarters. General Jim Mollison and Colonel Buck
Rawlings, who were in charge there, were always nice to our
gang of gypsies. Sometimes they'd even ship us out on planes,
if the planes happened to be going our way. We had to be at the
Office Candidate School at Miami on a Tuesday night to put on
a show. A plane was to fly us there on Monday, stay in Miami
Beach during the show, then fly us back. But on Sunday night it
began to rain, one of those semi-tropical Southern storms—
like standing under a waterfall. It rained through Monday. Not
only was it impossible to fly, there were electrical disturbances
too.

On Monday night I said to Colonel Rawlings, "I can't stay
here any longer. I better get going by car or we'll miss the whole
thing."

"I'll tell you what we'll do," he said. "I'll go with you, and if it
clears after we've left, I'll have Major Jim Dale sent out with a
B-25 to pick us up down the road. There's a landing field at
Crestview, Florida. We'll hope to meet Dale there."

We piled into two cars. Barney Dean and I were in one car
and Buck Rawlings was in the other. Going across Cochrane
Bridge, the water came up to our hub caps. We drove for a few
hours, then pulled into Crestview, Florida, where there was an
Army radio station and an auxiliary landing field.

We walked into the shack housing the radio equipment. We
found a woman in charge of the landing field and running the
place. She didn't seem to be in the Army; she wasn't wearing a
WAC uniform. There was also a weatherman there who was
running in and out and reporting on the weather.

Buck Rawlings walked in with his eagles glinting and de-
manded attention. "Could you tell me whether you've heard
from a Major Dale in a B-25 from Brookley Field?" he asked.

"No," she said, "I haven't."

Then she looked over Buck's shoulder and saw me. "Why, Bob Hope," she said. "Whatever are you doing in Crestview? My goodness, wait till I tell people you're here. I simply love you on the radio. I used to think you imitated Jack Oakie, but now I think you're just wonderful."

"Please, miss," the Colonel said, "we're trying to find a Major Dale."

"I told you I haven't heard from any Dale," she said.

There was no longer any question about whether or not she was a civilian operator. Colonels were just people to her and not impressive people at that.

"Would you please call Brookley Field and see if he's left there?" Rawlings asked. But Buck was out of luck. For that moment at least this doll was one of my real gone radio fans and calling Brookley was not on her agenda. I'm not boasting when I say this. Even Crosby has radio fans.

"It's amazing to see you're here in Crestview," she said. "How long are you going to stay?"

"How about being a nice girl and doing what the Colonel asks?" I told her. "We're trying to get to Miami."

Meanwhile, the weatherman was putting his coat collar up, running out and checking the balloons, running back in and turning his coat collar down again. The whole thing was beginning to play like one of Martin and Lewis' minor efforts.

My lady fan got on the phone, put through a call to Brookley, said, "No, the plane is not on the way"; then turned to me again and asked, "Where have you been?"

"We've been at Brookley Field," I said.

"Well, just imagine that," she said. "And you're here now. I can get you a room in town. Just wait'll Crestview finds out you're here," she said.

There was a flash of lightning and the lights went out. "Bob?" she asked. "Are you there?"

I said, "Yes."

"Light that candle on the desk," she told me. I lit the candle.

Now the joint was really eerie—Bela Lugosi's rumpus room. I felt a tap on my shoulder and I looked around.

It was a man who said, "Mr. Hope, my name is Milthrob. Do you know where I can sell a song?'" That wasn't his name, but Milthrob will do.

"Do you have a song?" I asked.

"Yes," he said. "I sent it to Major Bowes, but he sent it back."

It was then that I made my error. "How does it go?" I asked. He sang it to me there in the candlelight.

The girl to whom colonels were nothing said, "He's a big hit at the parties around here."

When the big noise at Crestview parties finished, I said, "That's pretty good. Do you have any more?"

"Oh, yes," he said. "I have another. It's called 'Julius Seized Her Before Luke Could Grab her.' "

I thought, *We're stuck anyway*, so I asked, "How does it go?" He sang that for me too. Then he said, "If I could only sell 'em."

Until then, I had been bored with Mr. Milthrob's words and music. But when he said, "If I could only sell 'em," I began to have a feeling of sympathy for him. I thought about how hard he must have worked on them, and about how much they must mean to him. After all, there'd been times when people thought my offerings corny too. For that matter, there are still some misguided people. I knew that there was only one chance in ten million that Mr. Milthrob's productions would ever find their way onto sheet music, but I decided to give him that one tenmillionth of a chance.

Barney Dean had been so frightened by the lightning and the wild gusts of rain that he hadn't left the car. He was waiting outside, sick of the whole thing.

"I have a little fellow outside in a car who knows about songs," I said. "You ought to sing them for him. He's in with the song writers, Johnny Burke and Jimmie Van Heusen. In fact, he's a director of their music-publishing company." I wasn't lying about that. Barney is tenth vice-president or something.

I stuck my head out and yelled, "Barney, come here."

"Leave me alone," he said.

"Come here, Barney," I said. "Come in here now!" When he came in, I said, "This is Mr. Milthrob."

"How do you do?" Barney asked. He's always polite.

"Mr. Milthrob has a couple of songs," I said, "and he'd like to sing them for you, wouldn't you, Mr. Milthrob?"

Mr. Milthrob nodded, filled his chest, placed his mouth close to Barney's face, and sang.

When Milthrob finished, I said, "Now sing the other one for him, Mr. Milthrob."

I watched Barney's face as he listened; I could see that the one ten-millionth chance I tried to give the song writer wasn't working. Barney was not impressed. As Milthrob finished his second number, a large percentage of the population of Crestview squished in. The girl who'd been snooty to Buck Rawlings had reached them on the phone. In no time the place was so packed that you couldn't put your hand in your pocket.

There we were, jammed in with whispering people; Milthrob was retesting his pipes; Barney Dean was lost in his gloomy thoughts; my lady fan was saying, "He looks exactly like he does in the movies, doesn't he?" We could have leased the whole thing to the producer of a film like *The Snake Pit*.

Major Dale and his plane did pick us up. We drove on into Jacksonville, hopped a train, reached Miami Beach at five o'clock Tuesday night, and put the script of our show together at the Ocean Surf Hotel.

The writers brought their stuff to me. I checked it and they ran upstairs to the typewriters and dashed it off. We just barely made the show. It was one of the few times we didn't have mimeographed copies. We were doing this show on a pier, and when I ran—I didn't walk—over there, it was only ten minutes before we went on the air.

There was a major at the door checking everybody. I walked

up to him and said, "Major, will you please just forget about the checking? Let anybody who wants to come in come in?"

"What's all the rush?" he asked:

"We'll be on the air any minute," I said.

He told the waiting soldiers, "Run in" and they ran to the seats. I ran out on the stage and said, "Boys, I don't have time to do anything in the way of a warm-up but I'll talk to you after the show. In two seconds we're on the air. Just love it, will ya," I said, "that's all. Good-bye. . . . How do you do, ladies and gentlemen, this is the Pepsodent show. Here we are in Miami . . ." and we were away.

Chapter 16

THE SOLDIERS' HUMOR—the humor they tried on you and the humor you learned to try on them—was a thing in itself. Like the time I walked out on the stage that had been set up at the race track in Bône, Africa. I was with a USO troupe and it was after we'd been to Bizerte and to Palermo, where we'd been scared to death by a series of rattle-bang, hell-popping air raids. I was wearing an old, dirty, green linen suit. It hadn't been pressed for months. And I was carrying a cane because I'd wrenched my knee jumping into a ditch during an air raid. I had a beat-up, dirty, dusty old straw hat.

When I walked out there with my shirt open, everybody could see that I'd been in a lot of trouble, that I'd been scared a lot, that I'd had it.

I said, "Good afternoon, everybody," and a fellow way in back said, "Hi ya, slacker!"

It broke the boys up. They looked at me in that travel-worn outfit and at my limp and my cane, and they laughed a large, economy-size belly laugh.

"It's amazing how you meet Crosby's relatives everywhere," I told the crowd.

That "slacker" crack was GI kidding. There were a lot of things in it. It poked fun at me for getting myself in such a wringer that I looked like a sad sack. It meant that they could see that somebody was going to have to pick me up with a blotter if the wear and tear I was running into didn't stop. It was the soldier's way of saying, "Thanks for bringing a little fun and some pretty girls over here where what we've got most of is camels, Arabs and fleas."

It was also a way of saying that they approved of the way I handled myself when I dropped in to pass the time of day with them in a hospital. You had to understand that the hospitalized ones wanted no sympathy. If you gave it to them, they'd roll over in bed and ignore you. So I'd walk into a hospital and if there were a lot of guys in traction I'd say, "Okay, fellas, don't get up." Then I'd walk into the next ward and say in a loud tone, "All right, let's get the dice and get started."

Or I'd say, "My brother is in the Army. He's trying to arrange a private peace with the enemy. He figures he's given the best years of his wife to his country. He's in the Air Force. He shot down five planes. They were all ours, but he's trying hard."

Through trial and error I'd sifted my gags down to a few that were pretty sure to fetch guffaws from servicemen. They fell into certain classifications. The fact that I'd been away from home a lot was good for a boff:

It's been suggested that I travel a bit. . . . That I wander from my happy home. This is not true. Just the other evening I said to my wife, "Dolores"— I knew it was Dolores, she introduced herself to me—"I've done an awful

185

lot of traveling but you've been very understanding about it . . . although you did rent out my room."

The fact that I was playing the USO circuit also seemed funny to them:

I don't have to close my eyes in the regular way any more when I try to sleep—I now have Venetian veins. . . . I said to the producer, "This is a man-killing schedule," and he said, "What are *you* worried about?"

Ribbing life as it is lived in Hollywood scored well too:

Yessir, that smog out there is getting worse. When you drive into a service station, the attendant asks, "Peel your windshield?" California is the only place you can plant seeds and have a gopher spit them back at you.

But I got my best results with gags tailored to the special problems, gripes and habits of the servicemen overseas:

How do you do, fellow tourists. This is Bob Hope, telling all you guys that I rushed here as fast as I could because I heard they were going to ration fraternization. I stopped off in Paris on my way here; they had quite a few artists there, sketching the girls in a show I saw. I thought I'd try it, but they threw me out—they said no fair tracing.

Last night I slept in the barracks. You know what the barracks are—a crap game with a roof. What a place to meet professional gamblers. I won't say they were loaded, but it's the first time I ever saw dice leave skid marks. A discharge—that's a little piece of paper that changes a lieutenant's name from "sir" to "stinky." . . . Soldiers are real strong. I walked in with a blonde on one arm and a brunette on the other. Two minutes later, no blonde, no brunette, no arms.

Right after we left Bône, Africa, we got to Algiers, where General Eisenhower had his headquarters. We told our Special Service man that if it could be arranged, we'd like to say hello to the General before we went back, him being the head man over there and all. We were rehearsing in the theater for a broadcast back to the States. They had crude equipment they'd brought down for us to use and we were trying to work out something. There was no band, just Tony Romano for the music.

A fellow came up to me in the middle of rehearsal and said, "A major would like to see you."

"We can't see him now," I said. "Would you please tell him to talk to our Special Service man because we're very busy."

The messenger said, "You'd better go."

I asked, "Why?"

"The major is General Eisenhower's aide," he said.

I yelled, "Recess!"

We got in a jeep and roared up the hill to headquarters. The first thing we knew we're standing in front of Ike. He greeted us by saying, "Sit down and tell me what's happened to you. I understand you've been bombed a little."

We told him about that. His personality was disarming. He put us at our ease and we had a good time. Finally, he said, "Well, you can get a rest here in Algiers because we've been very lucky. We haven't been bombed here for a month and a half. They can't get in we're so strong here. You'll get a good night's rest tonight."

"I hope so," I said. "And now we'd better go back and rehearse."

We did the show and that night when we went back to the hotel to have something to eat we ran into Quentin Reynolds in the lobby of the Aletti Hotel. "Come on up and meet the boys," he said. I didn't know who "the boys" were, but I walked into a room and met Clark Lee, H. R. Knickerbocker, and John Steinbeck. They were all living in one room.

We sat around and talked about the trip and home and everything, and it was real great. About three o'clock I went to bed and at four o'clock I heard a banging on my door. It was Jack Pepper asking, "Can't you hear that?"

"Hear what?" I asked.

"It's an air-raid warning," he said.

We found Frances Langford and rushed down to the wine cellar, which was used for an air-raid shelter. We're sitting down there when it started. The building shook and I thought: *This is it.*

The bombers kept trying to paste the battleships in the harbor, which was just outside the door. And all the big guns and the anti-aircraft guns, the ninety millimeters, were firing. I can't describe the racket. But I'll say this—I knew something was going on.

The next day I sent Ike a wire and thanked him for the rest. I said, "I'm glad I wasn't here on one of the nights when you had some action."

Also in the laugh department was a chain of events that happened in 1943, after I played an airfield outside of Tunis. I met a young colonel there, named Jack Austin. We visited a few night clubs, near the field, made out of bomb crates. At each of them I told a story. After each story I had a drink.

As we'd walked into the fourth club, I asked, "Where are you going tomorrow?"

"We're going over to Rome," he said.

"I'm going with you," I said. "They promised me I could go on a mission."

Nobody had promised me I could go on a mission. I just said it because there were drinks bubbling inside of me; I was winning the war alone, and I thought I could con the young Colonel into thinking I had permission to tag along with him. By the time we got back to the officers' club, I was so brave I was telling everybody the big things that Jack Austin and I were going to do.

The Colonel went outside and put in a phone call. When he came back he hauled me out of the crowd and said, "I've just talked to General Doolittle about you going on the mission tomorrow. He said to tell you to put down your glass and go to bed." This young Colonel, who looked like Clark Gable, drove me all the way back to Tunis in the headquarters car. As we got out in front of the hotel he said, "Get some sleep, dad." It aged me fifteen years, but I guess I had it coming to me.

We'd played our first radio show for servicemen in March, 1941, at an Army Air Force base at March Field, California. After that, with the exception of two shows I did at the NBC studio in Hollywood, when I couldn't leave home because of sickness, I did my regular Pepsodent radio show at Army, Navy and Marine bases until June, 1948. In September, 1948, Lever Brothers began to pick up the tab. During ten years we did over four hundred radio shows at camps and bases here in this country and all over the world. Pepsodent, who sponsored me until 1948 (and after that, Lever Brothers, who hired me for a Swan Soap hour) not only paid me the happy little sum our contracts called for each show, they paid for our travels too. I take it they got their money's worth, for, during my Pepsodent period, I was told that that dentrifice went from the sixth position in sales to first.

In addition to the four hundred radio shows, we played three or four shows for camps or bases every day (without benefit of broadcasting and, of course, without any fees) while we were on the road. Nor does the phrase "over four hundred" include the free shows we put on for the Armed Forces Radio Service. Those shows were called "Command Performance," "Male Call" and the "G.I. Journal." We averaged about one a week of these.

In addition to the payments from Pepsodent, Paramount and Sam Goldwyn also helped keep the Hope larder stocked during this time. In the years 1941 through 1951, inclusive, I appeared in nineteen movies for Paramount and two for Goldwyn. These included *My Favorite Blonde, Road to Morocco, The Princess and the Pirate, Monsieur Beaucaire, The Paleface, Fancy Pants* and *The Lemon Drop Kid*.

It was on a trip to Biak Island, and Hollandia, in Dutch New Guinea, in 1944 that I got the skin disease known as jungle rot. Drenching rains, like shower baths, are regular things down there. Of course, we have what we call "a light sprinkle" now and then right here in California. Light sprinkle. That's South Pacific for "Man the boats, the island has disappeared again."

In Guadalcanal it seems to rain every fifteen minutes. The whole island is musty, and the dampness breeds jungle rot.

Jungle rot is a horrible thing. I saw kids in the South Pacific who had it so badly they couldn't sleep unless they were given a hypo. They had it all over their backs. A few of them had it all over their bodies. Patty Thomas got it in her ear and had to have treatments for it. I got it on my feet. It still comes out on me on hot, humid, mucky days. There was one nice thing about it, though, if anything can be nice about that foul disease. It gave me a rest period every day. I'd go to the hospital and lie back while they painted my feet with a drug. They'd paint my feet and powder them and put my socks back on for me, and I'd be on my way to another show.

I had a flare-up of it in Washington, D. C., when I was there in the spring of 1953 to do a show at the Bethesda Naval Hospital. I asked a doctor, "Isn't there any way in which you can kill this stuff off?"

"In spite of the advances in medical science, we haven't conquered it," he told me. "It lies dormant under the skin. Humid weather brings it out."

I walked around that hospital feeling sorry for myself because the rot had given me blisters on my feet. I was conscious of them every time I took a step. But I had to visit the wards. You hate to go into a place like that and do a show in the auditorium and not go into the wards for those who couldn't make it to the hospital theater.

Someone told me about a Lieutenant Bill Owen, who was living in an iron lung there. In spite of that, he'd built up a disk-jockey job for himself in the hospital. I stood in back of a nice-looking youngster who gazed at me in the mirror over his head.

I was introduced to him and he said, "I'd like to interview you for my radio audience."

I said, "Go ahead."

We talked about a lot of things. Then he asked, "What's the most important question of the day?"

"The Korean war," I said.

"No," he said mentioning the title of a song that was popular then, " 'How Much is That Doggie in the Window?' "

"How do you know what the scoop is outside of the hospital?" I asked.

"I get around," he said, "by meeting a lot of wonderful people."

He'd been an interne there when he was stricken by polio. But it hadn't slowed him down or cramped his style. It had merely broadened his world. After talking to him I forgot my blisters. I walked out of that room. I felt childish even thinking about them and they didn't seem to bother me during the rest of my tour.

A lot of things qualifying for the "it's-a-small-world" department happened during the trips I made lugging my bags of gags around for servicemen. Before the roof fell in on us at Pearl Harbor, a boy used to hang around the Hollywood NBC and CBS studios mooching tickets. He was always asking me for pasteboards for my show. If I had any, I gave them to him. No matter whether it was a Lux show or a "Command Performance" show I was doing at CBS, he was there with his hand out.

Now we cut to Tunis. The year is 1943. I'm doing my first show in that area at the Red Cross Club for Lieutenant General Doolittle's 12th Air Force. The Club seats three thousand or four thousand. It's full. General Doolittle is in the balcony. I walk on, I look around. There in the front row is my loyal past, the ticket moocher. He just sits there, looks at me and winks.

I know what that wink means. It is saying, "You didn't have to help me get in here. I got to this place all by myself."

I got myself into a lot of places too. Sometimes I wondered why. When I checked in at Bougainville in 1944, I was living with General Griswold. In the middle of the night I was awakened by the sound of artillery not too far away. On that island our fellows were still fighting off Jap counterattacks against our base.

I was thinking of those stubborn Nips when I got up to go to the chic sale. Knowing that they weren't far away gave me goose pimples and I expected one of them to jump me any second. As I walked down a path to the latrine, something hit me on the head. I wrestled with it for a while until I discovered that it had leaves instead of hands. It was a low-hanging limb.

It was in 1944 on that same South Pacific trip that we reached Tarawa and did a few shows. While there we saw movies of the Marines landing on Tarawa six or eight months before. The audience was so quiet we could hear palms rustle. A hundred yards from the theater were rows of white crosses where some of the Marines that we were seeing on the screen were lying. After the picture we got up and walked back to our quonset hut past that cemetery. Those white crosses reached inside of us and squeezed our guts.

I tried not to play favorites with any one outfit. But in spite of myself, I found myself carrying a torch for the First Marine Division. In 1944 when I was in Banika in the Russell Islands in the Southwest Pacific with a USO unit, a Special Service marine officer came to me. "We've got the First Marine Division stashed away on a little island called Pavuvu. It's about twenty miles from here," he said. "They're training for the invasion of Peleliu. Nobody knows this but the men themselves. They haven't had any entertainment for nine months. If you'd come over with your troupe, it would be wonderful."

"How do we get there?" I asked.

"I think you ought to know first that there're no runways on Pavuvu," he said. "You'll have to go in Cubs; one of you to each Cub. You land on a road."

"We'll be ready tomorrow morning," I said. "I'll check with my people, but I know they'll want to go."

Frances Langford, Jerry Colonna, Patty Thomas, Bill Goodwin, and the rest of the gang had never turned down a show anywhere.

The next day we took off. Each of us was in a Cub with a pilot. When we reached Pavuvu, more than fifteen thousand guys stood on a baseball field, waiting for us. Looking down, I realized that fifteen thousand faces pointed at the sky is a lot of faces.

As we flew over, they let out a yell. It felt as if it was lifting our Cubs up into the air.

We did a show for them. While we were doing it, we knew that a lot of the men we were entertaining would never see the States again. If we hadn't felt the drama in that situation we'd have been pretty thick-skinned. We weren't that thick-skinned.

When we got into the Cubs to go back to Banika, all fifteen thousand of those marines lined the road and cheered each Cub as it took off. If I never get another thrill in my life, that one was it.

The First Marines went on to take Peleliu. Our USO unit finished its South Pacific trip and went back to California. Four months later I was asked to bring some entertainers up to Oak Knoll Hospital in Oakland, California, to dedicate a new surgical amphitheatre. We did a show for the people who packed into that amphitheatre. Afterward the colonel-doctor in charge said, "I hope you'll go through the wards and say hello."

In the first ward, a kid in bed put out his hand and said, "Pavuvu!"

"First Marine Division?" I asked.

"Yes," he said. "Every kid in this ward is from the First Marines."

It ought to be clear by now that I'm a softie about such things. My feeling about these matters was underscored when I talked with a boy in Espiritu Santo, an island in the New Hebrides group. The boy was badly injured. He was very weak and they were giving him a transfusion.

Walking up to his bed, I said, "I see they're giving you a little pick-me-up?"

His eyes went to the transfusion tube and he gasped, "It's only raspberry soda, but it feels pretty good."

Two hours later a doctor walked up to me in the officers' club. "Remember that boy who was joking with you?" he asked. "He just died."

I thought about how, in his last moments, he'd grinned and tried to say something light. I couldn't stand it. I had to go outside and pull myself together.

I've done a lot of work in hospitals but the things which happen in them get me down. I could never have been a doctor. Even in peacetime I've seen things in these big, white, disinfected joints which seemed unbearably sad.

Once I attended a Sports Celebrity Dinner in Philadelphia. Sonny Fraser, a good friend of mine, was being honored. He had the same disease that had killed Lou Gehrig. Sonny died at Temple Hospital in Philadelphia. Before he went, at that dinner he was awarded the Most Courageous Athlete Award. Later on, when I was in Philly to see the Villemain and Sugar Ray Robinson fight, I went to see him.

He looked down at his toes and said, "Look. I can move them." They weren't moving at all.

It still makes my eyes feel funny when I think of it.

When World War II was over and we went on into Korea, I went there too with another USO troupe. When I reached Japan I told the boys in Tokyo, "I know it's not on our schedule, but I'd like to do a show for the First Marines. I'm sentimental about them."

We went from Seoul to Pyongyang, did a show, then took off for Wonsan, where the First Marine Division was scheduled to be. As we flew into Wonsan we saw a lot of shipping in the harbor and small boats headed toward shore.

That's nice, I thought. *They're coming in to see our show.*

But when we arrived in the Wonsan airport, there wasn't a soul in sight. We wondered where everybody was. We just went over to the hangar and stood there. Finally the brass—Major General Edward M. Almond, Vice Admiral Arthur D. Struble and the rest—showed up.

"When did you get here?" they asked.

"We've been here for twenty minutes," I told them.

"Twenty minutes!" they said. "You beat us to the beach."

"How do you mean, we beat you to the beach?" I asked.

"We've just landed," they said.

They'd been attacking the place, but it turned out to be a bloodless invasion. When we landed at the airport there were guerrillas all around us, but we didn't know it, and the fact that we beat the Marines to the beach made the A.P. wire. But I didn't believe it until I talked to the newspapermen who were there.

Anyhow, when I walked out onto the stage in the hangar to do our show, I said to the First Marines, "It's wonderful seeing you. We'll invite you to all our landings."

After the show we had a cocktail party, with General Almond

195

and the Marine Corps General and Admiral Struble and a lot of brass, in a little tent. The party was complete with K-rations and beer and such items.

"Why don't you come out and stay with me tonight?" Admiral Struble asked.

"What do you mean, with you?" I inquired.

"Well, I have my flagship, the *Big Mo*," he said. "I'm in charge of the Seventh Fleet."

"I'm with you," I said.

We flew out to the *Missouri* by helicopter. They radioed ahead that we were coming, and as we landed and walked down the deck the sailors yelled, "Hi ya, Ski Snoot."

The Admiral took me to his quarters and said, "You'll probably want a bath and a change of linen."

I had those two things, then he gave me a big cigar. "The only thing I need to make this complete is a drink," I said.

"We're here on a battleship and that's one thing about our ships," he said, "we're not allowed to have liquor aboard."

Somehow the captain of the helicopter which had brought me out heard about my thirst and passed the word. When I went down to the Captain's quarters—it was the suite the Trumans used when they visited the *Missouri*—the officer who showed me around said, "If you feel like anything to wet your whistle just look in this case right here."

I opened the case. In it was a bottle of Scotch. I had a small belt, followed by dinner, then did a show for the crew of two thousand. I did every joke I knew, and every dance.

Then I went up to the ward room and did a few gags for the officers who hadn't been allowed to come down to the show on deck because they might crowd it up. Afterward I sat down with the whole ship's crew and saw Randolph Scott in a movie called *Colt Forty-Five*. There was so much shooting in it that when I stood up at the finish, I said, "I want to go home. This is too rough for me. It's rougher than the war."

196

The next morning the *Big Mo* radioed the shore. Marilyn Maxwell, a girl dancer, and a sister team of singers were flown out to us by helicopter, and we did another show. Then we took a helicopter to the *Valley Forge* and did a show on her flight deck for Admiral Hoskin and two thousand more guys. We helicoptered back to Wonsan, got into our C-54, whipped over to Pyongyang, did a show in the yard of the former Communist headquarters for a lot of troops who'd just been pulled out of the front lines.

Then we crawled back on the plane and that night were back in Tokyo. All in all it was one of the most exciting twenty-four hours I've ever had.

Just before we got on the plane to go back to Tokyo, a major said to me, "I wish I had a parka like yours."

"Brother, you've got one," I said, and gave him mine. The members of Les Brown's band—all forty-five of them—threw their parkas at soldiers too. They were nice parkas but we figured we didn't need them that much.

Even before my Wonsan landing, that Tokyo-Korean trip was quite a thing. Major General Ralph F. Stearley met us when we flew into Okinawa on our way across the Pacific.

"You'll be living with the brass here," he told me.

I thought, *So, I'm not going to be with the gang. This is not good.*

Then he added, "Rosy O'Donnell is here. I'm bunking you with him."

That put a different complexion on it. I knew Major General Emmett (Rosy) O'Donnell—now Lieutenant General. I'd played golf with him and I'd knocked around New York with him at places like Toots Shor's Saloon.

There had been a lot of looting on Okinawa, so when Major General Stearley took me to his house there a soldier was guarding it. In fact, there were two guards, one by day and one by night. As we neared his quarters, the day guard aimed his gun at us and didn't put it back on his shoulder and marched around the house again until he was given the password. The whole deal seemed menacing to me and once more I found myself wishing I was shacking up somewhere else.

When the General showed me into my room, there was Rosy. We said hello and Rosy said, "I'll show you where you're doing your show tonight."

We moseyed over to the ball field where we were to entertain the troops, then came back to the house. "Be careful going past the guard," Rosy said. "He took a shot at the chauffeur last night."

I opened my mouth to laugh, but he wasn't kidding. So I closed it again.

It had been raining, and the baseball stadium was so muddy that the girls in our troupe had to be carried bodily from jeeps to stage to do our show. There must have been twenty thousand volunteers for this carrying job. The competition was so intense that some of the losing candidates wound up with bloody noses, black eyes and trampled toes.

When Rosy and I got home that night, we sat around cutting up touches about Toots and about other people we knew in New York. Finally we went to bed. But I didn't sleep well. For one thing, I could hear the guard stomping around the house on the gravel outside.

Since we had to do shows not only on different sides of the island, but one in the hospital too, we stayed on Okinawa for two days. The second night there was a party for us at the officers' club. I left it late and got to bed about two-thirty. Rosy had gone back to Japan, so I was sleeping alone. The coffee, the drinks and the food I'd had were tossing around inside of me. However, I finally dropped off to sleep.

Two hours later I woke to go to the bathroom for a glass of water. As I sat up and switched on the bed lamp, I heard a noise. Turning, I looked through the window. Peering at me was the night guard. I smiled a toothy, forced smile at him. He smiled a fanged, snarling smile back at me.

Shall I get up now? I asked myself. *Can I get to the bathroom safely or will he take a shot at me? Does he think I'm a spy? Does he know who I am?*

I looked at the window and smiled again. Once more the character outside smiled back in a sinister way. I kept on looking. There was something about that face and smile that seemed familiar.

They were mine. I'd been smiling at my own reflection.

When we took off to fly into Tokyo, Colonel Lionel Leyden, a Special Services officer, stood in the aisle of our plane and made a speech. "Ladies and gentlemen," he said, "you're now in General MacArthur's command. It's the best damn command in the world. From now on, you're going to be treated as VIP's. Your rooms will have the smallest rats."

We called Colonel Leyden "The Coach." He never threw his weight around. He threw his talents around instead—where they did the most good. He was always in there in the background, helping. General Hoyt Vandenberg had given us two planes, for, with Les Brown's band, a group of writers, and a flock of entertainers, including the talented singer, Marilyn Maxwell, we were a sizable group.

The plane I drew was bossed by Colonel Harold Maddux. He was in charge of our project. If the other plane arrived before ours, it had to circle until we landed. Colonel Maddux had all the papers and credentials carried by colonels in charge of USO expeditions, and it was protocol that if any brass was waiting for us, Colonel Maddux had to meet them first. We reached one island—Guam, I think it was—during bad weather. Major Gordon Knight was in charge of our second plane—the plane with my writers.

Our plane was late in arriving over Guam, so Major Knight's plane circled and waited for us. They'd circled for half an hour when Major Knight said, "We're not going to wait any longer. Land!"

One of my irrepressible writers, Larry Gelbert, looked at him sorrowfully and said, "O.K., Private Knight."

I wish Colonel Maddux had been on hand to lean on during a landing I made in Alaska in 1949. In December of that year I attended the premiere of the film, *Twelve O'Clock High*. In it, Gregory Peck played a role based on the real-life story of Brigadier General Frank Armstrong, Jr. General Frank had been boss of an 8th Air Force group in England. I'd met him in London during the war and I knew that Armstrong's real story was far more exciting than the filmed version. He'd taken a below-par group, reorganized it and lifted it by the seat of its pants. Frank is a powerhouse.

He was at the premiere, too, along with Stuart Symington, who was then our Air Force Secretary, and General Curtis LeMay. The premiere was only a few days before Christmas. The next day the phone rang in my office at home.

It was Stu Symington. "How'd you like to come up with me to Anchorage, Alaska, for Christmas and meet the boys?" he asked.

"I figured on spending this one at home with Dolores and the children," I said. "I was away last Christmas."

"Why don't you bring them along?" he asked.

Before I could answer, I heard excited yelps of "Yes, Daddy, yes!" on the line. My two oldest kids, Tony and Linda, were listening in on the extension.

"Bring Dolores and your Tony and Linda with you," Stu said.

"Wait a second," I said. . . . "Dolores?" (By that time I knew she'd be on the extension too.) "It'll be thrilling," she said.

The kids were already flying around the house, hunting for galoshes and warm woolens; my hand was forced, so I said, "Stu, you're got a bet."

Frank Armstrong was still in Los Angeles, but he was heading north that afternoon, so Stu said, "Frank will fly you to Seattle. I'll pick you up there in my plane."

Stu's call had come through at ten o'clock in the morning. The next thing I knew, Armstrong himself was calling me. "I'll meet you at four o'clock at my B-17 on the Hughes Aircraft runway," he said. This meant I had about five hours to gather together an entertainment unit.

I called Jimmy Wakeley, the cowboy singing star, and asked, "What are you doing over the holidays?"

"I don't know," he said.

"Would you like to go to Alaska this afternoon?" I asked.

He took it in his stride. "Sure," he said.

"Pack your guitar and toothbrush and meet me in two hours," I told him.

I called Jeff Clarkson, Les Brown's piano player, next. Then I buzzed Patty Thomas. Patty was my dancing partner, who'd been with me in the South Pacific. And I asked them, "How'd you like to go to Alaska for a few days?" They both said, "Fine."

I had to let my writers know I'd be gone for a while, so I called Norman Sullivan. Norman's been with me for fifteen years. "You figure out the radio show for next week," I said. "I'm going to Alaska."

"You're doing what?" he asked.

I said, "I'm going to Alaska, Norman."

"When?" he asked.

"This afternoon," I said.

There was a moment of silence, then he came back with what seemed to me a funny line. "Oh, well," he said, "we'll move your pin on the map."

We all went up to Seattle together, met Stu Symington there, and took off in his plane the next day. With him Stu had brought an extra star for Brigadier General Frank Armstrong. Frank had been promoted to major general, but he didn't know it, and the fact that Stu had a new star for him in his pocket gave the rest of us a kick.

It was good flying weather from Seattle until we neared Anchorage. Then the whole area socked in. Keeping my voice chatty, I asked Frank and Stu, "We'll be able to land O. K., won't we?"

"Yes," they said, "but we'll have to go in on Ground Control Approach."

Because of the brass on board, our pilot was a lieutenant colonel. Symington picked up the intercom and said, "Colonel, switch the instructions you get from the ground out here into the cabin so we can all hear them."

As we squished through the soup, we heard the instructions coming through from the tower in Anchorage to our plane:

"You're a thousand feet from touchdown. . . . Let down to eight hundred. . . . A little more to the left. . . . You're now five hundred feet from touchdown. . . . Let down to three hundred. . . . Steer it just a little right rudder. . . . You're now a hundred feet from touchdown. . . . You're on your own. . . . You should be there now. . . . Good luck!"

We couldn't see a thing. It was twenty-eight below and the ground fog put up a dense curtain. It was even hard to see anything after we'd touched down. If anything had gone wrong with our ground-plane communications, it would have been a mess. Under such circumstances I can understand why a plane load of civilians will take up a collection and buy a pilot a watch.

When we got out a band met us. They were playing "Thanks for the Memory." Within half an hour Dolores and I were on our way to our first show at the hospital, and Tony and Linda were dividing their time between riding around in a sled and building a snowman. They gave us the full treatment up there—a tree, a dinner, and stockings. On Christmas Eve we were in church with our children.

Afterward we went up to the Air Force base at Eielson, and to Kodiak to do a show for the Navy. We did twelve shows in two days. I was so anxious to do them well that I worked up a sweat and caught a heavy cold that knocked out my voice. From then on I had to stand so close to the mike it was practically in my mouth.

When they put me back on the plane to go home, I couldn't talk; I just whispered to the mess sergeant on the plane, "Get me some soup and sleeping pills."

In 1948 Stu Symington invited Dolores and me to go to Berlin to take part in the Airlift Show. Along with Jinx Falkenburg, Alben Barkley (who was then Vice President), Irving Berlin, Elmer Davis and Jimmy Doolittle, we boarded Symington's plane. We landed at Weisbaden the night before Christmas, and did several shows there. They asked me to go into Berlin that night on one of the airlift planes, so Dolores, Jinx Falkenburg and I flew from Weisbaden to Berlin's Templehof Airport on an airlift plane carrying coal. Alben Barkley just went along to say hello to the boys. He appeared at most every show, as did Jimmy Doolittle. Alben's pretty smooth on his feet, very, very fast—in fact, one of the greatest extemporaneous boys I've ever met.

When we were playing Berlin, a fellow came around to see me on Christmas Day. "I'm a disk-jockey," he said. "I play records to everybody in the European Theater. And they all listen. I'd like you to come over to my place and say a few words on my show."

"I'll try to do that," I said.

That night we were invited to a big dinner by General Lucius Clay. And we met Beedle Smith, who was then Ambassador to Moscow. He'd just come to Berlin, and he swore he'd never go to Russia again. He was tired and he'd had enough of Moscow and his job. Mrs. Smith seemed fed up with the whole thing too, and to be back in American company meant a lot to her.

Afterward Dolores and I started home to our hotel. It was about two in the morning, but I thought of something. "I hate to disappoint that disk-jockey," I said to Dolores. "Why don't we go over there and surprise him."

We had his address written on a card so we got in a staff car and started out. They had a fuel-saving blackout on in Berlin and we'd driven only about five blocks when we ran out of gas. We walked the rest of the way through the dark streets of Berlin with a flashlight as our only light. Those streets were all bombed out and mostly rubble. There were people in that rubble (both alive and dead) and it was a weird experience.

At last we found the radio station where this boy was working. He was alone. The disk-jockey show was handled by a series of one-man shifts. When I walked in he looked up from his mike and said, "No. I don't believe it!"

Then he said into the mike, "Fellows, I've got news for you! Here's Bob Hope." Then he turned the mike over to me.

I started to talk, then I looked around. He was gone. The program was all mine. Later I found out that he'd gone to wake up the other shifts because he knew they wouldn't believe him in the morning when he told them that I'd dropped in at two-thirty A.M. to see him. After a while he came back and all the other boys came in, and we had coffee and kicked some conversation around. We sat there and talked about everything, the latest records, about our trip, show business. It all went out over the air.

Those drop-in experiences were the biggest kicks of all. During my 1950 Korean trip, I dropped in to the big Army PX during my first day in Tokyo. I heard a song blaring from the amplifiers in the music department. I thought there was something familiar about that tune—in a queer sort of way. Then I recognized it. It was "Buttons and Bows" being sung in Japanese, to Japanese music. My movie, *Paleface,* had played there and its key song had been a hit. Everywhere I went, the Japanese grinned at me, bowed, and said, "Buttons and Bows" as if that were my name.

When our unit got to Osaka, we were loaded into a staff car. Another car, carrying a Japanese band, followed us to the hospital where we were to do a show. There were seven Nips in that car. I don't remember all of their instruments, but I remember a trumpet, a sax, a clarinet, a trombone and a fiddle. They were right on our tails playing "Buttons and Bows" off key, bowing and grinning and hissing politely at me whenever we came to a traffic stop. It takes a heap of loving to like "Buttons and Bows" after being exposed to it in Japanese.

We did one show in Osaka in a huge swimming pool equipped with seats for forty thousand people. Swimming meets are the national sport of Japan and this thing was built like one of our football stadiums. Only ten thousand of our troops were on hand, so we only used one end of the pool, but two hundred or three hundred Japanese sat along the sides. I sang "Buttons and Bows," and every time I came to the title, the Japanese applauded. Those three words were the only ones they recognized. Our boys got a boot out of that, and every time I came to those three words they applauded too. Before long we were all laughing so hard I couldn't go on.

It was on this same trip that my gang was invited to lunch by General MacArthur and Mrs. MacArthur. What with Les Brown's band and a lot of entertainers, such as the Taylor Maids, Marilyn Maxwell, the dancer Judy, Jimmy Wakeley, Hy Averbach, and Bradley and Johnson, who did a dancing act, we had about fifty people with us.

I couldn't take my whole troupe because there was only room for twenty at the luncheon table. But everybody wanted to go to the American Embassy for lunch, so we drew lots to see who'd go.

I had four writers with me, Fred Williams, Charlie Lee, Larry Gelbart, and Chet Castleoff, and I decided I could take only two of them. Fred and Larry won the toss. The other two were left out. Chet wanted to go in the worst way and was very, very disappointed.

When he asked me if there was any way in which I could work him in, I said, "Chet, you can take my place and I'll stay home if you want to."

"No," he said, "I wouldn't do that. But I did want to see the General."

"It's tough," I said, "but only twenty people can go and we don't want to embarrass them. They only have seating arrangements for twenty of us, you know."

The lucky twenty went over to the Embassy and met Mrs. MacArthur and young Arthur MacArthur. Finally the General showed and we had a talk with him too. Presently luncheon was announced, and we sat down, but to my astonishment one fellow was left standing up minus a seat. Obviously, somebody had come who wasn't supposed to be there and I was pretty embarrassed. I looked at the General to see how he was taking it, and next to him—on his right—was Chet Castleoff.

The MacArthurs were nice about it. They had another chair brought in, tightened the circle and made room for the fellow who was still standing.

When the General made a speech and thanked us all for coming, nobody applauded louder than old Chet. When I spoke to him sternly about it later he grinned and said, "Well anyhow, I'll have something to tell the folks."

Chapter 17

THE ANSWER to people who ask me, "Why did you go on so many of those trips?"—if one is needed—is this: Wherever I go, boys say to me, "Hi, Bob! Saw you in Africa, Bob," or "Saw you in the South Pacific," or "Saw you in Japan," or "Saw you in Alaska."

Then there's the father who stopped me in a hotel lobby and asked me how his boy had looked when I'd seen him at Kwajalein. We both knew there were five thousand fellows there that day and that while I'd seen his son in the crowd, "seeing" in his case was just a stretching of the word. But it made him feel closer to his son to know that we'd been under the same patch of sky—for a moment.

This is also the reason why so many other entertainers did the same thing. Ask Jack Benny, Danny Kaye, Betty Hutton or hundreds of other USO troupers. They'll also tell you that you can work an audience and pull down twenty thousand bucks, but if the audience doesn't like you, you won't be happy with all that money. But if you work an audience for nothing and you're a hit and you feel that electricity crackle back and forth between you, you're happy. Being there is worthwhile.

Sometime during 1953 Colonel Layden of Special Services dropped by to see me. He was on his way to Korea again, taking the Horace Heidt outfit with him. He said that just because we'd signed a truce with the North Koreans didn't mean that our armed forces in Korea needed entertainment any the less. He told me that he felt that it was important to keep our soldiers' morale up now, because when they're not fighting is when they become restless and really get in trouble. When the fighting is going on they have plenty on their minds—but after a truce nothing, just boredom. So Colonel Layden said we were trying to shuttle a lot of entertainment units out there. My good friend, Johnny Grant, a Los Angeles disk-jockey, went over again. That was his third or fourth trip. He's not only been to Korea three or four times, but he's played Alaska a couple of times. He's always available. Not only that, but he's got talent, he tells a nice joke and he's happy and rotund.

The fact that he's got a lot of jelly to shake is *not* the reason why he's known as the road-company Bob Hope. The last time he went to Korea, I gave him the big hat I'd worn when I sang "Buttons and Bows" in *Paleface*. And I gave him some of my jokes because he said he needed them, and I figured I wouldn't miss them.

Servicemen audiences were so responsive that after the war it was hard for me to give up. I kept on trying to do my radio shows for big, special groups away-from-California—such as college students—until as late as 1950. But it became stale and people tired of it.

I wasn't tired of it. I loved it. After ten years of putting on a show that way, I'd almost forgotten any other way of doing it. It was only a couple of years ago that I stepped back into radio studios to do my stint.

My radio show wasn't the only part of my setup which wore itself out traveling. Larry Gelbart, who is a whip with an off-stage quip, volunteered to go to Tokyo with me in 1952 to help prepare scripts for me to use there. En route we stopped off at several islands—Johnston, Kwajalein, Guam and Okinawa. One night as we're riding through Tokyo in a staff car, Larry said, "Boy, I wish they'd start a war in Hollywood so we could go home."

After two or three days of looking Tokyo over, I met him in the hotel lobby. "How about this place?" I asked. "It's different, isn't it?"

"Yes," he said, "everything you see is marked 'Made in Japan.' "

While I'm talking about Larry, it might be as good a place to describe how I work with my writers. In the days when I was doing the "Your Hollywood Parade" radio show with Dick Powell, I worked with a writer named Wilkie Mahoney. Two or three nights a week Wilkie and I sat up late putting together my "Hollywood Parade" monologues. Wilkie would drop in, we'd figure out what we were going to talk about, then we'd sit down and kick it back and forth, with Wilkie at the typewriter tapping out the parts we thought usable. We kept on chopping away at it until we'd hacked out ten minutes of serviceable stuff. I talked about anything current and hot in my monologues—mostly Hollywood news, but anything as long as it was topical.

As time went by and my radio chores expanded and became more of a burden, my guiding radio and TV genius, Jimmy Saphier, suggested that I hire a staff of writers. The idea was for them all to submit material and for me to edit it. At one time twelve writers were preparing my scripts. Taken all together they represented quite a concentration of brains and talent.

When I started my world travels during the war, I had to let most of them go, but many of them are still going great guns in their chosen profession.

To name a few there were: Milt Josephsberg, now with Jack Benny; Milt's partner, Mel Shavelson, now working at Paramount; Jack Rose, also at Paramount; and Norman Panama and Melvin Frank, who are now important producers and directors.

As this book goes to press, I'm starting a picture, and Jack Rose and Mel Shavelson are doing the script. It's a departure from the usual pattern. The picture is the story of Eddie Foy, who, among other assorted Foys, fathered Eddie Foy, Jr., one of the stars of that current Broadway hit, *The Pajama Game*; Brynie Foy, successful Hollywood producer; and Charley Foy, night club impresario.

It's hard to impersonate a fellow like Eddie Foy, Sr. He had so much character, and his style has already been mimicked in so many ways by so many artists of stage and musical comedy. But the script has been written by Mel Shavelson and Jack Rose; both have had plenty of experience. It's one of the best scripts I've ever had the pleasure of distorting.

Eddie Foy, Sr. was a big star long before Orange Julius took over Broadway. When he and the Seven Little Foys played the Orpheum Time or the Keith Circuit, mothers from miles around brought their children to show them what the other half was doing to earn its bread.

The Foy family was one of the most colorful in theatrical history. Their home, in New Rochelle, was a combination house, museum and zoo. There are many great stories about the family and about its members when they hit the road, and Charley Foy has told me a few of them. Take the time when Eddie Junior was four years old and another baby brother came along. The new Foy was a Caesarean baby. He came home long before his mother, who had to stay at Woman's Hospital (on 110th Street, New York) for several weeks. However, she finally did come home, and asked to see her month-old baby. He couldn't be found. After a long search, he was finally found in the barn. Eddie Junior was very jealous of the little stranger and wanted to get rid of him. He took him out to the barn (along with his father's make-up kit), blackened the baby's face, put a red wig on him, and laid him on the straw bed where the goat slept. He figured that no one would know him disguised that way.

During the period when the boys were growing up, Eddie Senior got a letter from the Royal Tailoring Company. It requested his permission to use his name in connection with sales promotion. The usual release was enclosed for him to sign. He would receive half a dozen suits in exchange for the permission to use his name. Bryan and Charley seized this opportunity. Without letting their father know, they went down to the company and came home with three suits of clothes apiece. Less than two months later, a popular magazine of that day carried the message in a full-page ad: "EDDIE FOY WEARS ROYAL TAILORING CLOTHES."

Eddie Senior hit the ceiling. He got in touch with his attorneys, Malevinsky, Driscoll & O'Brien, and told them to sue. He thought he had a great case until his wife told him the facts, squared Bryan and Charley with their father, and kept them from being disowned.

There was the time when Jack Britton (one-time welterweight champion of the world) put on a benefit for the family of a motorcycle policeman who'd been killed. Britton was training at Port Chester, New York, and all the fight champions of the day came up and performed at this benefit. The Foys were rabid fight fans and, on this occasion, Charley and Bryan acted as corner seconds. After the show, three carloads of fighters, referees, managers and seconds started back to New York, thirty miles away.

The autos were open jobs, and the occupants were freezing. So Bryan Foy suggested that the crowd stop off at the Foy home in New Rochelle for coffee and to warm up. Then, since everyone was dead tired, he suggested that they spend the night, provided they keep quiet and not disturb his father. There were eighteen rooms in the house, but it was a big crowd and the beds were loaded, three to a bed. Sometime during the night one of the fighters, a fellow who weighed about 220 pounds, got up to go to the bathroom. When he came out he forgot where he belonged and wandered into Eddie Senior's room, just across the hall.

He saw him lying there in a big bed, all alone, and asked, "Hey, you bum, how did you get such a big bed all to yourself?"

The Foys commuted between New York and their New Rochelle home. One wintry night they took the last train out of New York in a terrific snow storm. The train left at midnight and it was two hours late reaching Larchmont, where connections were made for New Rochelle. There was no service to New Rochelle after one o'clock. There were no taxicabs available, and no means of getting home.

Eddie Senior went over to the car barns, woke up the night watchman, gave him five dollars, and persuaded him to get out a streetcar and take them home. When they got there, they took the watchman in for coffee. By the time he was ready to return, there was four feet of snow in front of his car and it was impossible to move. The morning papers came out with headlines: *STREETCAR STOLEN FROM CAR BARN!*

In 1912, when Eddie Senior was playing in the show, *Over the River*, he had a Ford car which (for lack of a garage) he kept in the auto salesman's showroom. When the watchman closed up, he left Eddie's car out front, so Eddie could drive it home to New Rochelle. On one wall of the showroom was a lifesize picture of "Eddie Foy and the seven little Foys."

One night after the show, both the weather and the car were cold, and Eddie was trying to get it started. He was cranking the car, and his sons were cheering him on. A tall man and a lad of thirteen watched them from across the street. Finally they came over.

"Mr. Foy," the man said, "I recognized you from the picture

212

in the showroom. I think I can help you get this car started. My name is Henry Ford and this is my son, Edsel. I make these cars."

After cutting up some further touches about the car, Eddie said, "You know, I've done you a lot of good, advertising your car. But whenever I need a bolt or nut, your company sends me a bill for each little piece of metal."

Ford replied that he would send Eddie every bolt and nut he could ever use on a car. Eddie took this as a polite way of telling him that he was sending him a new car, and he rushed home to wake the rest of the family and tell them the great news. They awaited the car anxiously. About a month later, a box (three feet by four) arrived, C.O.D., sixty dollars due. In it were enough bolts and nuts to last a lifetime, with tags on each one to tell where it went.

Eddie Foy Senior broke up the act when his son Charley was nineteen and Bryan Foy was twenty. The mother of the Little Foys had departed this world years before, and it was about time he fell in love again. A few weeks before he was to be married, his fiancée came up to Toledo to see him. The boys were there and saw the girl, but since she was wearing a heavy veil, they didn't recognize her. But she knew who they were, and she kept looking at them. The result was that they followed her when she left. She finally ducked into a store to get rid of them.

Later, she told Eddie Senior about it. He called the boys in, gave them blazes, ending up with, "Leave that woman alone. She hasn't done anything to you—yet." The boys were baffled, until they met her again a month later when Eddie Senior married her.

Other writers from my radio days were Norman Sullivan—who's still with me, along with Howard Blake, both very useful and handy guys—and Jack (Screwy) Douglas. I also had a trio of boys named Jack Huston, Al Schwartz and Sherwood Schwartz, Al's brother.

I divided them into teams. My show went on the air on Tuesday. On Wednesday we rested. Thursday we met to knock out a few ideas for the next show. Then the boys went home and began to write. Each team wrote a spot and brought it back for further sweating. The commercials divided our show into three spots: monologue, middle section, and sketch. I called my monologue a speed-comedy monologue. I did as many as twenty-four jokes in it in four minutes.

My idea was to do it as fast as I could and still have the listeners at home get it and let the live audience in the studio laugh too. Unless the live audience took the play away from me with their laughter, I raced. At that time there was nothing like my speed-comedy monologue on the air.

I'd decided that if I wanted to compete with all the other shows on radio, I'd have to have something different and ear-catching. I didn't open with a commercial or a band number, which was the usual custom. My announcer said, "The Pepsodent show, starring Bob Hope, and here he is"; and I said, "Ladies and gentlemen, how do you do, this is the Pepsodent show, we'll get you by the skin of your teeth," and within seven seconds I was away and into my first joke.

This was our formula and it brought us a lot of success. Our Hooper climbed until we were hailed as radio's box-office champs.

But to get back to my writers. We'd meet in my office at my house, where we had a blackboard on which we wrote ideas as they came up, so we wouldn't forget them. At our first meeting, each boy read the stuff he'd written. The others gave their reaction to it. We ribbed the bad material, laughed at the amusing stuff, and had fun.

On Sunday night I took the material my writers had turned in down to NBC and previewed it before a live audience. Those previews ran for an hour or an hour and ten minutes, sometimes even an hour and twenty minutes, while my writers and the producer checked each gag to see which of them pulled the biggest laughs. Then we packed the best material into a half-hour show. That way, when we were on the air on Monday nights, we really flew.

A representative of the advertising agency, who handled one of the accounts for which I shilled, once made a little speech to my writers. Our Hooper rating had just come in. It was a fabulous nineteen.

When the agency man was through, he said, "And now that our rating is nineteen, I think I'll go home."

One of my writers said, "Fine. That's how we got that rating."

The ad man gave him a look with an injector blade in it. My writers never needed a pencil and paper to compose memorable cracks—memorable to me, that is. One of my writers, Johnny Rapp, who used to write "Baby Snooks" for Fannie Brice, came back from Las Vegas once with adhesive plaster on his face.

"What happened?" I asked.

"I visited the gambling rooms and lost a bundle," he said. "Then I went back to my hotel bathroom to commit suicide and accidentally shaved myself."

Another of my writers, Fred Williams, was stopping at the Waldorf-Astoria in New York with me when we happened to look out of the window and saw a couple of fellows walking on the roof. I got the desk clerk on the phone and asked him who the roof walkers were.

"President Truman is making a speech to the United Nations in the grand ballroom today," he said. "Those men on the roof are Secret Service men. They're guarding him."

Later, when we got in the elevator, there was a chap in it who was obviously a Secret Service man. He might as well have worn a neon sign on his hat spelling out his occupation.

Fred turned to me and said, "The President doesn't play piano badly enough to need all this protection."

Fred was once a newspaperman in New Orleans, but he'd become bar-happy and it had cost him his job. He couldn't have been a more delightful companion when sober. He had a wonderful sense of humor and I had a great affection for him—when he was off the sauce. He was funny when he was tangling with the red-eye, but only in retrospect. He'd do such outrageous things when he was happied up that I'd get mad at him and almost pop a blood vessel. Then, when he switched back to being his amusing self, the insane things he'd done would strike me as hilarious and I'd laugh until I almost had hysterics.

Fred's dead now. He was killed last year in an accidental fall from a freight car on which he was hitching a ride. But, taken all in all—the good with the bad—I loved the rascal.

He was the mainspring of some of the most unbelievable experiences I've ever had; I don't think Freddie would mind my talking about them here, although they involve a mention of his high alcoholic content. I think he would enjoy reading about his adventures and misadventures if he were still around to read them. In fact, I think he'd resent it if I left him out of my story.

In 1947 I took Freddie on the trip I made with Dolores to appear at the annual film command performance for the King and Queen of England at the Odeon Theater in London. While crossing the Atlantic, Freddie was a thorough gentleman. He had his own stateroom de luxe and a new dinner jacket.

"I've never had it this good," he told me. "I wonder what Red Skelton's writers are doing. They'd never understand this type of living."

On my second day in England I met a friend who told me, "I've just run into your boy, Fred Williams. He asked me if I knew where he could find some whiskey for a sore throat. I sent him over to the Embassy Club and told them to give him a bottle of Scotch."

"He's not supposed to have any!" I said in alarm.

"Sorry, old boy," my friend said. "Didn't know."

Two hours later I had a call from Fred. He was tighter than anybody on that tight little island. In fact, he was thinking of running for king. "This is going to be my greatest command performance," he said. "I think I'll sit in the royal box."

I knew then he'd be no use to me as a writer for some time, so I said, "Get some rest somewhere and take it easy, Fred, and don't get into any trouble."

The night of the command performance I was having trouble myself. Dolores couldn't work the zipper on the beautiful dress she'd bought for the occasion and I was trying to give it the magic touch when I got a call from Norman Siegel. Norman was head of Paramount's Hollywood publicity department, and he was handling our press relations.

"I'm calling from the Odeon Theater," he said. "What do you think has just happened? Freddie Williams came in and fell flat in the lobby, right in front of the King and Queen."

"What did you do?" I wanted to know.

"We took him to the Green Room," he said. "He's there now, acting as a self-appointed master of ceremonies."

The Green Room is a room backstage in which the actors relax between shows. Sure enough, when Dolores and I arrived at the Odeon, there was Williams, very happy indeed. I had to go upstairs to work on a routine I was to do with Bob Montgomery. Bob and I were walking up and down, rehearsing our lines, when Freddie appeared and walked up and down between us.

"Do me a favor, Freddie?" I asked. "I've never asked you for a favor but do this one for me, will you?"

"You have but to name it, my liege," he said.

"Go home," I said. "Just go home."

"I can't do that," he said. "I want to keep on looking at you. You're so beautiful in those tails."

At last I talked him into going home. When he disappeared, I heaved a sigh of relief.

After the command performance we were supposed to stay in London for three or four days, but Army Special Services asked me to go to Germany to do a few shows for our soldiers there. By this time Freddie was convalescent and I thought that if I took him with me to Berlin and Munich, it would get him back on the alkaline side and straighten him out. After three or four days, we came back to England before returning to the U.S.A., and I was in the Savoy Hotel with Freddie when the phone rang.

It was Norman Siegel again. "How're things?" I asked.

"Everything's just dandy," Norm said, "but I just have one little squawk to make. You are being charged with a cape and a gown. Fred Williams rented a gown and a cape for the girl he escorted to the command performance. No one has seen gown, cape or girl since."

I turned to Williams, who was standing beside me, and asked him reproachfully, "You wouldn't do a thing like that, would you?"

"You wanted me to go first class, didn't you?" Williams asked. Whimsical, that Freddie.

"Have you got the girl's name?" I asked.

"I tried to call her today, but she's moved away," Freddie said. "She's probably flying over London in that cape. She had her witchy side."

During World War II when Freddie was drafted to serve with the Armed Forces, I lost track of him for a while. But I got a call from him from Lowry Field, near Denver, where he was based.

"Is it possible for you to get me shifted to the Air Force base at Santa Ana?" he asked. "They have the radio department of the Air Force there, and I could make myself useful doing scripts."

My youngest brother, George, was working at Santa Ana as a writer. Also, I'd played a lot of shows at Santa Ana and I knew a couple of officers there, a Captain Jones and Colonel Eddie Burkmeister. So I said to Freddie, "I'll see what I can do."

I put in a call to Captain Jones, who told me, "Sounds as if we can use him here. Give me his serial number."

Not long after that I got a call from Williams. "I've been transferred to Santa Ana," he said. "That's where I belong, writing for the radio."

Knowing Fred, I asked, "Where are you *now*?"

"I'm in Hollywood," he said, "but that was a wonderful thing you did for me and I want to thank you for it."

Three or four days later George called me. "Where's Williams?" he asked. "He came down here to the air base at Santa Ana and signed up, but we haven't seen him since. The brass is pretty mad at him."

A little later, Williams called me to ask me how I was feeling. How *he* felt was no secret. I could smell the maraschino cherries and the bitters over the phone.

"They're sore at you down at Santa Ana," I said. "Why don't you go down there and go to work?"

"Are they really mad at me?" he asked. "If they are, maybe I'd better not go back there until they cool off."

I hung up in disgust. Three or four days later, George called me again. This time he said, "Williams still isn't here. They're going to hang this fellow when they catch him."

"I can't help it," I said. "I've done everything I can for the idiot."

Several days went by and Williams was once more on the phone. "Guess what happened?" he asked indignantly. "They've transferred me to a Montana base."

Then he made a Williamesque remark to end all Williamesque remarks: "They can't do that to you!" he said. I loved that "you."

I said, "I hope you draw a tour of duty in Siberian waters. For what you're doing you should be in the Russian Navy."

I didn't hear from him again for a long time. Then one day the producer of my radio show called me to ask, "Did you promise a general in Colorado Springs you'd go up there and do a show for him?"

"I don't remember doing it," I said, "but I meet so many people I could have."

The mystery soon evaporated. Ten minutes later, Williams called. "Bob," he said, "I'm in trouble."

"Naturally," I told him.

He ignored my interruption. "I'm up here in Palo Alto on

leave," he went on. "I'm stationed at Colorado Springs and I called up my general and asked him for an extension of leave, and I told him I was you."

"Give that to me again, slowly," I said.

"I called up my general and I told him I was Bob Hope," he said, "and I asked for an extension of leave for Private Fred Williams."

I was fascinated in a loathsome sort of way. "What did the General say?" I asked.

Williams laughed merrily. "He said, 'Tell him to go right ahead, Bob. How many days does he want?' I didn't want to be greedy, so I said, 'Five.'"

Then Freddie asked me, "When do you want to do the show for us?"

I said, "You mean you promised I'd do a show?"

"Yes," he said, and hung up.

I figured falsifying a thing like that to a general in wartime could mean a prison term for my screwball pal. So I rounded up my gang, got into a plane, flew to Colorado Springs and did a show to keep Williams out of the pokey.

I thought I'd taken care of him for the duration, but he was transferred to Yuma, Arizona, and before long he was in jail there. This didn't stymie our Freddie. The USO had no busier booker than my pixilated friend. He called his commanding officer, Colonel Anderson, and told him, "If I can get out I can bring the Bob Hope show here."

Once more I decided to bail Freddie out by doing a show. In Yuma, when we got off the plane, there was the Colonel waiting for us, with Williams beside him, fresh out of jail. I greeted the Colonel and Freddie, and together we reviewed the troops. I remember thinking the whole situation unbelievable.

After the show, the Colonel said, "I want to thank you for a good time. And now we have arranged a dinner with you at the officers' club."

"How about Freddie?" I said.

"Well, all right," the Colonel said, but he said it hesitantly.

We had a wonderful meal of venison. While I was digging into it, I looked up to see Freddie at the bar, happily slapping a major on the back. He had fueled his burners from the officers' club private stock. *He's not long for this world,* I thought.

When dinner was over, we went outside. "Your plane doesn't leave for an hour and a half," the Colonel said. "How about coming up to my cottage and having one for the road."

It seemed a sound idea, but I said I didn't like to leave my buddy, Williams.

The Colonel said, "Bring him too."

This time his voice had icicles hanging from it. Fred came along and sat next to me. The Colonel was trying to talk, but Freddie gave him plenty of competition. What with Williams' jabbering, the Colonel was out in left field.

Finally he turned to Fred and said, "Mr. Williams, may I speak to Mr. Hope?"

He put a lot of emphasis on that word "may."

Fred glanced at the Colonel tolerantly and said, "Oh, go ahead, Colonel."

Then he turned to me and whispered in carrying tones, "He outranks me, you know."

Before long it was plane time. When we got into the car, there were three people in front: the driver, Freddie and the Colonel. Fred was smoking a cigarette and dropping ashes on the Colonel's shoulder. The Colonel sat there, watching him, saying nothing. But I could see that his mind was busy. It was my guess that he was working on a plan to transfer Williams to the Aleutians.

Fred was a great one for assembling one-man followings of strays. Once, when he was with me in New York, he brought his newest pal up to my room.

"He's very nice," Fred said. "He used to be a dietitian for the Salvation Army, but he had a little trouble with them and they unfrocked him."

Before long, I had to go out. When I came back I stepped over a body lying in front of the elevator in the hall. For a moment I thought it a heavily brocaded rug. Then I took another look. It was Williams' newest pal. He was stretched out in the Waldorf on the twenty-second floor in front of the elevator, snoring and wearing a blissful smile.

At the end of my stay, I had only a few minutes to make a plane, so I asked Fred to check out for me. I'd been back to California two days when the manager of the Waldorf called me to ask, "Mr. Hope, when do you want me to check you out?"

"I *am* checked out," I said. "Mr. Williams checked me out."

"Mr. Williams moved into your room when you left," the manager said. "He's had a couple of parties there and I thought maybe you'd want to check out soon."

"What's the bill?" I asked.

When he gave me the figures, I said, "Just pack Williams in his bag with his head sticking out and carry him to the station. Make sure you get him on the train."

That Williams was a beaut. When he wasn't building good will for you in his own way, he was great. He must have been or I wouldn't have put up with his whims so long—or miss him so much.

Chapter 18

LOOKING BACK over the last few pages, I see that I've been so full of the Williams epic that I've forgotten to tell how I got into an ad-lib contest with King George VI at the Odeon Theater. When Dolores and I were invited to London to attend the showing of the annual command-performance film for King George VI and Queen Elizabeth in the fall of 1947, the film chosen for that year was *The Bishop's Wife*, starring Loretta Young. Cary Grant and David Niven. I've already mentioned some of the slap-happy things that happened on that trip, but the high point of the expedition for me was the chance to kick the conversational gong around with the King.

When Dolores and I boarded the plane in California, Jean Hersholt came to the airport and gave me a book to present to Princess Elizabeth, the gracious and high-hearted lady who is now Queen of England. This book had been made to look like a stamp album. In it were autographed photographs of every important Hollywood movie star. Each photograph resembled a stamp. But when I arrived in England, Princess Elizabeth was in Scotland on her honeymoon. Norman Siegel rushed around asking people if I oughtn't to present it to Princess Margaret. Some said I should and some said I shouldn't, so the whole deal was temporaily lost sight of.

After the command performance, we visitors went into a room just off the foyer in the Odeon Theater to pay our respects to their majesties. They greeted us cordially.

The King said to me, "I enjoy your *Road* pictures. You must have fun making them."

Then the King and Queen went up stairs and the rest of us stood around razzing the girls about the curtsies they'd made. Dolores had almost fallen on her face when she'd bobbed hers.

Suddenly Norman Siegel rushed in and asked, "Where's that book of autographed photographs? They're waiting upstairs for it."

After a frantic search, it was found in the manager's office. I ran upstairs with it and handed it to Princess Margaret. "I think you'll enjoy this," I said, and began to show her the photos.

The King watched us leaf through it, then slipped me the royal needle. "Look at him," he said; "he's hurrying to get to his own picture."

"Why not?" I asked. "It's the prettiest."

He grinned, then asked, "Is Bing's autograph there too?"

"Yes," I said. "But he doesn't write. He just made three X's."

"Why three?" the King asked.

"He has a middle name," I reminded him.

We kidded back and forth like this and next day the headlines in the *Daily Express* said: THE KING AD LIBS WITH BOB HOPE. It was the only time I've ever had a King working as straight man for me. I almost asked, "King, would you be interested in a screen test?" but I remembered in time that he had a fairish job of his own and with no dues to pay to the Screen Actors Guild.

That was one of the big moments of my life, but if I had to

choose between it and my first hole-in-one, it would be a near thing. I'd have to study the photos to see which finished first. Which brings me to golf.

I'm finding out that that's the way things happen in this autobiographical racket. You're going along talking about one thing, and you turn a corner and there's another subject, staring you in the face.

Books on how to improve your golf game are always popular, but I think I've got something a little different along those lines. So far as I know, no one has recommended the routine I'm about to outline for cutting down a golf score.

Two years ago I was driving to Pebble Beach from Palm Springs to play in Bing's pro-amateur tournament at Pebble Beach. I got into my car with Freddie Williams, and we started for Los Angeles. Between Beaumont and Riverside I was pushing it along at about seventy-two. The highway was wide open, nobody in sight, but it was raining a little and I went into a skid.

We turned around, bounced into a ditch, rolled into an orchard and ended up against a tree. Both of us were thrown out. I felt that there was something wrong with my left shoulder, so I stood ankle-deep in mud and practiced my golf swing. The swing wasn't so hot. We left the car and hitch-hiked back to Riverside, and I went to see a doctor. He stretched me out on an X-ray table and took some pictures.

When he'd looked at them, he said, "You're not going to play any golf for eight weeks. You've got a fractured clavicle."

Following that layoff, I went back East, stopping off at the Bob-O'-Link Golf Club in Chicago, where I'm a nonresident member, to have a crack at the course. I got together three friends, Dick Snideman, Dick Gibson and Hugh Davis, and we teed off.

I had a seventy-four for the eighteen holes. It's one of my best scores. The payoff was that on the eighth hole—158 yards—I had a hole in one. You may think that a busted clavicle is a hard way to improve a score, but if you're willing to try it, it could work. It did for me.

I've had some bad rounds in my life—real stinkers—and I've had some amazing ones, too. In fact, I have a lifetime record of four holes in one.

And while I'm being modest about my golf, it seems a good time to tell about the time I pinned Ben Hogan's ears back. I've been playing with Ben since 1942, when we did an exhibition at Topeka, Kansas, for the Bond Drive. When he was here in Hollywood to make the movie version of his life, *Follow the Sun*, he came over to the Paramount lot to talk to Sid Lanfield, who was directing the picture. While Ben was around the studio he asked me, "Want to play some golf tomorrow?"

I said, "Yes."

My handicap was four but I hadn't played for quite a while, so I rushed out to Lakeside to see Ike Buehll, head of the handicap committee there.

"Ike," I said, "you know I'm not really a four-handicap any more. I've been shooting high scores and you ought to give me a couple more shots."

"I'll have a look at the cards," he said.

When he had a look he said, "Well . . . you've got a couple of eighty-ones. I'll make you a six."

The next day Hogan came out to the club and had lunch with me. A lot of people saw us together in the dining room. As a result we drew a middling size gallery on the first tee. We played the back nine first and coming up to the seventeenth (which was our eighth hole) I was two under par on my own ball and one up on Ben. By this time we had quite a gallery with us, and Ike Buehll walked out to see what was going on.

The seventeenth hole is about four hundred and fifty yards. My second shot landed on the green. As I walked up to it, Ike looked at me and said, "You liar!" I tried to tell him I was playing way over my head because I was so scared.

He growled and said, "That was a great scene you put on for me, Actor."

Ben and I were betting a ten-dollar nassau. I shot a seventy-four; a thirty-four, a forty, and collected. It's the one and only time I ever collected from Ben and Ike Buehll hasn't talked to me since.

Caddying was one of the few things I *didn't* do as a boy in Cleveland. In my early twenties I'd tried to play golf, but I just couldn't cut it. I lacked patience. I stood in one spot on a public course in Cleveland and let three or four foursomes go through me while I flailed away at the ball. Afterward I burned my clubs. I didn't touch the game again until I landed in the bigtime in vaudeville and a couple of lads on the bill persuaded me to play. After that, I couldn't leave it alone, and vice versa.

When I took Dolores abroad for the first time in 1939, we made a special trip to Scotland to play the St. Andrews golf course. While there, someone told us, "Don't miss the cemetery."

I'm glad that we didn't. The stones are sensational. One epitaph reads: "Here lies Sandy McTavish, in heaven. His handicap was seven."

Another headstone, erected in memory of a famous amateur golfer, is the image of a man in the middle of his backswing.

Despite such tributes to the game, self-interest sometimes rears its scaly head on a golf course instead of the pure sporting instinct. A producer in Hollywood was playing golf one day with two of his actors. This producer has a poor opinion of "moral victories." He likes to score. Option time was near and the two actors were letting him kick the ball out of the rough without penalty. When he reached the eighteenth tee he took a terrific swing at his ball and it trickled about four feet.

He looked at his two actors, and one of them said, "Hit it again, sir. I was thinking."

He teed up another ball and drove again.

This is a true story. I know the people involved.

Ordinarily golf puts a premium on quietness, but not all galleries know this, especially the gallery who followed Bing and me when we were playing a tournament at the Tam O'Shanter in Chicago. This tournament was sponsored by George May, an industrial consultant who was presenting the gate to the War Bond Drive. A manufacturer of men's clothing, including novelty sports apparel, had asked each of us to wear those gaudy Hawaiian shirts that hang outside of your pants. They are called aloha shirts and are covered with fish, tropical flora and hula maidens. Bing was used to these little pretties, but mine was a shock to me. However, we both wore them and they dangled down over our pressure-cooker-size stomachs.

Our gallery was the largest I've ever seen. At least twenty-five thousand people had flocked out to the golf course. Most of the country's good golfers were playing, but not all of the crowd were there for golf. Some of them were interested in radio and motion pictures and Bing and I had those people in our gallery. There were the usual hecklers and wise guys that Bing and I draw.

On one tee, as I was about to drive, one smart cookie made a crack about the aloha shirt flapping around my hips. "Hey, Bob," he said, "your slip's showing."

When the snicker subsided, I turned and looked him over. "Your father's slip is showing, too," I said.

We had no more trouble with bright boy. He hid under a divot and sulked.

The galleries that follow celebrities golfing are more numerous and more unruly than those which follow golfing celebrities. About five years ago I was playing in the Celebrities' in Washington, D. C., with General Omar Bradley and Sam Snead. The crowd gave us very little room. On the first hole I hit a good drive, then took a four iron from my bag and shanked my second shot. In other words, I hit the ball with the shank of my club and it streaked off to the right, laterally. It's one of the most miserable shots in golf. I'm very good at it. My ball thudded against the leg of a man in the gallery. I was concerned. But when I rushed up to him, he was laughing.

"I hit your leg," I said breathlessly. "Doesn't it hurt?"

He tapped his leg. It gave out a hollow sound. "Wooden," he said.

General Bradley kept score that day, and at the last hole the results were announced. They said, "Sam Snead, sixty-five." Then I heard them say, "Bob Hope, amateur, seventy-one." I was the leading amateur. I don't say that General Bradley would deliberately cheat for me, but he's a very nice man.

I was once in a foursome at the Forest Hills Country Club in Bloomfield, New Jersey, with Babe Ruth and two golf greats, Vic Ghezzi and Craig Wood. The Babe was a left hander at golf and when he hooked one it was like a right-hander slicing. It was hard to get used to the switch. It seemed to confuse the spectators and they were in constant peril of being beheaded at all times. Between us we winged at least eight people out of a gallery of ten thousand.

I've hit so many people that I carry golf insurance. But I've been lucky. Bing and I were playing in St. Louis once when I hit a little girl on the head with a ball. She ran across the green just as I connected, and it hit her on the noggin and she fell down. I had the shakes for a couple of days after that until the little girl was declared out of danger.

I won't forget the time when I was playing with Joe Louis, Fred Astaire and Jimmy McLarnin at my home club, Lakeside. Joe's not a great chatterer on a golf course. But when he does talk he says something. On the fifteenth hole I drove with a seven iron. The ball landed in front of the green and rolled into the cup.

Joe looked at it and said, "Man, that went in the hole!" It wasn't gabby, but it summed things up.

Joe played one round at Lakeside with Bing. He plays good golf, but he came to grief on the seventeenth hole. He knocked his ball into a trap, walked down into the sand, missed another, and said, "Oh, Joseph!"

That was all he said during the eighteen holes. It was his idea of cussing.

I could do a book about my high spots in caddies. I've had some wonderful ones. My regular caddie at Lakeside, Grant Leonard, is more than a caddie. Eight or nine years ago he won the PGA California Open. Having him caddie for you is like taking a golf lesson. You might call him a caddie-consultant.

Then there's Scorpie George Doyle, one of the greatest in my area. He's a caddie with the nerve of a talent agent. If he's caddying for a fellow who doesn't play well, Scorpie will walk up to him after the second hole and hand him a card. The card asks, "Why don't you take lessons?" Scorpie takes a chance in doing this, for the player might brain him with a club. But chance-taking doesn't worry Scorpie. He's the kind who says, "Good try!" after a bad shot. Still and all, his clients think he's a valuable man to have in their corner.

Jimmy Demaret once told me about a caddy who worked down in Valdesta, Georgia. This caddy used to come up to the N.Y.A.C. Wing Foot Country Club every summer. He was quite a character. One day up at Wing Foot, Jimmy asked him, "Sam, when are you going back down South?"

The caddy thought a minute, then said, "I'm going back when the weather fits my clothes."

Of the memorable things which have happened to me on a golf course, the round I played with Ike Eisenhower in 1953 is the topper. In 1953 I was in Winnipeg, Canada, when Stu Symington called me long distance and asked, "Can you be in Washington on Derby Day?"

"I was planning to be in Churchill Downs with Bill Corum that day," I told him.

"Better switch it," he said. "You're going to play golf with the man in the White House."

I went down to do a performance at the Blue Grass Festival at Lexington, Kentucky. I spent Friday—the day before the Derby—at Churchill Downs, then flew to Washington to be there on Saturday. The President, Senator Bush of Connecticut, Stu and I made up a foursome. Ike and I were partners.

You're never lonely playing with Ike. Three or four Secret Service men ride along in your golf bag to make sure you don't swing your clubs too wildly. I pulled J. Edgar Hoover out of my bag three times. But playing golf with a President is handy. If you hit a ball into the rough and it stops near a tree, the tree becomes a Secret Service man and moves away.

When I played with Ike in Washington, I asked, "What do you want to bet?"

"I usually play for a dollar, dollar, dollar," he said.

For those who don't understand such basic matters, this means that a dollar is wagered on the first nine, another dollar on the second nine, and another dollar on all eighteen holes.

"Funny thing," Ike went on, "I've just lent a million and a half dollars to Bolivia, and here I am playing for a dollar, dollar, dollar."

Chapter 19

I'VE MENTIONED some of my radio adventures with Honey Chile Wilder and the time I stole a live audience the first time I went on the air from Hollywood. I've also mentioned how the success I scored on the air led to a loan-out to Sam Goldwyn and this loan-out raised my fee per picture to a hundred grand. But radio has played a much more important part in my life than I've shown by the space I've given it.

In the beginning, Louis Shurr handled me for a few radio spots. But I wasn't signed to him exclusively and I could free-lance if I felt like it. While I was on the Woodbury show, I met a young agent named Jimmy Saphier. I not only got to know him, I liked him. I found him a shrewd boy who knew the business, and my kind of guy.

I went down to the RKO Building one day, walked into his office and said, "I want you to handle me for radio."

It was an unusual thing to do. Agents usually grab actors instead of actors grabbing agents, but it turned out fine. That was sixteen years ago. We're still together.

On the Atlantic Refining Company show I did in 1935 and 1936 with Honey Chile, we had with us Frank Parker and Red Nichols and his Five Pennies. Then in May 1937, I went on the air for Woodbury soap. When I wound up my radio work for Woodbury early in the fall of 1937, I was off the air for a couple of months. Mann Holiner, who'd been handling the Woodbury series for the Lennen and Mitchell advertising agency told me, "I hate to lose you. I feel that you're finally finding yourself in radio. I wish I had a sponsor for you."

"What about Old Gold?" I asked.

"I've been trying to sell you to Old Gold," he said, "but they're not buying you."

"Why not?" I asked. "You say I'm ready."

"I'm the only one who thinks so," he said.

Luckily for me, that wasn't one hundred per cent true, because in December, 1937, I found myself lined up with Lord and Thomas, an advertising agency owned by Albert Lasker. It was Lord and Thomas who gave me my monologue spot in the Lucky Strike radio show, "Your Hollywood Parade."

Every week our sponsor, George Washington Hill, who was Mr. Lucky Strike himself, insisted that he wanted to hear more fiddles. More fiddles were added, until each time you turned around on stage a fiddle hit you in the back.

Mr. Hill not only sponsored the show, he kibitzed it. He insisted that our music have certain rhythms. There was a rumor that he played the drums at home, keeping time with our radio orchestra, and that we had to use certain kinds of rhythms so he could keep up with us. That was only hearsay, but even if it was true, it was jake with me. Hill was a great merchandiser, who understood what advertising was all about, and he had a rhythmic beat when it came to signing our pay checks.

In 1939, when I'd been on the air for Pepsodent for one season, Albert Lasker invited me to Chicago to meet Kenneth Smith, who was then one of the principal owners of Pepsodent. Lasker himself was also a Mr. Big in Pepsodent. He not only owned Lord and Thomas but a sizable chunk of Pepsodent too. Another Lord and Thomas executive—who shall be nameless here—took me out to Ken Smith's yacht on Lake Michigan to have dinner on board.

When we left the pier in Chicago in a launch, he pointed to

the Smith yacht and said, "I want you to remember one thing: Amos and Andy built that boat."

I'd done well by Pepsodent, but I guess he didn't want me to get a big head or delusions of grandeur. I certainly wasn't blasé about my Pepsodent record. I still get such a boot out of even an ant-sized triumph I almost bust. But in trying to make sure I had humility, this character rubbed me the wrong way. They called humility "sincerity" then; salesmen even wore "sincere" neckties.

Anyhow, I said, "When I finish with Pepsodent, Mr. Smith will be using that yacht for a dinghy."

We had dinner on the yacht. Lasker congratulated me on my season's work and handed me an envelope. In it were two round-trip tickets to Europe for Dolores and me, plus twenty-five hundred dollars spending money. After that, I *really* began to brush my teeth with Pepsodent.

Dolores and I played a date at the Paramount in New York for a week, while we were waiting to sail. Woody Herman and his orchestra worked with me. And I was glad to get back and see all the people at the Paramount, including Bob Weitman, the manager. It was always one of my favorite houses.

As for our act, I told a lot of jokes about picture business and radio and Dolores never sang better. But a strange thing happened on our second night. I was backstage when I heard a fellow in the audience giving the bird to somebody who was on. My hackles rose and I said to the stage manager, "Who is that louse out there?"

"I don't know," he said.

"Well," I said, "it better not happen when I'm out there, that's all. I'll kick his teeth in."

About five minutes later I went on. I had barely started my routine when the razzberry happened again. This time it was really juicy and wet. I said in a loud voice over the P. A. system, "What wise guy did that? I'd like to have you come backstage and have you do it back there. It would be a pleasure to see you backstage."

The only answer I got was another razzberry. Then the razzberrier began to laugh. It was a nasty, chuckling sound and I said to Bob Shapiro, the manager, "Would you find that fellow and bring him back to me? I want to barbecue him for my night lunch."

The audience was beginning to laugh, not with me, but at me. And I was really sizzling. For a while the razzberries stopped and I went on with my act. I tried to forget it and tried to make the audience forget it. Pretty soon I introduced Dolores. Then in the middle of her first number it happened again, bigger and louder than ever.

Now I was burning on Dolores' account. At the end of the show I called Bob Weitman backstage and said to him, "If you don't investigate and find out who's doing it you can include the Hopes out of your show, as Sam Goldwyn says."

He gave me a funny look and said, "We've been investigating

like crazy. Do you know what it is? It's a short circuit in the sound system. It's two wires rubbing together. It sounds exactly like a bird, and it's going back into the horn." -

"Well, fix it," I said.

"We have," he told me.

He only thought he had it under control, for when I went out for the next show, the last one of the evening, the same thing happened again. When the audience laughed I said, "Ladies and gentlemen, that's just a short in the sound circuit."

Then they really roared. They wouldn't believe it, and now everybody's broken up, the band is laughing and even I'm enjoying it since I know that it's not some oafish clown making insulting noises. "It really is," I said. "It's a sound thing in the circuit."

They had engineers working on it all night. But the next morning when I opened my mouth for the first show it happened again. We all collapsed in spasms of mirth, the audience, the performers, everybody. Finally they fixed it, but while it lasted that hidden razzberry was a great thing. It got so many laughs I was tempted to keep it in my act as a permanent.

Chapter 20

My FIRST REAL BRUSH with TV happened in 1950–51. I was in Palm Springs when a friend of mine, Hugh Davis, who was then executive vice president in the Chicago office of Foote, Cone and Belding asked me if I'd like to do a television show for Frigidaire.

"I don't think so," I said. "I'm busy enough. Besides, I don't know much about that medium."

"But how much would you want if you did do it?" he asked.

To get him out of my hair, I said, "You can't pay me enough."

"What do you want?" he asked.

"Fifty thousand," I said.

I was sure nobody would pay me that much. Hugh took off for the East and three days later called me from Chicago. "Would you do a television show for forty thousand dollars?" he asked.

I asked, "For myself?"

He said, "Yes."

That meant all I had to do was supply myself and my material. It didn't include paying guest stars.

I said, "O. K.; I'll have Jimmy Saphier make the deal."

Jimmy arranged for me to do the first show for forty thousand dollars, and four more for twenty-five thousand dollars each. That was the year the Internal Revenue Bureau gave me the award as the best supporting actor.

We did that first show from the New Amsterdam Roof in New York; Frigidaire paid one hundred and twenty-five thousand for the talent on display, which included Bea Lillie, Douglas Fairbanks, Jr., and Dinah Shore. To my surprise, I was as nervous as a cat. I'd been in front of cameras and microphones for years, but I was as jumpy as if I were just starting out in show business.

After seeing me on a TV screen, one critic remarked, "Comparatively speaking, TV is still a baby but it doesn't need that much changing."

However, when the other votes came in it was decided to let me stay on. In fact, Frigidaire and Foote, Cone and Belding were so happy about the way that show worked out that they paid me twenty thousand dollars each for the next four shows too.

I've been asked by a lot of people if there's much difference between working for TV and for radio, if, for example, there is a difference in tempo. I honestly think that the secret of TV is being relaxed, casual and easy. I used to work very fast on radio because I found out when I was working for service audiences that they wanted it fast. They didn't want situation comedy; they wanted jokes and they wanted them right now; they wanted them to go bang, bang, bang. I was successful with them that way. I carried this technique over into my first days on television, but it wasn't too successful. With that particular type of material and a civilian audience, I was ahead of them, and working too fast for them. I've slowed down for television, especially with my monologue.

The truth is that when you're right in the room with those who watch you and listen to you, as you are in TV, practically sitting in their laps and muttering into their ears, your personality is more important than anything you can say. If you say something with a little hook on it—and it doesn't have to have much of a hook—you're home because it's the personality which counts. What I'm trying to put across is, whatever you say on

TV, it's as much the *way* you say it as *what* you say. If you've got an Arthur Godfrey personality, you can walk on and say, "The people in Washington, D.C. (or St. Louis) are doing something about the weather today; they've decided to endure it." For California you could say, "Out here we have four seasons, all in one day!"

Godfrey is one of my favorite people. When I'm in New York I pop in on him, surprise him while he's working, and we have a ball. In fact, one of my favorite pastimes is busting in on Arthur Godfrey. I met him while I was doing a show for Chesterfields in Durham, North Carolina. North Carolina, that's Doris Duke with highways. That was three or four years ago. We became buddies and stayed up half the night having fun together. Things were so rosy and bubbly that toward morning he said, "I should go back to New York, but if you'll go on the air with me I'll stay here and do it tomorrow."

"I'm your guest," I said.

He had his girl call up New York and say, "Arthur is going to do his portion from Durham with Hope." Arthur is a law unto himself. He's very popular. He gets five thousand fan letters a week, one from each sponsor. So they let him broadcast from any place where he feels comfortable.

I must have gotten a bad piece of ice that night before or something for I woke up very late. I turned on the radio to see what time it was and as I turned it on I heard Arthur say real slow, about three words a minute, "Bob Hope is supposed to be on with me this morning. But I don't know whether he's going to make it because when I left him last night he took a brisk walk around the hotel and fainted."

I was in the suite above his in the hotel. So I put on my bathrobe and went down to Arthur's suite. He was in his bathrobe, too, and was looking just as dog-eared and rumpled as I felt. The two of us sat there doing a nationwide broadcast in our bathrobes and thanking God we weren't on television.

A couple of years ago, when the great TV panic was on in Hollywood, they were firing the cowboy stars at Republic and the horses were playing the banjos. Half the people you saw on the street had a beautiful tan. The rest had jobs. As for me, I was the only one at Paramount still making Easterns.

In its early days television was such a novelty that its addicts looked at everything. Every family felt that it owned a movie theater. Some families even put popcorn machines in their front halls. There were a lot of television sets in cocktail bars. That worked out fine. If the customers didn't like the program, they breathed on it and melted the screen.

Things are better now so far as the movies are concerned. The novelty of three-D brought people back into the movie houses. But the actors soon ran out of things to throw at the audience, and the audience began to throw things back. Nowadays the public shops for better TV shows. They're willing to tear themselves away from their twenty-one inchers to see a good movie. Of course, when color TV comes along, that'll be another story. Video will be a novelty all over again. Maybe someday TV will have a three-D, too, and Ed Sullivan will walk right out of a set into your living room and sit on your lap. With three-D TV I may get a letter from a lady in Pomona complaining that my nose tore a hole in her sofa.

But I love knocking myself out in radio, TV and the movies, because I know the applause is genuine. The noise that sounds like hand clapping is the income tax department smacking their lips.

I'm not trying to scratch anybody's back or thump anybody's drum when I talk about the influence of TV because I'm in both television and movies. I've been very lucky in pictures and I have a nice five-year TV contract with NBC, with two more years to run. But television is so much like vaudeville it frightens me sometimes. I feel like the murderer returning to the scene of his crime.

Talking about high points, it seems the right time to mention the testimonial dinner the Friars Club gave me last year. Once a year the Friars put on a Celebrity Night. It's flattering to be their guest of honor. Of course, they really put it on because the club can use the dough. But it's a compliment just the same—if not to you personally, at least to your drawing power—because they pick somebody they think can fill the grand ballroom at the Waldorf with paying guests at fifteen bucks a plate.

Jesse Block, of the great vaudeville team of Block and Sully, is an officer of the Friars. He made like a whirling dervish arranging the dinner. And my own public relations operative, Mack Millar, who's been with me for twenty years trying to persuade people to acknowledge the existence of Bob Hope, came up with the idea that the Cerebral Palsy Fund be cut in on the proceeds. Trying to build good will and keep it that way for an entertainer or for anybody in public life is a ticklish business.

And anybody who can stick it out as long as Mack has stuck it, without having the public tar and feather his employer along the way, must be a character with good judgment. In addition, Mack is one of those parties who, when he gets an idea about something that can do you good with the people in the radio, TV, movie and personal appearance audiences, sinks his teeth into it and refuses to give up until he's put it over.

But to get back to that Friars dinner, among those at the speakers' table that night were Stu Symington, Alben Barkley, Barney Baruch, Milton Berle, George Jessel, Mayor Impellitteri, Fred Allen, and my home-town mayor, Thomas Burke, of Cleveland, now a United States Senator. He took Bob Taft's place.

Jessel led off by saying that the Friars were saluting me because I was an "average American who makes three million dollars a year." This is a slight exaggeration. I'm not average.

Barney Baruch tried to add a few years to my life by saying, "May the Lord take a liking to you, but not too soon."

Milton Berle was never Berlier. His idea of praising me was to call me "America's second greatest comedian."

When George Jessel, the Toastmaster General of the United States, introduced Fred Allen, he said, "If rank spelled the order of importance among comedians, the next speaker would be a field marshal. I first met him in the days of the lost art of vaudeville. He was a juggler who told a joke when he missed a trick. He hasn't missed many since."

I myself knew Fred when he was a vaudeville juggler. He played all of the regular vaudeville circuits, spouting a line of bright patter. But with the exception of the public in New York and Chicago, he was so subtle his patter went through the heads of his customers and came out the other side in a shower of bone dust. He never cut into my following. He was too literate.

I think that most of those who attended that Friars dinner will agree that Fred stole the show. He is one of the real wits of our time. He even writes his own stuff. It was Fred who quipped, "I hear that in deference to its new TV star, Bishop Sheen, Du

Mont is manufacturing a set with a stained-glass tube." When he got around to me he said, "Born Leslie Townes Hope in London, our guest of honor went to Hollywood—a place where, after you struggle for recognition, you put on dark glasses so you won't get it."

When I stood up to speak, it was one of the few times I've ever been flabbergasted. I stood there frozen for a minute or two, with my mouth open like Marilyn Monroe's but not half as attractive. I forgot most of the ad-libs I had prepared.

Speaking of cerebral palsy, I've been up to the top of my well-rounded head in Cerebral Palsy work since 1949. That year I was playing a personal appearance tour at the Paramount Theater in New York with Jane Russell and Les Brown. We were there for two weeks doing six and seven shows a day to take care of the extra customers. That was the moment Bob Weitman, in charge of the Paramount, chose to tell me that Leonard Goldenson, head of the United Paramount Theaters, wanted to start a money-raising drive for the victims of cerebral palsy. Bob said that there were a half million children and adults who had been afflicted by this scourge, that Leonard wanted somebody to spearhead the initial campaign, and that he wanted to ask me if I'd do it.

"I don't see how I can give it the time it deserves," I said, "and it wouldn't be fair to obligate myself to a program as important as cerebral palsy unless I go all out."

"Talk to Leonard about it anyhow," Bob said.

Bob had me cornered in the men's room backstage at the Paramount, so I gave in and said that the next day I'd go up to see Leonard. When I saw him and he talked to me, he was full of hopes and plans for the things that could be done to help afflicted people. When he got through telling me about them, and asked me to take the post of national chairman, the first thing I knew, I was saying, "I'll help."

I hopscotched back to the Coast by way of Cincinnati, Rochester, New York, Owensburg, Kentucky, Kansas City, Topeka and Wichita. In those places I stopped off to look at the set-ups they had for helping the cerebral palsied. Some of them were fine. In Wichita they had what is perhaps the best clinic in the world for this purpose, The Institute of Logipedics. It had been built and was being supported by gifts long before anyone thought of putting on a national drive.

But some of the places set up to do a job for the palsied weren't fancy. In one city, the clinic was in a garage. It had bars attached to its walls so the kids could hang onto them while they tried to learn to walk. The people in charge had made an effort, but they didn't have the things to work with they needed. It's tough to help kids (or adults, for that matter) who've been stricken by palsy. It's slow and tedious work. You labor for years and years and years to get any results at all.

Early in 1954, I made a short film at Paramount for cerebral palsy. Having done it, I handed over the post of national chairman to Bill Ford, the younger member of a certain Detroit Ford family, and I became the honorary life chairman. It's a kick to think that within five years this project has become the nation's third largest beneficial charitable foundation.

Bing is honorary vice chairman. Arthur Godfrey is an honorary chairman, and every chance we get to do something, we do it. If we can work a benefit for the cause, we pick up the ball and run with it.

Before I stagger out of this high-points-of-my-life swamp in which I'm bogged down, I might add that there's such a thing as a high point in pan mail as well as in fan mail. Some years ago I did a joke in one of my pictures, *Paleface*, which made a moviegoer in Tulsa, Oklahoma, reach for his pen. The offending line was: "All day long I work with beautiful girls like Paulette Goddard, Madeleine Carroll, Dorothy Lamour; then at night I go home and dream about Indians. I don't know what's wrong with me."

When the picture was released, I got a beef from the party in Tulsa, who had Indian blood in his veins and who didn't think my joke funny, me funny or the movie funny. But I thought he was funny, so I framed his letter. It hangs on my dressing-room wall.

Tulsa, Okla. 3/10/43

Mr. "Boob" Hope
Hollywood, Cal.
Dear "Boob":—

So you're the No. 1 *"Funny* (?) man"* of radio and screen, eh! Well, that's what *you* think. In reality, you're the No. 1 "Joke" (and I do mean JOKE) man of them all. You big "Fat Head", you go around over the country making fun of the Indians and you think you are smart and cute.

Well, brother, you'll never see the day when you are just half as smart as our beloved Will Rogers (an Indian) was nor will you ever see the day when you are half as popular as Will was. It's too bad that Will is not alive today to "take you around the horn" about your silly cracks about Indians. To listen to you, one would think that it is a disgrace to be an Indian . . . Well, you big "boob" you've got a lot to learn. There's thousands of Indians who are a darned sight smarter and a darned sight more civilized than you. What you deserve is a good sock on those "lantern" jaws of yours and hope some Indian will have the satisfaction of giving it to you. Maybe it would take some of that conceit out of you. . . .

Yours very truly,
A MEMBER OF THE APELA INDIAN CLUB, TULSA, OKLA.
And darned proud of his Indian blood.

Of course, most Indians will hold still for jokes just like anybody else. The Irish, the Jews, Southern colonels, Englishmen with droopy mustaches, vaudeville acrobats, Baptist deacons, bankers, Republicans, Democrats, Mae West and Henry Ford—to name a few—have all taken a kidding from time to time. If the kidding isn't malicious, if it's good-natured, no one objects. Not even Indians. I know. During the making of *Paleface* they chased me for eight weeks but they didn't really mean it.

The fact that they are traditionally deadpan makes them

fair game for jokesmiths. Two of my pet stories would be no good if Indians were chatterbox extroverts. One of these yarns grew out of something that was supposed to have happened when I was on location during the making of *Paleface*. The producer, the director and the assistant director all worried about the weather. After all, it controlled their shooting schedule. If they thought bad weather was due, they scheduled interior

shots. An Indian standing nearby saw them brooding and he announced, "Tomorrow sunshine in the morning; rain in the afternoon."

Sure enough, it was sunny in the morning and it rained in the afternoon. The assistant director was so impressed that he asked the Indian, "What happens tomorrow?"

"Tomorrow sunshine all day," the Indian said. "Rain late."

He hit that one on the button too. The next day his forecast was: "Rain all day." He still batted a thousand.

Figuring that he'd save the studio money on its shooting schedule, the assistant director put the Indian on salary. Three or four days later they asked him, "What's for tomorrow?"

"Don't know," he said.

"What do you mean you don't know?" they complained.

"Radio broke," he said.

End of joke. But I'd like to think it did happen.

My other Indian story involves a director who hired three hundred Indian extras for a film he was making in Arizona. Before his first scene he lined them up and made a speech. "Gentlemen," he said, "I have one request of you. This is a serious scene. Please do not laugh."

Those who heard him said that those three hundred stone-faced Indians almost broke into a chuckle.

Speaking of Indians, I've invested in a lot of different enterprises, but none gives me more fun than my affiliation with the Los Angeles Rams football team and the Cleveland Indians ball club. The Rams are a team to be proud of. They're world's champs, or close to it, every year. They can make you forget a lot of troubles when you're sitting in that huge Coliseum watching their magic.

I'm really getting quite a kick out of being one of the owners of the Cleveland ball team. There's only one thing wrong. Since I started backing the Indians, Roy Rogers won't talk to me any more. Even Trigger turns his back on me now.

The Indians are really going after the pennant this year. I finally made them forget that silly notion of trying to get Manhattan back first.

Naturally, I'm quite an important figure around Cleveland, now that I'm part owner of the Cleveland Indians. But it hasn't changed me a bit. I still have to sneak in. I attended the opening at Cleveland last year, but I didn't see much of the game. In the first inning, I yelled, "Throw the bum out!" and they did.

Crosby owns part of the Pittsburgh Pirates, and he's really lucky. He's got something to fall back on, in case Gary ever cuts his allowance. It's funny the way Crosby bought into the Pirates. He was burying his money in the cellar one day, and there they were.

Not only people in Tulsa interpret jokes differently from the way you hope they'll interpret them. I'm really on the spot when I do political jokes. I would never do a joke to hurt any campaign or any party. I can't afford to go out and start knocking Democrats and knocking Republicans, because I'm usually selling a product everybody buys and I don't want to alienate part of my audience. It's pretty hard to do a comedy show and stay in the middle and please everybody when you're kicking current subjects around all the time. Will Rogers used to get away with it. But he was supposed to be a cracker-barrel type. I've got a lot of crackers in my barrel but there was only one Will Rogers.

In 1944 I was asked to attend the White House Correspondents Dinner. I was down at Brookley Field and again I had a problem with transportation and weather. I was sitting down there trying to figure out how to get a plane to Washington, when General Mollison got a wire from General Arnold. It said: HAVE PLANE COMING NORTH TO WASHINGTON TONIGHT. MAKE SURE HOPE IS ON IT.

I took off, ran through a hail storm and landed at the Washington airport about nine o'clock. The show had started at eight-thirty. By the time I got there it was nine-thirty. Fred Waring, Jascha Heifetz, Ed Gardner and others were on the bill. I was supposed to be master of ceremonies, but I arrived so late Ed Gardner had taken over my job and all I could do was go on at the finish and do a spot.

F.D.R. turned out to be the greatest audience I've ever worked for. I'd prepared a lot of special stuff for him. I did the joke about Fala being the only dog who had been housebroken on the Chicago *Tribune*. My readers who remember the slight coolness between the *Tribune* and F.D.R. will understand that. The head table was against the wall. The rest of the people there were facing us. Every time a joke was told everybody looked at the President to see how he reacted. He'd bang his hand with the cigarette holder in it on the table and roar. Then everybody else would knock themselves out laughing too.

I said, "I think I should apologize to our President for some of the things I've said on the radio. Especially about Mrs. Roosevelt. Like when Mr. Churchill and Mr. Roosevelt were conferring on world strategy in the middle of the Atlantic. The way I put it, 'World strategy means where and when will we attack the enemy and what'll we do with Eleanor.'"

In those days Eleanor jokes were a big item. She'd come in and say, "Good-bye, Franklin." And he'd say, "Where to now, dear?" And I'd used a plane joke: "Nothing passed us on this flight. We went so fast, only Eleanor passed us going both ways."

F.D.R. laughed at the Eleanor jokes too, but I said that I thought I ought to give her her just due. Mrs. Roosevelt had done a tremendous job during the war. I knew she'd been criticized for traveling so much, but you only had to be out in the field and follow her into a hospital, say in Guadalcanal, to realize how much good she was doing morale. Because when they said, "Mrs. Roosevelt is coming tomorrow," or they asked, "Who do you think was here yesterday—Mrs. Roosevelt! I got her autograph!" it made them feel important, and not forgotten back home.

My experience with the large shots in politics is that they can take joshing themselves, but their followers can't. I got along fine bouncing my heavy-handed humor off Harry Truman. In 1945, when I was in Washington to do a Victory Bond show, President Truman was there. It was about two weeks after he'd walked into the White House. Next day I got a letter from him, thanking me for what I'd done for the Bond Drive and asking me to drop in at the White House after dinner. I asked if I could bring my entire show: Vera Vague, Jerry Colonna, Frances Langford, *et al,* because I knew they'd want to go, and I didn't want to go over to the White House and leave them out of it.

The President said he'd be delighted if we'd do a show for him. So I went to the White House with all my people. We walked into the Gold Room and there was the President and his family sitting with his staff.

There were about thirty-five or forty people in all. As I walked in I said, "Man, this looks like Missouri already."

The President laughed and we did a show for them, and they enjoyed it. Punch and cookies were served and the President said, "Twice a year we have formal parties here, dancing and everything, after which the President takes the people around on a tour of the White House. Follow me and I'll show you how he does it."

So he took us on a personally conducted tour of the White House. He couldn't have been nicer or more cordial.

In the 1948 election, everybody thought Dewey would kill Truman. Like others, including Mr. Gallup (who went into hiding afterward), I felt sure that Dewey was going to win. But the stagehands and the union guys on the sets at Paramount kept saying, "You'll find out."

About nine o'clock the morning after the election I was sitting in my dressing room. It was noon back East, and Dewey was conceding defeat. A joke I'd heard when Al Smith lost to Hoover came back to me. Al's enemies had made political capital of his Catholicism. The feeling was (especially down South) that if Al won, the Pope would hop the next ship to the U.S.A. and take over. When Al had his brown derby bashed in and his cigar trampled on, some wag was supposed to have sent a one-word cable to the Vatican with Al's name signed: "Unpack."

So I sat down and sent a wire to Truman. I didn't think he'd mind if I was flip because I'd met him so many times. My wire also said "Unpack." Matt Connolly, Truman's secretary, kept my message under a sheet of glass on top of his desk for a long time. For that matter, I could have sent the same telegram to Dewey. He had his suitcases ready to go, too.

Chapter 21

MY APPEARANCES at the Palladium in London are certainly among the higher points of my life. Right now the Palladium is the greatest vaudeville theater in the world. Week after week it pulls a reserved-seat audience. In spite of the fact that we accuse the English of being slow, its audiences are very fast on the pickup. They still love variety the way millions of people once loved the Orpheum and Keith circuits in this country.

So many American acts play there that they call the Palladium the Real American Embassy. Palladium audiences are not stiff about being kidded. They loved it when I did such jokes as: "I came over on the *United States*. It's a wonderful ship. It cost us ninety million. That's money we had left after Churchill's last visit." Or "You have to hand it to Churchill. If you don't, he comes and gets it from us anyway. But I don't want you to think I'm knocking your wonderful statesman, because I know you people worship the ground his cigar drags on."

Val Parnell is the managing director of the Moss Empire Theaters in England. He is also the business manager of the Palladium. This genius behind the Palladium is without doubt the greatest showman in England, and this restricts his territory too much. In 1951 when I played the Palladium I used the line, "Parnell has brought more Americans to England than Eisenhower." It drew big laughs and lots of applause.

The Palladium is the only two-a-day, reserve-seat house in the world (still playing vaudeville) where the audience doesn't pay to get in because it's interested in the movie that's playing there and the live acts are tossed in as bonus entertainment.

Val Parnell has done an amazing job of building and upholding the Palladium's reputation. He's a shrewd booker of talent. He knows show business from A to Z, and he has a great sense of humor. Last year, when I opened there, I did a joke about the British jet Comet, the new plane which flew from London to Rome in two hours. I said that the British were working on an even newer plane, but that they were having trouble because the blueprint kept taking off from the drafting tables. The joke only fetched a fair boff and I asked Val if they didn't understand the term "blueprints" over there.

He looked at me, and asked, with a twinkle in his eyes, "Who do you think made the blueprints for America?"

A couple of years ago one of our great Yankee tenors played the Palladium. Parnell caught a few of his shows and detected a number of flat notes. About the middle of the week the tenor said to him, "I don't feel so good. I think I have wax in my ears. I'm going to have them blown out."

"I wouldn't do it," Val said. "You won't like what you hear afterward."

In spite of what you heard about Martin and Lewis not liking the London critics (they claim a British newspaper critic is a columnist who uses lemon in his tea and forgets to say "when"), they were a hit over there. As for myself, I intend to keep going back to the Palladium as long as they'll have me.

English audiences are very kind to American humor, because it's so fast in contrast to their own comics who usually go in for character and situation comedy. They call me a "dasher" because I don't stand there and play it slowly, and because I like to get as many laughs in half a minute as possible.

It's only natural that I have a weakness for the British. The phrase "our British cousins" is more than a phrase to me. I have forty of them. I even have a feeling of kinship for those few Englishmen who are *not* descended from my grandfather.

A case in point is the Reverend Butterworth. I was introduced to him during the making of *The Lemon Drop Kid* when he was visiting the Paramount lot as a guest of Cecil B. DeMille. I happened to mention that I'd been born in London, and he told me about his pet project in England—Clubland, a club for young boys in the East End of London. It's partly a club and partly a school which teaches boys a trade. It had been bombed out during the war, and the Reverend Butterworth told me that if he couldn't raise money for rebuilding, he'd have to close it down and a lot of kids would lose their chance at a useful education.

"I may be in London next year," I said. "If I am, I'd like to do a benefit for you."

I didn't know then whether I would be in England or not, but later I was asked to play the Prince of Wales Theater in London. I told Lew Grade, my agent in England, "Have them make the contract between the Reverend Butterworth and the theater. I'll play two weeks at twenty grand a week, but only if the club gets all the dough."

When they called the reverend in to sign the contract, it was the first he knew about it. It gave him quite a jolt. He's very sentimental. I was told later that he cried. When my ship docked, he was waiting for me. When I opened, he sat out front every night, beaming and enjoying every word, although before the two weeks were over my gags must have made him gag.

Near the end of my second week, he said, "Don't forget. I want you to come to Clubland and see the place. We'll have it ready for you."

On Friday of my last week I went there before my first show. In every department—woodcarving, gym, table-tennis room—the kids were working or playing so hard they didn't look up. Apparently they'd been told to show me how much they loved their equipment, and they were doing it.

"What happens when I'm gone?" I asked the parson. "Do they fall asleep exhausted?"

Even he could see they were overplaying, and he chuckled. "Afterward," he said, "I've promised them you'd do a show for them." So I worked out for them upstairs in the auditorium.

In 1952, when I went back to London to play a Palladium engagement, the Reverend Butterworth invited me to Clubland again. They had roofed over a couple of buildings and had set special stones into the walls to honor those who'd helped the rebuilding project. They even had a restoration stone in my honor, right across from a stone in honor of Queen Mary, who was one of the sponsors of the club.

That stone got me and I thought I'd like to do another show for the reverend. Bing was in London, and I asked him if he'd do a Clubland benefit with me at the Stoll Theater. "I'd like to," he said, "but I'm not sure I can make it." However, on the chance that he might be there, I booked a benefit. I didn't actually promise the people that Bing would be on hand, but somehow the idea got around that because Bing was in town, we'd naturally be at the Stoll together.

When I walked out to do the first part of my act, the audience yelled. "Where's Bing?"

"It's pretty late for an old gentleman to be out," I told them. "He's probably in bed, sipping his hot milk."

They let out a groan of disappointment. I kept on talking, and Bing walked out and leaned against the proscenium arch, smoking his pipe. It was the first time he had ever been on the stage in England, and they gave him a tremendous ovation. He stayed out there and sang for forty minutes. They wouldn't let him off.

We pulled in several thousand dollars for the Reverend Butterworth. Leaving England, I took the launch at Southampton to board the *Liberté*. Who should be on the launch but the reverend. He said he had something to show me, and taking me to the upper deck, he pointed to a spot on shore. "There's the place we're buying for a summer camp for our boys with the money you and Bing earned for us," he said.

The only criticism of such gestures on my part comes from the gentlemen who handle my personal-appearance bookings. They call me "Free Talent Hope." According to them, I'm such a pushover for benefits they're afraid I'll begin to turn down paid dates. One of these citizens who handles my finances told me recently, "I'll bet that anybody can call you up and insult you, and when they're through insulting you, all they've got to say is, 'We need some free talent for a worthy cause; we're having a little benefit and we'd like to have you on hand,' and you'll show up."

I couldn't think of a snappy comeback to that. For one thing, things like that *do* happen to me.

Among the big, fat chunks of advice which have been dropped into my lap about the things I should cover in this story, I've been told, "Why not give the public a few samples of your ad libs; the kind of off-the-cuff remarks and comebacks you make if somebody in one of your audiences needles you, heckles you, or asks you a prickly question?"

I've got my share of ego, but not that much. I don't want to say in print, "Look at me, folks, I'm a bright boy. I say the funniest things. Why only the other day I said . . ." and so on and so on. To me, that comes under the heading of bright sayings of children as reported by their parents, with me being both parent and child.

When some yokel backs me into a corner and lets me have the

needle, or when I'm standing on a stage and somebody in the audience slips me a loaded question, I can defend myself. But this doesn't make me unique. Almost anybody with average intelligence gets off a few nifties in a day or a week's time, but if they're smart, they settle for letting their friends quote their cracks instead of working them into the conversation themselves.

Anyone who's listened to my radio shows knows that during part of each of my daytime broadcasting sessions, a mobile microphone is passed around and anybody in the house can go into a Q. and A. routine with me. There's no script involved. Nothing is prepared. It's simply a contest of wits, based on the fact that audiences like to fence with a comedian.

I've been in training for this kind of match ever since I joined Hurley's Jolly Follies in my tossed-salad days. Rated off the background of such training, I'd have to be the dope of the world not to have some verbal and mental agility. If I hadn't, I'd be an idiot, and you can't be an idiot and be a comedian. You can be a comic, which is not the same thing. Any of the top comedians can handle ad libbing and do a slick job.

You've got to know the entire scam. You've got to channel this kind of give-and-take the way you want it channeled. If you don't, you're in trouble. And if you are tired mentally and physically, you ought to stay out of such situations. Your tiredness will show up every time, unless you're lucky.

In all honesty, I think I have pretty good timing. At times I have good material; at other times I have great material. But I know how to cover up the merely good and make it sound better by timing. In fact, timing is my greatest asset, especially on radio or television.

I know how to snap a line, then cover it, then speed on to the next. You have to get over to the audience that there's a game of wits going on and that if they don't stay awake, they'll miss something, like missing a baseball someone has lobbed to them. What I'm really doing is asking, "Let's see if you can hit this one!" That's my whole comedy technique. I know how to tele-graph to the audience the fact that this *is* a joke, and that if they don't laugh right now, they're not playing the game and nobody has any fun.

At least, that's my comedy technique for personal appear-ances. I have other comedy styles. In pictures, I work with broader material and use my face a lot. I have a pretty flexible face (part of it was put out by the Goodyear people) and I can mug it up with anybody.

In radio, you can't expect to have brilliant material all the time, something different every week, so you use different tech-niques to make the most of the material you have. Lots of times you're forced to give out with a joke that isn't as funny as it might be, so you use different techniques to bolster it. If nobody laughs perhaps you squeeze some humor out of apologizing for it. Or you can play it as if you think it's terribly funny and you can't understand why the audience doesn't follow you.

They like that, but only if they feel you're not making fun *of* them, but are having fun *with* them.

I also have a sneak attack, where I make a line seem nothing. This is called a throwing-it-away technique, which is the oppo-site of hitting a joke too hard. Anybody can learn a lot about this technique by studying the work of such artists as Helen Broderick (one of the greatest throw-away comediennes), and Bea Lillie, who tries to hide funny lines from you instead of ramming them down your throat. Such master chefs of comedy dishes as Broderick and Lillie don't lay their stuff out baldly on a platter. You've got to spot the tastier morsels for yourself, and reach out and spear them with your fork as they're served.

The worst thing a comedian can do is to let an audience think that he's sore at them. It antagonizes them and he can get into trouble that way. He should remember that if they don't react the way he thinks they ought to react, it's his fault. Either he's not selling his material, or it was bad material in the first place.

During one of my broadcasts, a fellow in the tenth row on

the aisle took a flashlight picture of me. NBC doesn't allow any cameras in a studio during a show, and the ushers came down the aisle and tried to take his camera away from him. Every eye in the house was looking at this big conflict, and I was standing up there loaded with gags which had been polished and shined for the occasion, and I might as well have dropped a small can of Yami yogurt on the mike for all the good my intensive preparation was doing.

Thank God we were being taped, so I could cut out all the wrangling before it went out over the air on a nationwide hook-up. "Get back in your stalls," I told the ushers, "and let this man have his camera until after the show's over. After that you can tear up the whole studio if you want to, but let's get the laughs first."

So the ushers retired to the military police schools from which they'd graduated.

If you flip your lid when things like that happen to you, you're dead.

People have asked me, "Aren't there lots of different kinds of audiences and don't you have to use different kinds of jokes for those audiences?"

Not to give such questions a short answer like "yes," it goes without saying that fresh material has to be tailored to fit each new, special audience.

Suppose I'm to do a show about my boyhood. The jokes I use will fall under the heading of "back home" jokes. I've covered that subject so many times it's stale to me; however, it's possible to take a "back home" routine and switch it to a present-day one. Suppose I've once used a gag about the days when Dad had a Stutz Bearcat with a built-in ukelele. I can update it by saying, "Things are different now. Simmons is putting out a mattress that makes up into a sport roadster."

When I go to Washington to play the White House Correspondents' Dinner, it's nice to have a line or two on tap to the effect that "Washington is not really crowded. Only when four fellows get into the same cab at the airport, they find it roomier to change into their tuxedos on the way to the hotel."

Let's say I'm playing to a New York night club audience. Such an audience knows so much about show business and Broadway and Hollywood and radio and TV that I can play those themes the way Borrah Minevitch plays his harmonica. They read about show business, they're close to it. If I mention a Neilson rating, they know what I mean, whereas hinterland audiences might not dig it.

Or let's suppose—although it's a horrifying idea—that I'm called upon to toss out a few gags at a book critics' convention. Let's suppose further that a publishing firm like Simon and Schuster has just brought out a book of mine. Such a situation would put me in the position of a Frenchman who's been sentenced to death, but who's joshing the boy who triggers the guillotine by making remarks about the blade being sharp or dull. There I am, with my neck out in more ways than one, but I'm determined not to be dull myself, even if my humor is a little strained. So I pin a fixed smile on my puss and go with something like this:

Ladies and gentlemen—and critics. You all know what a book critic is. He's a fellow who gets his books for nothing and still complains. And they can be rough. I know one critic who has a fountain pen that writes under blood. My new book is upsetting the publishing business. Simon won't talk to Schuster. S. and S. not only insinuates that I had a ghostwriter, they brought the book out on Halloween.

Or suppose I'm before a group of newspaper photographers. Maybe something like this will do:

I know when I first started in the business I had a chance to get a good break on the cover of a picture magazine one week. I got a bit sassy with the editor and they made a last minute switch and I wound up on Field and Stream with a pheasant in my mouth. But I like photographers. They always take six or eight pictures, and if they like you, they print the one with your

eyes open. Everyone in Hollywood is afraid of photographers. They can really make it rough for you. They took a picture of Crosby once and you should have seen it. It came out looking like Crosby. The newspapers have always had a good word for me. I can't tell you what it is. But believe me, it's a good word. . . . Louella and Hedda have sort of a friendly rivalry. Friendly rivalry, that's Hollywood for "you fire your food taster and I'll fire mine."

If I'm asked to emcee an Academy Award show, it means that I sit down with my writers for two or three weeks and think about it. We ask ourselves, "What should we talk about? What's great, and especially, what's late and timely? We start thinking in terms of such lines as, "Well, here we are at the annual

Academy Awards affair. It's the twentieth year they've had the Academy Awards. Bette Davis has nineteen Oscars, and what I'd like to know is, who sells her her brass polish?"

It's no deathless line, but it's a beginning.

For my money, the No. 1 joke of them all is the topical joke, a quip based on today's newspaper headlines. When you use one, everybody is with you as soon as you tee off. A case in point was the week when Jimmy Roosevelt was billed in the papers as the Ding-Dong-Daddy of Beverly Hills.

That week, on my morning show (where I submit to queries) a fellow asked me the following question: "What will we do with my little brother, who lives in Regina, Saskatchewan? He's only eight years old and already he has four girl friends."

"I hope he doesn't sign any letters in which he mentions their names," I said, then I looked at the audience and said, "I'm not going to mention anybody's name, either."

They got it. In one second I had a message going back and forth between me and the audience. I hadn't mentioned any name but they knew what news item I was kidding about. I ended by adding, "Oh, well, this little fellow couldn't do *that*. He's too busy to write letters."

One Tuesday, shortly after Hemingway's plane crack-up in Africa, I was due on the air at five. At three o'clock we were still writing our show. We had four or five Hemingway jokes, and stuff about Molotov at the Paris Peace Conference. They played great. The point is, we were prepared to junk Hemingway and Molotov if something else hot happened at four o'clock.

Take the time I was covering the Democratic Convention and a fire broke out on the floor. The fellow on the podium said, "I suggest we adjourn before something serious happens here."

There they were, only trying to nominate a President of the United States, and there's a little fire in some waste paper and the man thought that was the really important thing. You don't have to be a genius at recognizing current and topical comedy material when you see it or hear it to have a bell clang in your mind at something like that.

Second in usefulness are local jokes. When you play Chicago, you've got the stock yards and the Windy City to talk about. "Where else," you ask, "can you lay an egg and have the wind roll it in front of another comedian?"

The gags I did for servicemen during the war were really local jokes in the sense that they were all based on the special situation, of men being away from home, lonely, and having their own special gripes and diversions. Those gags might not mean much to anybody else, but they meant something to the sailors, soldiers, marines and fliers because they were aimed at them.

There are all kinds and types of comedians who're giving laughter to the world, just as there are all kinds and types of jokes and audiences. The first laughsmith to earn his cakes with a joke was the court jester. He went in for broad, hokey stuff. Red Skelton, for example, does a lot of broad, hokey characters and he mugs a lot. In reality Red is a practitioner of the type of clowning that's been going on ever since the first jester inflated the first pig's bladder.

On the other hand, Groucho Marx is strictly a verbal comedian. In spite of his mustache and the way he throws his eyes at you, what he's really doing is making with words. In addition, he works hard to perfect the timing of his words.

Danny Kaye's art lies in his special git-gat-gittle songs and the things he does with his hands, his voice, his face, his whole body. It's sheer genius and magic in action. He's hard to explain, but he has a great style, even if it can't be put on paper. Danny has been practically adopted by the British. I used his dressing room when I was over there. It was a modest affair; just two mirrors and a throne.

Then there's the complaining comedian. He comes out grumbling about the low blows life is giving him. People like that because they like to think somebody else is having it tougher. If you talk about your hardships and sneak in your humor along with your beefing and growling, it makes you very human. Like Danny Thomas. He's always suffering, and he gets off to a much better start than the guy who comes out with a big laugh thinking he's a hit already, and practically saying, "Well, here I am. Let's go! I'm a very funny guy." That way is the forced way. The Thomas way is the natural way. His pitch is, he's got problems just like everybody else, and he's talking them over with the audience.

Jimmy Durante plays an obvious mug who can't handle big words, but who can handle a lot of laughs. He's got a happy personality and he makes you think he's having more fun than anybody else. If he can go along for the first couple of minutes, O.K., then let the audience think he's all at sea and has forgotten his lines, they eat it up.

Jack Benny is a master of all of the comedy ingredients; material, situation, building a situation, putting it together, and selling it with expert timing. His timing is wonderful. In fact, he goes beyond being a comedian. He's an artist. That's the only way I can explain Jack. He has a Chaplinlike way of creating sympathy for himself. He's always the patsy, always on the spot. Somebody's always making him miserable, or beating him down, or calling him a tightwad. Handled properly, this kind of material is mighty effective.

Donald O'Connor is a fresh, appealing personality with more talent than anybody under fifty ought to have. They say that Donald appeals to the mother-instinct in girls. All I know is my mother never squealed at me that way. And Jackie Gleason is a delightful rough-house comic who makes a robustious contribution to comedy.

Sid Caesar is a great student of comedy. How he's done the job he's done every week I'll never know. He should be decorated. That's the trouble with television. You take "I Love Lucy"; it still has a top rating, but now people are beginning to say casually (when they ought to be ecstatic because they've got a chance to look at that show for free), "Oh, Lucy's all right."

Lucille Ball is a very gifted girl. She has a natural ability for clowning. I could say the same about Joan Davis, a vaudeville graduate with a practical knowledge of how to play a comedy scene. And Cass Daley is a riot.

Then there's Herb Shriner, who has good off-beat stuff. He's very pleasant, has a nice easy approach, the way Bob Burns used to be. And Wally Cox's Mr. Peepers is a cross between Chaplin and Harold Lloyd. Godfrey is just Godfrey. No matter what the papers say about him, he's still Godfrey. And that's good enough for millions of people.

It's my hope that NBC and all the other big networks will eventually protect such people and make them stop killing themselves off. I think it's dangerous to use them up so rapidly. The networks will wear out all these great performers, then they'll ask, "Whatever happened to those folks?"

The public is rich right now as far as free entertainment goes. All they've got to do is switch on their sets and presto! Jack Benny, or Sid Caesar, or Cass Daley, or a great football game enters their homes. My hunch is that the public is being spoiled through being overentertained.

And while I'm listing the cream of the comedy crop, one of the greatest comedians I've ever seen was the late Sid Fields, an English boy who captured London during the war years when he appeared in "Strike a New Note," a Val Parnell production. Sid was as whimsical as our own Frank Fay, and he could create sympathy like Chaplin. He was one of Eisenhower's favorite diversions when Ike was in England. A lot of our G.I.'s who were stationed in England during the war will never forget him.

In 1946, when he visited America and Hollywood, we gave him a testimonial dinner at the Masquers' Club in Hollywood. He drew a large gathering of celebrities, among them Ronald Coleman and Jack Benny. Everybody loved Sid.

I was master of ceremonies, and after we'd talked about Sid for a couple of hours, he got up to speak. He was all choked up. "The things you've said about me were wonderful," he said. "I never expected to come to a strange country and receive such friendship." He tried to say more, but he was so close to tears that he sat down. He almost put Bette Davis out of business. In fact, that's where Johnny Ray got his whole idea.

Chapter 22

MY FRIENDS and co-workers do a lot of talking about how I'm supposed to have an amazing amount of energy. There's nothing amazing about it. I relax in snatches, wherever I am, the way a cat does. I can sleep riding from a train to a hotel, sitting up in the car. I've heard people talk about how many shows I did for the servicemen during the last war, as if that was something remarkable. It was no hardship. If you go out in front of an audience of twenty thousand boys who are fighting a war and you entertain them and they laugh at you it makes you feel good because you're doing it.

Looking forward to a trip such as a ride to London to play the Palladium with a new act is stimulating. It's like having somebody back a tank up to you and give you a transfusion of nervous energy. In the last twenty-five years of my life, I've always been looking forward to some new excitement in New York or in some small town, in Africa, Australia, Japan, or Alaska, or even playing a benefit here in Los Angeles such as a Boy Scout Jamboree.

People ask me, "Why do you like it?" That's easy. I do it because if I sat home and didn't do it, I would worry about the chance that I'd missed something.

They also ask me why I have a daytime radio show, a nighttime radio show, and a TV show, too. "Isn't it a little rough?" they ask. This schedule is a pretty rugged one, but the training I've had helps. I used to do four shows a day in vaudeville, then drop into a night club and if anybody asked me to get up and do something, I got up and did it. I might do thirty or forty minutes off the cuff. I thought nothing of working from twelve noon until one o'clock next morning. After that maybe I'd get up early and play a little golf.

Stamina depends on whether you can relax between the times when you're putting out. I can. I can't relax when things are going badly, but I've been lucky. They don't go badly often. I'm just like anybody else when it comes to mentally helping the pilot take the plane off the ground and mentally checking his instruments. But on a plane ride I can only be concerned for a limited time, then I fall asleep.

I'll never forget my first plane trip, about twenty years ago. A little old lady sat next to me. She was so calm and casual that I asked her, "Do you take these trips all the time?"

"Yes," she said, "I do. I'm hired by the airlines to make people like you think this is safe."

But something peculiar seems to happen to me whenever I try to take a real long rest. I wanted to get away for a while in the summer of 1947 after making a picture. I only intended to go to New York but I went down to Puerto Rico and ended by going all through South America. I took Dolores and Tony and Linda with me.

I took Doctor Freddy Miron too. Doctor Miron is a masseur at the Lakeside Country Club, where eight years ago I was made an honorary life member, along with Bing. (There are only three life members. So it's quite an honor.) The Doctor holds some kind of degree from Battle Creek, Michigan—Doctor of Massage, for all I know—anyhow that's how he got the title "Doctor."

Freddy Miron is a little fellow of Spanish descent, who came to California after studying massage at Battle Creek. Eventually he became a trainer and masseur for such stars as Doug Fairbanks, Senior, and Joan Crawford. He also rubs a few directors and producers, among them Dave Butler. If he can handle Dave's blubber, he's pretty good.

I met him at Lakeside Country Club and employed him to lay his talented hands on me every night to put me to sleep. He not only makes me feel drowsy; he gives me the latest golf returns from all over the world.

I asked him to make the trip with us because he speaks English with a Spanish accent, and Spanish with an English accent and I figured I'd need an interpreter. I'm glad I took him along because at every stop people I couldn't understand jabbered at me.

Our kids got a kick out of the trip, although they were only seven and six. When I fell asleep on the long trips, I'd wake up and see Tony coming out of the pilot's compartment wearing the pilot's hat. I could almost see his head swelling until it was big enough to fit it.

Looking back, it seems quite a fast trip, because Tony had his birthday on July first in Buenos Aires. Two weeks later we were in Elkhart, Indiana, visiting Dick and Helen Snideman, two old friends of ours, ten thousand miles away from Buenos Aires. Linda had her birthday there. Fast as it was, too much happened while we were on it.

When we reached Montevideo, and I got off the plane, I said to the local Paramount representative who met us (there's a Paramount field man in almost every big city), "Where am I going to stay? I'd like to check in at the best hotel."

"You've been taken care of," he said.

Honey Chile Wilder, the girl I'd introduced to radio back in my early days on the air, had married a chap named Albert Cernadas in the Argentine, and Honey Chile had arranged for us to stay at his summer place. I didn't know what kind of a place it was, so I asked the Paramount man, "Do you think we ought to go?"

"Yes," he said, "I think you ought to go."

When we got there, we found that it was one of the country's show places. We had it to ourselves. If we thought of something we wanted an arm came through the wall and gave it to us.

The estate was equipped with a big swimming pool, a private zoo, and a private theater. In that theater I saw a print of Bing and myself in *The Road to Utopia* with Portuguese voices dubbed in for ours. It was a queer experience to hear Bing and myself yelling jokes at each other in another language.

Also they were just showing my film *Monsieur Beaucaire* in Montevideo. In fact, they were having the preview that very night. The man from Paramount asked me if I'd put in an appearance at the screening. "I'd be glad to," I said.

He added, "I think it would be nice if we stopped at the radio station first so you can say hello to the people here over the air waves."

It turned out to be an old-style studio with glass partitions separating the artists from the audiences, similar to the ones they once had at the old NBC studios on Fifth Avenue in New York. A great South American singer, Pedro Vargas, was holding forth. I'd worked with Pedro once in Washington.

He looked through the glass, saw me, stopped in the middle of his song, and said, "Bob Opey! Bob Opey!"

That's the way they pronounced my name in South America. They say Bing Cromby, Dorothy Lamourah, and Bob Opey.

There were about four hundred people in the studio audience. They all looked at me, and Pedro waved at me to join him behind the glass wall. When I went in he said, "They want to take you into another studio and do an interview with you."

"O.K.," I said, "but who's going to be the interpreter?"

Then I remembered Freddy Miron, the Battle Creek Spanish Don with the educated fingers. I introduced Freddy Miron to Pedro.

"Let the interviewer ask Freddy the questions," I said. "Then Freddy can ask me. I'll give him the answers and so on and so on."

We went into another glassed-in stage and a fellow shot some Latin-sounding stuff at Freddy. Freddy listened, then asked me, "How do you like it here in Montevideo?"

"I like it fine," I said, "but it's the wrong season for me to be here. I'd hoped to see those beautiful things who lie around on the beaches in Bikinis, and it's too cold for them. They might get chapped."

Freddy turned to the fellow and gibbered my answer to him in Spanish. He got a big laugh from the crowd. Then the man asked Freddy to ask me, "Did you see the soccer game here?"

"Yes," I said through Freddy, "I saw it this afternoon and I liked it. I'm going to borrow some legs from Marlene Dietrich and come back here and play it sometime."

Freddy repeated this and once more he got a laugh. He was taking it very large. I tapped him on the shoulder and said, "Smile at me once in a while, will you? You're getting all the laughs. You might at least give me a beat-up grin. After all I'm giving you the material, you know."

This sort of thing went on for five or six minutes. Freddy was really living it up. He loved it. He was probably wondering: *How long have I been this funny?* When we went downstairs he said to me, "Do you think Paramount will do something for me? I really wowed them out there."

It was Freddy who gave me a toast to use when the glasses were being held aloft: SALUD Y PESETAS Y TIEMPO PARA GASTARLAS. It means, Health, Wealth, and Time to Spend it. We changed it to: SALUD Y PESETAS Y MAS MUJERES EN BICICLETAS, which means Health, Wealth, and More Women on Bicycles. The revised version was much more successful.

The "restful" part of the trip soon evaporated. I took Dolores and the children to Rio de Janeiro, where I went out to the La-Gavia Country Club, which has a tropical setting. It's cut out of the jungle. You can hear monkeys chatter and you see strange animals walking across the fairways. Sometimes they're part of the foursome with you. On the fifteenth hole I stooped down to pick up a ball. I brought up a handful of red ants and they started to eat on me. They bit out a few fillets. A couple of days later I developed an infection and a doctor had to lance.

No wonder I think *not* resting is less painful.

In April, 1952, I flew to Honolulu for a week's vacation. I was really enjoying it when I ran into a string of requests to play benefits, at places like Schofield Barracks and the Glockarina Bowl. Those requests came from people like Admiral Radford and I couldn't very well turn them down. Besides, as I've already admitted, I'm a patsy for entertaining the troops.

To top it off, I dropped in at Don the Beachcombers. I had some of his famous rum drinks compounded of jet fuel, put on a cocoanut hat, went to the Queen of the Surf Club and in no time at all I was doing a master of ceremonies job. Nobody asked me to, but the way I felt they couldn't have stopped me. I had a few more rum sodas and a steak and wound up in bed with diverticulosis. That's a block in your colon, and it shouldn't happen to a dog, even a Russian wolfhound.

It laid me low for two days. I thought I was going to die. It was typical of the way my "rest" trips usually turn out. The doctor said, "I want you to get right on a plane for California and take it easy on the way back." But I'd promised to play the Honolulu penitentiary and the convicts were expecting me. They'd carved wooden bowls for Dolores and me. I didn't want to disappoint them, so I stopped off there on the way to the airport.

The trusty who let me in smiled a welcome and said, "I belong to the radio guild in Hollywood."

"Well," I said, "they're bound to get some of us."

A couple of years ago I went to Palm Springs to relax. My phone rang and a voice said, "This is Father Keller." Father Keller is the big mind behind the Christopher Movement. The Christophers are trying to spread religion in general. They don't make any special effort to try to spread the Catholic Religion, they just try to spread good to the whole world.

"I want to see you," he said.

"That's fine," I said. "I'd like to see you too."

"I'm making a little movie short for the Christophers with Ben Hogan," he said, "I'd like to have you come over and say a few words."

"I'm here for a rest," I said.

"This won't take long," he said. "I'm going to ask Bing too, and I know *he'll* do it."

I don't think I'd have done it for anybody else, but Father Keller's doing such a great job, that I said, "Okay, I'll meet you out at the golf club."

The next day Bing and I joined him there. The "few words" wound up as an hour and a half of dialogue between golf shots. The entire country must have seen this film by now because every time Hogan wins a tournament, they run it on television. It was called Faith, Hope and Hogan. I imagine they labeled Bing Faith because of his role in *Going My Way*.

It's not restful when I'm home either but I'm immunized to that. In fact, I'd miss it if the whirligig slowed down. Mornings, when I'm working in a picture, there's a sort of morning round-up in my dressing room beginning about eight o'clock. This invasion is led by Tubby Garron, an ex-café-singing-waiter. He's a fabulous character who proudly calls himself The Biggest Liar in the World. Be that as it may, there is no doubt that he can talk faster than anybody in the world. His ordinary conversational tones have more decibels than those of circus sideshow pitchmen. He's not only one of the greatest song pluggers in that whacky business, he's the self-appointed master of ceremonies for this morning get-together of my friends, associates and co-workers.

Two other members of this group are Monte Brice and Barney Dean. Monte is a veteran of picture business. In his time he's been an assistant director, and a director. Now he's a writer. When we need a line fast, or a gag to toss into the hopper, or a piece of business to glue the action together, he writes it right on the set. I've already described the kind of portfolio Barney Dean holds at Paramount.

In addition there are Len Henry, the dialogue director, and Charlie Cooly who does everything for me I'm too tired or too busy to do for myself. And there are the make-up men, Charlie Berner and Harry Ray. Sometimes their boss, Wally Westmore, walks in; in fact, anybody who happens to pass by. The costume boys come flying in and the film cutter, Chuck West, is likely to sit in too.

My dressing room (it's really two small rooms thrown together) isn't very big. It gets pretty crowded. In fact, we're thinking of putting in oxygen tanks to take care of the breathing.

Everything goes on while I'm making up. We relay the latest international scoop back and forth, we hack away at the latest films, we spring what we think are the latest jokes, and we go into what's wrong with the Cleveland Indians.

Around twenty minutes to nine we break it up. A red light flashes on, everybody disappears and Len Henry starts to give me the dialogue for the first scene. Luckily for me, I'm a quick study and it doesn't take me long to sop up my lines. It all depends on the scene. If it's a long scene I wood-shed it the night before at home. But usually scenes are broken up into short takes. "Wood-shedding" is shop talk for getting off by yourself and doing your homework, like Lincoln reading by the fire. It might be better if some of my stuff went into the fire, too.

Some of the requests put to me have their comical side, although this doesn't mean they're not worth while. Mrs. Ida Mayer Cummings runs the annual benefit show in Hollywood for The Jewish Home for the Aged. This show is one of my favorite benefits. When I first reached California in 1937, I was asked to take part in it. I played it the next year, too. I've kept on playing it every year since, unless I'm out of town. This benefit usually occurs in February, but Mrs. Cummings begins to call me in November. Once she starts, she keeps my telephone line so busy I can't make an outside call without going through her.

She rounds up a lot of different artists, but in view of what happened year before last, she must get a little confused at times. When she called me then, I said, "Yes, Mrs. Cummings, I'm going to be there—if nothing happens."

"Don't say 'if nothing happens,'" she begged. "Don't let anything happen. I've got to have you."

This was her regular routine. Then, when you show up, you find fifteen other stars there, any one of whom could have handled it alone. Nevertheless, you're happy to be there.

"You've simply got to come," she said. "I haven't got anyone else."

"Mrs. Cummings," I said, "I'm absolutely going to be there." I'd talked to her from my office. Then I walked into my house, and a half hour later my daughter, Linda, said, "Daddy, Mrs. Cummings is on the phone."

When I went to the phone, she said, "Hello," and I said "Hello."

"Are you coming to the benefit?" she asked.

"Yes, Mrs. Cummings," I said.

"That's fine," she told me. "Can you bring anybody else? I'm stuck for talent."

"Maybe I can get Jane Russell," I suggested.

"Can't you bring a comedian?" she asked. "We could use one."

I hadn't realized that Mrs. C. was a kidder. Then it dawned on me. She had her calls mixed, and had forgotten whom she was talking to. All she knew was that she was determined to get a large assortment of comics lined up.

"I'll see if I can bring a comedian," I said.

She didn't know she had talked to the wrong person until Hedda Hopper printed the story. That "Can you bring a comedian?" got a big laugh all over town.

It is only fair to say that, when you think how much good the

Jewish Home for the Aged does, Mrs. Cummings' persistence is understandable. Mrs. C. can certainly be excused for her confusion. In rounding up her annual show she does the work of nine people. My hat's off to her.

Sometimes the people for whom I do benefits show their appreciation in strange ways. A couple of years ago I went up to Duluth to do a charity show. When it was over, the sponsors of the show gave me a live bear. We did a radio show there, too, and one of the characters in the show was named Pierre, so we nicknamed the bear Pierre. I brought him back in a chartered United Airlines plane. Pierre wasn't housebroken and the pilot almost bailed out. He was up front in the baggage compartment and it got real gamey up there. They used more oxygen than usual on that trip.

When I got him back to my home in San Fernando Valley, my kids wanted to keep him but I said, "No bear. He might not have nice table manners, either. When you hand him food, he could polish off your fingers."

Some other citizens who were grateful for a little help I'd given them had also given me a white mule. I nicknamed him Bing. I solved my animal boarding-house problems by presenting both Bing and Pierre to the Griffith Park Zoo in Los Angeles.

One of the oddest offers I've ever had was made to me Christmas before last. I was invited to attend a private party in New York. The invitation had some novel social overtones.

I was offered ten thousand dollars to accept. But I said, "I don't work parties. You better get yourself another boy."

"We don't want you to work," I was told. "We just want you to put in an appearance. The man who's throwing the party wants to have some celebrities there."

I figured I could be different too. I suggested that I'd be glad to telephone him during his party for five thousand dollars, but he wouldn't buy that idea and the whole deal fell through.

Speaking of benefits, I was playing golf at Lakeside one Sunday with my wife, in a temporary escape from radio, television and movies, when I looked down the fairway and saw a man walking toward me with a briefcase. Looking closer, I saw that it was none other than Chef Milani. Chef is quite a man on radio in Hollywood. He gives out cooking recipes and other suggestions for use in the kitchen. He is an Italian, sentimental and emotional. He'd called my home to ask me if I'd play a benefit for the Italian war orphans in Montebello, a community on the other side of Los Angeles, and I'd said, "I'll try." But when my secretary relayed it to him, he'd seemed reluctant to take that for an answer.

I greeted him and he walked around a couple of holes with us. After a certain amount of throat clearing he said, "I would like to know whether you are really going to play this Montebello benefit?"

The fact that he had chased me out to my playground to repeat his request annoyed me. Chef's a sincere guy, all he wants to do is good, but the golf course is one place I don't expect to be bothered, and I didn't like it.

"I've told you if you'd wait I'd give you a yes or no," I said. "You don't have to come out here to the golf course to see me. I have an office for things like this. I'd like to go to your benefit. It's a worthy cause and I know you want to put it over and I'll let you know about it."

He stood there while I teed off; then he began to cry. It spoiled my whole day to see a man sixty years old crying and I was sorry I'd talked harshly to him.

I walked back to the tee, grabbed him, and said, "Chef, I love you. I love you, Chef. I'm going to play the benefit. I'll be there, Chef. Stop it!"

He threw his arms around me and gave me a big Italian kiss and a hug that would scare a bear. It was quite a thing. The caddies stood around astonished at seeing one man kissing another man.

The result was that I showed up at Montebello and did the benefit in an open park on a platform. There were more people

on the stage than in the audience. Or it seemed that way to me. Chef had about five thousand people out. In addition, his relatives were on the stage. He does a great job and he's a fine guy, even if he is a touch sentimental.

Charlie Woit, who manages the Hope Enterprises, gets unhappy when I do something for free. The Hope Enterprises is a holding company set up to handle the business end of my pictures. I'm a partner in every other picture I make for Paramount and my share is handled by Hope Enterprises, which puts up half the money to finance the film. It also handles my personal-appearance tours.

Our first tour of this kind grossed six hundred and eighty-seven thousand dollars in thirty days. We grossed about forty thousand dollars selling the programs alone.

On our one-night-stand tour in 1949, we had eight or ten publicity workers (known to the trade as flacks) ahead of us beating the drums, and we had our own chartered plane, a DC-6. They'd have crowds of several thousand at the airport to greet us and they'd arrange radio blurbs. We did a fabulous thirty-two shows in thirty towns in thirty days.

When I got off at an airport I always tried to come through with some kind of laugh. But at one spot, a local moppet took care of the laugh production. I walked down the steps with Doc Shurr, and a woman with a little boy—he must have been all of five—pointed at us and said, "There he is, darling!" This kid ran over, grabbed Louis Shurr's legs, looked up and said, "Bob Hope!"

The crowd loved it.

During my vaudeville days I made the jump out to St. Louis to play the Fox Theater there. I was just beginning to show some interest in golf, and I visited a driving range. Next door to it was a watermelon stand run by a man who called himself Sam the Watermelon Man. Walking over I began to eat some of his fruit.

"You're playing at the Fox, aren't you?" he asked.

"Yes," I said. "But it's so hot I wish I had some of this down at the theater."

"That's easy," he said. "I'll bring some down to you."

The next day he brought me some and I walked out on the stage eating it. We were doing four shows a day and anything we could do to vary the monotony of our routine was relished by the band, anything that wasn't in the act or that they hadn't heard.

I said to the audience, "Sam the Watermelon Man brought this to me. He's got the greatest stuff you ever bit into." In return for that plug Sam kept us in watermelon all week.

Sixteen years later I went back to play a personal appearance date at the Kiel Auditorium in St. Louis with Les Brown and Doris Day. We drew ten thousand, five hundred people and took in thirty-three thousand dollars for one performance, the most money we ever made in one show. As we got off our plane before the show, we were looking around for the cars we'd hired and watching the mayor sign the big map we'd had painted on our plane (we asked the mayor of every city we visited to sign it; it was a good front-page publicity gimmick). Who should show up with a fleet of cars but Sam the Watermelon Man. He had a big sign on one car: SAM THE WATERMELON MAN WELCOMES BOB HOPE. What's more he had motorcycle police as a convoy. Nothing would do but we all had to get into his cars and ride to our hotel with him.

En route he said, "How about coming out to my place after your show?"

His loyalty after sixteen years got under my skin, so I said, "Sure, Sam."

That night after the show Les Brown and Doris Day and our whole company went out to Sam's. He seated us at a big table in the middle of a grandstand he'd had built. Around us were three hundred people who'd bought tickets to watch us eat watermelon. When we finished Sam gave me a microphone and begged, "Say a few words Bob, will you, huh?"

When I was through Doris got up and sang a song, Les Brown said a few things; in fact, everybody in the show got up and did something. Sam even had special spotlights ready for us. In short he milked a few thousand bucks worth of talent out of us and all we got out of it was watermelon. I took ten per cent of the seeds home for my agent.

It's my hunch that talk about business is dull to most people. I notice that when Bing told the story of his life, he devoted only a couple of paragraphs to his coin-snaffling projects. I'm two or three businesses back of Bing. Bing will soon have his own cities —Bingville, Crosbytown, Groanerburg—and install one of his sons in each as mayor. He won't have to worry about Gary. They've already named a city for Gary in Indiana.

But it's not Charlie Woit's fault that Bing is a length or two ahead of me as a tycoon. Charlie's very thrifty and very serious about the Hope Enterprises, which is a good thing. None of the stockholders—there are eighteen of them—approach commercial affairs with the frozen pusses of habitual financiers. Last year we had a meeting in my office to listen to a report on earnings and losses. In the opinion of my off-beat stockholders, Charlie Woit was much too thrifty in watching out for the best interests of all concerned. As proof, they offered the food served at the stockholders' luncheon. I'd told Charlie to order lunch for our pack of Wall Street wolves, and he'd ordered it from an industrial caterer. They brought over box lunches. The stockholders sat down to boiled ham, potato salad and one roll each. They'd read the favorable reports on how we were doing and some of them were shocked that we had a lunch which had been apparently re-routed from San Quentin. My own cook could have put out a super meal for them for ten bucks extra, but Charlie is a "no" man. He says it so often that he's still with us.

If everybody had as little sales resistance as Dolores' grandmother, Nana, the Hope Enterprises would never have to worry. Her name was really Nora Kelly; Nana was her nickname and she lived in the Bronx. When I was on the Woodbury hour she sat in front of her radio all alone, applauding loudly. When she died, at seventy-six, they opened her closets and carton after carton of Woodbury soap fell out. She'd wanted the Woodbury Company to think I was moving their stuff. She'd done her part to keep it selling.

Chapter 23

SPEAKING of Dolores' family, it may surprise those who read this to hear that I'm a strong family man too. I'm no angel. I've known very few angels. My mother and Dolores are two. But I'm still married to the same girl I married twenty years ago, which is four or five under par for the Hollywood course. Until recently, I tried to keep my family out of my publicity. For that reason, not much is known about them. As late as a year ago I'd be willing to bet that the majority of moviegoers, radio listeners and TV viewers didn't know whether I had any children or not, or how many brothers and sisters I've had.

The truth is, family has always meant a lot to me. The Hopes, of Eltham, England, and Cleveland, Ohio, had a strong clannish instinct. We stuck together. The thing joining us was the need for all of us to help Mom. There's a theory that facing tough times binds people together. I know it works that way with men in the same Army or Marine outfit or on the same destroyer, PT boat or submarine. Well, the Hopes, of Cleveland, had many a battle on their hands.

After working and working and trying to make ends meet, my mother at last began to complain of a backache. I asked, "Why don't you go down and see the doctor, Ma? Let me take you."

"No," she'd say, "I'm too busy. I'll be all right. I'm better to-day."

What was really in her mind was that she felt she had so much to do to make sure all of us were happy that she didn't want to take time out to go to the doctor. Of course, that wasn't true any more, but the years had grooved her mind that way. After I'd started to work in tab shows, I sent her a little money now and then. When I got a few good breaks in vaudeville and started to make important money, I told her, "You're through working now. I want you to stop. I'm going to buy you a house." So I bought her a house up on Yorkshire Road in Cleveland Heights.

"From now on," I said, "you and Dad just sit back and enjoy yourselves."

I was thrilled that I could buy them a house. I was away from Cleveland, on the road, but my brother, Fred, lived only a few blocks away. My oldest brother, Ivor, lived up in the Heights section. My baby brother, George, was around part of the time.

Finally, we did get Mom to go to a doctor and a great specialist at the Crile Clinic in Cleveland examined her. When he'd read the X-rays, I went to see him to hear the verdict.

He shook his head, "I'm afraid my news is bad," he said. "It's cancer."

She had no chance. It was beyond repair. We just saw her wither away. There was no point in operating. There was nothing anyone could do but try to keep her from having pain. They gave her hypos and pills, but I used to hear her moan anyhow. I have photographs of myself carrying her out into the backyard like a child. At the end she weighed about seventy-five pounds. But she never gave up.

It was murder that this should happen just when I was really able to take care of her. Of course, she enjoyed her new house for three or four years, but after she was gone that seemed nothing. She died while I was playing in *Roberta*.

Dad only lived three years longer. He died while I was in *Red, Hot and Blue*. He pined away. He acted lost. He'd come to New York and visit me, and we'd have a ball, but the purpose in his life was gone. He'd been knocked off his pins and couldn't get up again. He never got used to living alone.

He died of all kinds of complications when he was about sixty-six. That is not old. He was a very strong man. Being a stone-mason doesn't breed weaklings, but he just gave up.

My brother, Sid, was a victim of the same dread disease as my mother. There was nothing the rest of us brothers could do about it except try to give him some enjoyment and happiness, and lie to him and tell him that he was going to pull through. This worked until a fellow came to his house and tried to change his religion by telling him, "You know you're going to die, don't you? You've got cancer. You ought to get on our side of God." We could never find out who the fellow was. Sid wouldn't tell us.

But when we made our next visit and I told him, "You're going to get well," he said, "Don't lie to me. I know I'm dying. I have cancer. I just want to ask you one favor. Take care of my kids."

Sid's five beautiful kids moved in with my brother, Fred. They're at a place called The Pines, a summer resort and restaurant not far from Columbus. They all work there when they're not going to school, and they're happy. Anyhow, we've tried to make them happy.

You'd think that with such a family history, I'd brood about cancer moving in on me too. But the only thing I worry about is the possibility that someday my physical motor may wear out. I've had one little scare that way. Three years ago I was at the Long Beach Auditorium. The Officers Reserve Association was presenting me with a jeep that had been in Korea. Jane Russell was on the bill with me. I'd rushed down there from the studio in a hurry. I didn't have time to eat and I got there late. I sat down and the show started. When I got up to walk to the other side of the room, I began to lose my balance.

This is it, I thought. *They told me I've been working too hard. I guess I'm done.*

My heart was really giving out a Cugat beat. I grabbed a chair, and asked Jane to get me a glass of water. She took a look at my pasty face and ran for it. They sent for a doctor and he called another doctor. When they checked my blood pressure it was 180 over 95.

I'd had a thorough physical examination a month before because, having signed a three-year contract with me for a lot of moola, NBC had taken out a million-dollar policy on my life. They wanted to make sure I was going to be there for that third year. Their doctors had voted me 1-A, which made it even more astonishing to me when I fell over at Long Beach.

When the doctors were through looking at me, they said, "You're going to get in your car and go home." They had Charlie Cooly drive me home. "Drive him slowly," they told Charlie, "and call his doctor."

All the way home I sat there feeling kind of balmy and wrapped up in a haze of silly happiness about the whole thing. I thought: *Now I can really take time out and see the world—by boat this time.*

I had mental pictures of native boys carrying me off in Tahiti and in New Zealand, and letting me look at all those countries quietly and lazily and just sitting around and watching the people play whatever games they play there.

When I got home my doctor rushed over and took my pressure and said, "You're okay now. But you'd better get a cardiograph tomorrow."

I said, "Fine. I'll do it tomorrow when I get to Palm Springs."

At Palm Springs the doctor made me lie down and plastered a lot of metal and wire gadgets on me. When he finished he said, "Uh-huh."

"Uh-huh what?" I asked.

"Man," he said, "you'd never get a million-dollar policy now!"

That scared me. So the next morning I got into my car and was rushed back home to my own doctor again. He took me over to his cardiograph man and I had another heart examination. This man went over me good and when he was through reading his wiggly lines he said I was perfect. I've never had another attack. You explain it. I can't.

Most of the brood of Hopes, who arrived at Ellis Island in 1908 wearing two suits of clothes to save luggage, are still bound together in some way. Fred owns and runs an annoyingly successful wholesale meat business in Cleveland and Columbus, Ohio. He's so energetic he needs two cities to give him room for his activity. He's a vitamin with legs. I use the word "annoying" because he refuses to cut me in on his meat business, although I've hinted that I'd like to invest in it. My youngest brother, George, who was once one of the stooges in my vaudeville act and who later had a fling at radio-script writing, works for Fred as a salesman.

My oldest brother, Ivor, is more broad-minded about declaring me in on his way of making a living. Ivor is president of a Cleveland metal-partition-manufacturing company, and he cut me into the deal. In fact, I'm the majority stockholder. It was only fair that Ivor let me in with him. After all, I tried to give him a leg up when he was head salesman for the Sanymetal Products Company in Cleveland. Sanymetal was opening a new factory in East Cleveland. Ivor had been telling them about the vaudevillian in his family, so they said, "If he's so good, why don't you bring him to the factory opening?" I happened to be in town at the time playing a date, so I went out to do a show for Ivor's employers, hoping that as a by-product they'd be grateful to Ivor.

When I got there, the workers had already blottered up a few seidels of beer and some of them were a little sluggish. I didn't mind. I'd played to some soggy audiences before. When I was introduced, I hurled a fistful of crackling nifties at them, but nothing happened. It was a staring contest. They stared at me and I stared back at them.

No one had warned me about it, but they had soundproofed the factory so expertly that the audience couldn't hear me. They didn't have a microphone, so what I said went into the walls. After ten minutes, I went into the walls myself, along with a few termites, and disappeared. It wasn't a matter of quitting. It was a matter of getting out without being killed. I think they demoted Ivor to errand boy.

My brother, Jack, who was named after my Uncle Jack, came out to visit me in California in 1937. I asked him to stick around. I needed someone I could trust to help me take care of my business and my joke files. Along with Charlie Cooly, who helped me get my first big job in Chicago at the Stratford Theater, when I was starving to death, Jack handles my phone calls and acts as a buffer between me and people who get me on the phone because they've made a bet with a pal they could, or strangers who ring me to tell me that they think Milton Berle's latest show is his greatest, "and how're you doing?"

If I made Brother Jack sound a little like a plumber's helper in the above description, it's really not fair to low-rate him in that way. The fact is that he is one of the big wheels in the production of my TV shows, and I couldn't have a more loyal and valuable boy on my side.

But no matter how strongly I feel about the word "family," Dolores feels even more deeply about it. When we found out that she couldn't bear children, she began to bend my ear about adoption. We were getting along fine and I wasn't too keen about the idea. I was content with a wife and show business and golf, but after five years of being nudged by Dolores, I was talked into visiting The Cradle in Evanston, Illinois, and meeting Mrs. Florence Walrath, who was then its managing director. There's a lot that isn't known about the way an adoption agency such as The Cradle works, but in my opinion they have a wonderful system and I'd like to share my knowledge.

The time comes sometimes when a natural parent or parents realize that adoption is the best security they can give their baby. The best security, that is, if they select the right kind of agency to handle the adoption. When the baby is accepted by the agency, the natural mother signs an agreement called a "relinquishment." This agreement promises the natural mother that her baby will be placed in the finest available home, as long as it follows the religion the natural mother follows. The selected agency is the sole legal guardian of the baby until it's legally adopted.

Many people think the idea of such an agency is to find babies for prospective parents. That's not the way it is. It's the other way around. So even before Dolores dragged me to The Cradle, The Cradle had looked *us* over with a microscope and had decided that we might do for one of their babies.

When we arrived, we had a long talk with Mrs. Walrath. Then, and only then, were we told they had a baby girl about eight weeks old *we might suit*. They brought her into the showing room. Dolores could hardly tear herself away, but we finally made our way down to Mrs. Walrath's office.

"How do you like her?" she asked Dolores.

"She's beautiful," Dolores said.

Then Mrs. Walrath asked me, "What do you think?"

"Oh, she's all right," I said.

Mrs. Walrath took Dolores aside and said, "I don't think that Mr. Hope is serious about wanting a child."

"Don't mind him," Dolores said. "He's just trying to appear disinterested. He's afraid he'll seem soft."

Fortunately for me, Mrs. Walrath was able to see through me the way Dolores sees through me, and we got the happy news that the little girl was to be ours. That's how we got our Linda. Once we had her home, I was enthusiastic about the whole business. Everything began to revolve around her, and she wound herself around me like a small blonde boa constrictor. So we wired Mrs. Walrath to watch out for a baby brother for Linda. A year later she called up to tell us, "I think we have the boy for your family." I happened to be going to New York, so I said, "I'll stop off at Chicago and take a gander."

When I got there, Mrs. Walrath took me to see the baby. He was held up to the plate-glass window in the nursery. Someone said, "He looks just like you."

I looked at his face. His nose was a little ski snoot like mine, so I said, "That's for me." And that's our Tony.

Dolores and I often talked of adopting several children, but the war stepped in and stymied that, as it did so many other things, for I was never home long enough to fill out and sign the other applications which were needed. But in 1946 we stopped off at Chicago and lunched with Mrs. Walrath. I could see that look in Dolores' eyes again, and she begged Mrs. Walrath, "Please find us another baby." So before long we went back to The Cradle once more, this time to be looked over by a two-month-old girl doll.

"I have a surprise for you," Mrs. Walrath said. "There's a baby boy too."

When we saw him, Dolores wasn't sure, and I left her there, wondering what to do, and went down to Mrs. Walrath's office to talk over the legal details with the lawyer. But when Dolores came in a little later, still puzzled about what decision to make, I'd already signed for both babies. That's how we got our Nora and our Kelly.

Of the five thousand, four hundred and nine babies that The Cradle has placed, there are eight Cradle babies out here in Hollywood. The Hopes are proud to be Cradle parents. I wish I could really tell you what The Cradle means to me here in Hollywood, where all day long the talk is box-office and autographs and premieres and who'll get the Oscar. "The town of make-believe," they call it, but don't get the idea everything is make-believe in Hollywood. There's nothing make-believe about our children. They are real.

Before I sign off on The Cradle, there's another story I want to tell. When I went to Chicago in 1952 for a television show, Mrs. Walrath was living at a place called The Mather House. A generous man named Mather had left money to establish a home for elderly ladies. When they enter it they turn over any money they have to the common fund. After that they live in the home for the rest of their lives.

Mrs. Walrath asked me to come out and have lunch with her. All the ladies were on deck. They're very proud of the place. They have a right to be, because it's beautiful and they go first class. We had a gay time and I made a speech. After lunch, when we were having dessert, a bird flew in through a window. It fluttered around and was finally trapped in one of the curtains. A few cracks were made about this invasion. My contribution was, "He'll probably be on the menu tomorrow."

But the best crack was made by one of the ladies. "Mr. Hope," she said, "this is in honor of you. You're used to getting the bird." Maybe it wasn't a line for the ages, but I thought it was cute.

We named our youngest girl "Nora Avis" for Dolores' grandmother and my mother. Kelly is "William Kelly Francis" for my father and Uncle Frank Hope. Dolores selected "Anthony" for our oldest son, and we call him "Tony" for short. "Linda Roberta" was my own special choice for our oldest daughter.

Being our kids, Linda, Tony, Kelly and Nora are naturally closer to show business than most children. We discourage them from getting any closer. But the truth is, Nora's a natural-born ham. She doesn't care whether she has an audience or not. She just goes and hopes that an audience will show up.

If I'm going to do a song with a girl on a TV show, I'm likely to start rehearsing the song at the family table. I'll sing it to Nora, using her as a foil. She plays up and, much to the amusement of everybody, gives me the full treatment, with the right set of facial expressions. She's only seven, but she reacts the way an ingenue reacts when she's listening to a juvenile pushing lyrics at her. I'm sure she's waiting for me to come home and tell her there's a spot for her in one of my pictures.

Linda is fourteen now and has been taking harp lessons for more than a year. I didn't know whether she was doing good with the instrument until my fiftieth birthday party on May 29, 1953. Then she walked into the living room, where she keeps the harp, and played "Thanks for the Memory." It was the best present I had. Her fingering was a little slow, but she hit all the strings vibrating in her daddy's heart.

Tony's a natural clown, but, as yet, we don't know what Kelly's going to turn into, though he's coming along fine. During the first couple of years, we thought he might fly away like Peter Pan. Kelly is crazy about Space Patrol and Buck Rogers, and all those

other TV characters. In fact, he's ashamed of me because I've never been to the moon.

During the summer, Dolores likes to have our children's day planned to include some work along with their swimming and playing. So Tony gets out and works with the gardener. This means that he has to get up very early, and by the time I get up he's already exhausted. Dolores also thinks up chores for the others too. Linda is the best table setter and unsetter in our part of the San Fernando Valley.

Linda's a nice girl if I do say so. She's appealingly innocent. Not dumb, but innocent, which to me is a winning trait. Certainly she's not like the fourteen-year-old daughter of one pal of mine. Not long ago my pal went up to his daughter's bedroom and found a pile of pulp magazines there. They were heavy with sexy photographs.

He stalked downstairs and said, "I was just up to your bedroom and I'm shocked at the kind of stuff you read."

"Really, Dad," she said, "you're too old to be digging those crazy comics."

In addition to the other members of our family, the Hopes also have a Scotty dog. Her name is Princess. The fact that Princess is still with us is a victory for the infiltration tactics used by Linda. I banished Princess after her first month with us. After watching this pooch undo most of the work done for us by an interior decorator we'd hired, I told Linda, "You'll have to get rid of this menace. She's ruining our carpets and chewing the furniture. She thinks she's a flop-eared, sabre-toothed termite."

But I was bucking something stronger than I knew. At such times a little girl can be as tough as concrete. Linda hid Princess in a secret place for a while, then sent her over to hole up with her Aunt Mildred until the heat was off. Little by little, she began to bring Princess back for week ends.

I'd ask, "What's she doing back here?"

Linda would say, "She's homesick, Daddy."

Finally I gave up. We have Princess with us now permanently.

I've had a couple of dogs myself. The first one was a great Dane named Red Sun. I saw him at the San Diego Dog Show in 1941 and I admired him so much that a friend, Ernie Ferguson, gave him to me. But the first Red Sun died of heart failure and Dolores bought me another Dane that I called Red Sun too. In 1944, when I was playing the Los Alamitos Naval Air Station, they served a dinner featuring beef. It was during the wartime meat shortage and the service bases were the only ones eating steer with any regularity. Butchers were weighing it out for civilians on jewelers' scales at so much a carat. I couldn't demolish all of the meat on my bone. There were quite a few carats left. So I said to Commander Scribner, who was in charge of the station, "I wonder if I could take this bone home—er—for my dog?"

"I'll have it put in your car," he said.

When I got home that night I said to Red Sun, "Wait until you see what you got for me."

I opened the rear of the car, took the bone out of its box and held it up to gloat over it. Before I could stop him, Red Sun opened his big trap, snatched it and was loping around the yard. I grabbed a flashlight and chased him, cornered him and split it with him. It seemed the best way out.

Like any father, I have moments when I wonder whether I belong to my children or they belong to me. There's a little thing which happens every morning when I go to work. As I step out of the door they say to me, "Do your funny dance, Daddy." So I have to do a routine which consists of a couple of shuffle steps. Halfway to the garage I have to stop and do it again. This gets me to the escape hatch.

I also have a pair of imaginary characters they pressure me into playing for them, and if I do say so myself, I kill them with this one. One of these imaginary characters is Scandinavian. The other is a semi-Mortimer Snerd.

I also used to do a little girl for them too. I'd rap under the table, and an invisible little girl would say to them, "Go to the window." They'd rush to the window and another invisible little girl outside the window talked to them. I did both voices. It was nothing to make Edgar Bergen lose sleep, but it was good enough for my prejudiced audience—until they got wise and yawned when I did it.

In 1944, just before I went to the South Pacific to do a series of USO shows, I took my family up to Pebble Beach for a week while I played golf and had a little rest at the Del Monte Lodge. Linda and Tony were six and five, respectively, then. I was breakfasting with three buddies, Dave Butler, Vic Hunter, and Dick Snideman, when my kids came in with their nurse and sat at another table.

I said, "Good morning, children," and Tony said, "Good morning, Bob Hope."

This was supposed to indicate to anyone listening that I was a stranger to him. I'm afraid that was true, for in those days, what with flying all over to entertain the troops, I wasn't home long enough to get to know him. Still, I thought it was a fresh performance for a five-year-old.

I got up, walked over to him and said, "That kind of stuff is O. K. when we're alone, but if you don't mind, just say, 'Good morning, Daddy' when we're in public."

Linda looked at me and said confidentially, "We know, Daddy. We're supposed to let you get the laughs."

I've never been topped that thoroughly before, or since. I was frayed. I hardly knew how to get back to my table.

At breakfast at our house, Nora sits on my left at a large, ranch-type table in the breakfast room. We take most of our meals there, unless we're having company. The day after Nora goes to see one of my movies or watches me on television, I'm a celebrity to her. She eats her meal looking at me with her eyes big and full of admiration.

She smiles at me and asks, "Was that a real monkey you worked with last night, Daddy?" or "How did you get out of that shipwreck, Daddy?" Whatever's happened, she brings up some point in the story or some gag in the show and asks about it.

This chatter is her way of letting me know that she saw me and that she thinks I was great. The next day she's forgotten the whole thing and I'm back to just being that man who sits on her right. But for twenty-four hours I've been king.

Isn't it wonderful how kids are so anxious to be grown-up? Nora, already she's using perfume. It's called Pablum No. 5.

Sometimes my kids are brought to watch me make a picture at Paramount. When they were very young, I didn't allow them on the set unless I was doing something I thought they'd enjoy. If I'm doing something off-beat or if I'm dressed in a peculiar costume, it frightens them. Once I was dressed as an old lady, and they cried and took on something terrible until I removed my wig. It scared them, because, although they recognized my features, they knew something was wrong with the trimmings I was wearing around those features. One day when Nora dropped in to see me work at Paramount, Claire, our script girl, said, "So you're Nora!"

Nora gave her her full history in one fast line. She said, "Yes, I'm Nora, I'm seven years old, I'm in the second grade and I don't get many A's."

Kelly has given us lots of worries. During his first year in school he was a pixie character—real unpredictable. When he felt like it he got up and walked around the room. If he wanted to go on tour, he just left his desk and walked. When I got home after work I'd ask him, "How many times did you walk away from your desk today?" and he'd say, "Only three or four times today, Daddy."

"You'd better cut down on it, old boy," I'd say, "because some-day when you get up and walk around, you're going to run into me standing there, and I'm going to spank you all the way back to your desk."

The sisters of St. Charles Kindergarten, where Kelly goes, have been very understanding and tolerant about his ambulatory weakness. I sent a note to one of them. In it I said, "Be tough with this little boy, because we want to get him straightened out. If you have to, lick him or smack him. In fact, every time you do, I'll give you twenty dollars."

The sister sent a little note back to me, "I don't think that will be necessary," it said. "Kelly is improving. Besides," she'd added, "you couldn't afford it."

When our kids began to grow up, we fixed up a play room for them and gave them rooms of their own. While we were at it, Dolores and I decided to redo the whole house. We tore out one entire downstairs wall and put in glass, so no matter where we are, we can look out at the garden and enjoy the California sun —if it shows up. This remodeling set us back ten times the original cost of the house, and with the tax situation the way it is, I had to go into hock to do it.

One of my heads kept asking me, "Do you know what you're doing?" My other head would ad lib back, "You only live once and you have maybe twenty-five more years to enjoy yourself, so why not live it up until the sheriff comes and wheels the whole thing off to be sold?"

So that's what we're doing—living it up. And it's a joy and a pleasure. When you've worked long enough and hard enough, I think you have the right to baby yourself a little. Not that our place is any Pickfair. People still drive by, look at it and ask, "Is *that* all Hope has to live in?"

My office adjoins my house. It's a different project, separate and distinct from our house. In fact, it's on a different property. It was put up (and is owned) by Hope Enterprises. But it's handy. The people I want to see on business can walk in and out without disturbing anybody. Otherwise, I'd have to go into town and fight the traffic. And I can have my writers out there for story conferences. It's a nice set-up.

One of my friends, a fellow who did the B pictures at Paramount in my early days there, used to tell me, "No matter what you do, don't buy a big house. Keep within your budget. The danger out here is in living beyond your income. Then, if your private gold mine caves in, it's not only brutal, it's tragic." When he lost his job at Paramount, he'd expanded his scale of living to such an extent that he couldn't retrench, so he committed suicide. I've often wondered if, when he gave me that wise counsel, he was trying to advise himself or me.

Anyhow, I know that if your overhead's too big and you quit pictures or something happens to your contract, you're just standing around asking the people on the Greyhound buses if they'd like to bid on your home as they whiz by. During my first two or three years in California, I played it cagey. I wanted to make sure I had a house that wasn't too big to hook onto the Super Chief if I needed to move it East.

Our first house on Camden Drive we rented from Rea Gable, Clark Gable's second wife. It was a nice little house and we enjoyed it. Then we rented a house in Beverly Glen. It was still on the modest side. Our next was a house on Navajo. None of them were large. The original cost of the house we're living in now was thirty thousand dollars and with it came three acres of property.

The Hopes fling one big party every year. Last year we invited two hundred and fifty friends. It begins New Year's morning. We serve brunch. After that we take everybody who wants to go to the Rose Bowl Game in chartered buses. At least, we take all those who're still able to go, because usually they arrive feeling the effects of New Year's Eve and, what with the Tom and Jerries on the buffet, some of them like it at our house and just want to lie down.

Our party begins at eleven o'clock. We leave for the game around one-thirty or a quarter to two. The buses are supplied with any kind of refreshment anyone can want. You'd think such a bus ride would be a great spot for a comedian like me, for, after all, a busload of people is a captive audience. But the two men who really take over are Jack Clark, a song plugger, and Shot-Gun Britton, a make-up man. Shot-Gun is Jane Russell's make-up man. He's from Hardin-Simmons University in Texas and is real funny. He's got a Texas twang and he and Jack Clark whip it back and forth like a couple of Groucho Marxes.

I wish I could quote some of their quips, but I forget their outstanding nifties—by that time I've had a Tom and Jerry or two myself. However, their material is real insane. When we come home, jollity and jests continue.

One year while the party was in full blast, one of my writers, Wilkie Mahoney, looked the house over. He hadn't seen it since we'd remodeled it. He took in the swimming pool and my one-hole golf course, and he said, "Just think, this whole thing was built on 'Who was that lady I seen you with last night?' "

Dolores has a wise and loving touch with our children. I'm lost in admiration of the job she has done with them, and with the job she's done keeping me in line. A lot of children whose fathers are in show business grow up too precocious, too wise, too fresh, too unfunny. That's not true of our four. Dolores sees to that. She also sees to it that they're having a devout rearing. Among our neighbors is a family named Dailey. One day Mrs. Dailey overheard our littlest one, Kelly, ask our next youngest, Nora, "Is everybody in the world Catholic?"

"Yes," Nora said, "everybody but Daddy. He's a comedian."

I was surprised and pleased when I heard that. I have no trouble convincing them that I'm their daddy, but sometimes I have trouble convincing them that I'm a comedian. Them, too, I mean.

Index

Q

Queen Mary, the, 167-168
Queen of the Surf Club, Honolulu, 272

R

Radford, Admiral William, 272
Raft, George, 166
Ranger, Ralph, 132
Rapp, Johnny, 215
Rawlings, Colonel Buck, 179-182
Ray, Harry, 148, 274 .
Ray, Leah, 129
Raye, Martha, 133, 137-138
Red, Hot and Blue, 122-124, 126-128, 283
Reid, Wally, 32
Reynolds, Quentin, 187
Rialto Theater, New York, 129
Richman, Harry, 114, 115-116
Ritz-Carlton Hotel, Boston, 114
RKO Studios, 109, 118, 119
RKO "Theater of the Air," 109
Road to Bali, The, 140, 142-143
Road to Morocco, The, 141, 189
Road to Rio, The, 141, 142, 144
Road to Singapore, The, 139, 141, 142
Road to Utopia, The, 161, 270
Road to Zanzibar, The, 139
Roberta, 41, 103, 106-109, 111-112, 125, 128, 283
Roberti, Lyda, 107
Robin, Leo, 132
Robinson, Edward G., 166
Rockefeller, John D., Sr., 27-28
Rockwell, Frank, 111
Rogers, Roy, 153, 247
Rogers, Will, 245, 248
Romano, Tony, 162-165, 174
Romanoff, Prince Mike, 114, 115-116
Romanoff's restaurant, Beverly Hills, 115
Rooney, Pat, 103
Roosevelt, Franklin D., 248-249

Roosevelt, Mrs. Franklin D., 249
Root, Johnny, 38
Rose, Jack, 210
Rosequist, Mildred, 36-39
Ross, Shirley, 132, 133-134, 137
Runyon, Damon, 136-137
Russell, Jane, 137, 243, 275, 284, 297
Ruth, George Herman (Babe), 229

S

St. Andrews golf course, Scotland, 227
St. Charles Kindergarten, California, 295-296
St. Claire Theater, Cleveland, 40
Sanymetal Products Company, Cleveland, 286-287
Saphier, Jimmy, 209, 232, 237
Savoy Hotel, London, 218
Sawbridge, General Ben M., 173
Sax, Sam, 129-130
Say When, 114-116
Schenck, Marvin, 104
Schertzinger, Victor, 141
Schwartz, Al, 213
Schwartz, Sherwood, 213
Scott, Randolph, 196
Selwyn, Billy, 132
Shapiro, Bob, 235
Shavelson, Mel, 210
Shea, Mike, 65-66, 67
Sherin, Ukie, 56-57
Shore, Dinah, 111, 238
Short, Hazard, 107
Shriner, Herb, 265
Shubert, Lee, 99, 100
Shubert Brothers, 99, 101
Shurr, Louis (Doctor), 117-118, 122, 129, 131, 146-147, 155-157, 232, 279
Sidewalks of New York, The, 60
Sidney, Louis K., 104, 106
Siegel, Norman, 217-218, 224
Simon and Schuster, publishers, 260